HTML5
FOR
DUMMIES®
eLEARNING KIT

by Frank Boumphrey

WILEY

John Wiley & Sons, Inc.

HTML5 eLearning Kit For Dummies®

Published by
John Wiley & Sons, Inc.
111 River Street
Hoboken, NJ 07030-5774
www.wiley.com

Copyright © 2012 by John Wiley & Sons, Inc., Hoboken, New Jersey

Published by John Wiley & Sons, Inc., Hoboken, New Jersey

Published simultaneously in Canada

For general information on our other products and services, please contact our Customer Care Department within the U.S. at 877-762-2974, outside the U.S. at 317-572-3993, or fax 317-572-4002.

For technical support, please visit www.wiley.com/techsupport.

Wiley publishes in a variety of print and electronic formats and by print-on-demand. Some material included with standard print versions of this book may not be included in e-books or in print-on-demand. If this book refers to media such as a CD or DVD that is not included in the version you purchased, you may download this material at http://booksupport.wiley.com. For more information about Wiley products, visit www.wiley.com.

Library of Congress Control Number: 2012941785

ISBN 978-1-118-07475-6 (pbk); ISBN 978-1-118-23650-5 (ebk); ISBN 978-1-118-26142-2 (ebk); ISBN 978-1-118-22259-1 (ebk)

Manufactured in the United States of America

10 9 8 7 6 5 4 3 2 1

WILEY

About the Author

Frank Boumphrey was introduced to programming by the British Army, which took him away from his favorite occupations of blowing things up and jumping out of planes and tried to make him into a mainframe programmer.

Burnt out by thinking in hexadecimals, he left the army and went to medical school, spending most of his career at a large Midwestern medical institution and ending up as a professor and chief of spine surgery. Along the way he helped introduce the MRI to the medical world.

He maintained his interest in programming and was early involved with the Internet and exchange of medical information electronically. In this role, he was a user of SGML and an early adopter of HTML, which he used since its inception. This led to a second career in consulting on medical documentation and electronic record keeping. He recently retired from this second career.

He was at one time president of the HTML Writers Guild and, as such, served on several W3C working groups, including the XHTML group (he was an editor of the Recommendation) and the CSS, RDF, XForms, and DOM groups. He also sat on the W3C advisory committee.

He has written several web-related books, and this is his second *For Dummies* book.

Frank and his wife Rona shared their house with several cats and occasionally resident children. They have several children and grandchildren.

Dedication

The editors at Wiley dedicate this book in lovely memory of Frank Boumphrey, who passed away soon after he finished writing the manuscript for this book, and in honor of his family. Frank's good humor and the joy he took in writing and revising has left a wonderful and lasting impression on us all.

Publisher's Acknowledgments

We're proud of this book; please send us your comments at http://dummies.custhelp.com. For other comments, please contact our Customer Care Department within the U.S. at 877-762-2974, outside the U.S. at 317-572-3993, or fax 317-572-4002.

Some of the people who helped bring this book to market include the following:

Acquisitions, Editorial, and Vertical Websites

Sr. Project Editor: Rebecca Huehls

Sr. Acquisitions Editor: Katie Feltman

Copy Editor: Jen Riggs

Technical Editor: Ronald Norman

Sr. Editorial Manager: Leah Michael

Vertical Websites: Rich Graves

Editorial Assistant: Leslie Saxman

Sr. Editorial Assistant: Cherie Case

Cover Photo: ©iStockphoto.com / Tommaso Colia

Cartoons: Rich Tennant (www.the5thwave.com)

Composition Services

Sr. Project Coordinator: Kristie Rees

Layout and Graphics: Andrea Hornberger, Jennifer Mayberry

Proofreaders: Lindsay Amones, Rebecca Denoncour, Lauren Mandelbaum

Indexer: Potomac Indexing, LLC

Special Help:
Chris Minnick, Pat O'Brien

Publishing and Editorial for Technology Dummies

Richard Swadley, Vice President and Executive Group Publisher

Andy Cummings, Vice President and Publisher

Mary Bednarek, Executive Acquisitions Director

Mary C. Corder, Editorial Director

Publishing for Consumer Dummies

Kathleen Nebenhaus, Vice President and Executive Publisher

Composition Services

Debbie Stailey, Director of Composition Services

Contents at a Glance

Table of Contents

Introduction

*I*f you've been thinking about taking a class online (it's all the rage these days), but you're concerned about getting lost in the electronic fray, worry no longer. *HTML5 eLearning Kit For Dummies* is here to help you, providing you with an integrated learning experience that includes not only the book and CD you hold in your hands but also an online version of the course at www.dummieselearning.com and practice files you can download at www.dummies.com/go/html5elearningkit. Consider this Introduction your primer.

About This Kit

Each piece of this eLearning kit works in conjunction with the others. Whether you pop the CD into your computer to start the lessons online, follow along with the book (or not), or go online to see the course, this kit teaches you how to

- ✔ Build the framework for an HTML document using general best practices for HTML and following new practices in HTML5.

- ✔ Use the most current tags and elements as you add text, pictures, links, and multimedia content to your web pages. These tags include HTML5 multimedia tags that offer native support for playing audio and video.

- ✔ Make forms that use new, semantic tags for forms along with long-standing form elements such as text boxes, drop-down lists, radio buttons, and submit buttons. Find out about new features in HTML5 that improve form validation.

✔ Create and apply CSS rules to web page backgrounds and elements. You see how CSS can transform the look and layout of HTML content.

✔ Add the most current CSS3 styles that newer web browsers support. These styles expand the selection of fonts and design elements, such as rounded corners and shadows, that web pages can now use without complicated hacks.

✔ Design HTML and CSS that's flexible enough to display well on computer monitors, tablets, or mobile web devices like smartphones.

✔ Set up form attributes that send data to a server, and validate forms by combining HTML5 and JavaScript.

✔ Explore scripting and animation features, such as swapping images on a web page, adding geolocation, and creating basic animations on the `<canvas>` element.

How This Kit Is Organized

In addition to containing seven lessons, this book has a CD and a companion website, which offer six lessons. I describe all these elements here:

✔ **Lesson 1: Getting Started with HTML5:** This lesson introduces you what's new in HTML5 and explains how to create the framework of an HTML5 document. You learn some best practices for creating HTML, such as adding an ID to every element. The development cycle for HTML5 is evolving, so you discover who's involved and basic tips for handling the differences among browsers that are typically in different stages of adopting HTML5 standards.

✔ **Lesson 2: Filling the Body with Text, Pictures, Links, and Multimedia:** This lesson is all about filling the body of a web page with content. HTML5 introduces new tags that describe common elements on a web page, such as a header and footer. You learn what the important new tags are and where they go, as well as how to use the existing tags that have withstood the test of time.

✔ **Lesson 3: Creating Forms:** Forms are important to many, if not most, websites. This lesson focuses on how the underlying HTML in a form works. Find out how to create a form of your own using basic form elements, including some elements that are new in HTML5.

✔ **Lesson 4: Creating Basic CSS Rules:** CSS adds the razzle-dazzle to web page content — okay, if not dazzle, exactly, at least color, backgrounds, fonts, layout, and more. This lesson is your introduction to CSS, explaining the basic parts of CSS rules and how to create CSS rules that change the appearance, background, and positioning of web page elements. Discover the concepts of inheritance and cascading, so you understand how HTML and CSS work together behind the scenes.

✔ **Lesson 5: Styling Pages with CSS:** Delve deeper into specific CSS properties in this lesson. For example, discover all the different properties that modify fonts and text, including the new @font-face rule that enables you to explore a broad range of downloadable font files. Customize the corners of boxed elements by rounding them or even make different curves around each one. Create shadows and glows, customize borders, and more. The upshot is that you learn basic CSS along with new features in CSS3. You also combine media types and media queries so that your website displays well on a variety of devices, following the best practices for the mobile web and CSS3.

✔ **Lesson 6: Adding Interactivity with Scripting:** In this lesson, both the book and the course explain how you set up form attributes so a form can share data with a web server. Both also introduce the topics of swapping images on a website and adding geolocation features so a site can detect where a user is located and present information based on that location. In the book, you find additional infomation about the building blocks of JavaScript and more detailed explanations of how to combine JavaScript elements to make example scripts work. The book also points you to example files at www.dummies.com/go/html5 elearningkit that you can download, modify, and display in a browser, so you can develop a better understanding of the way the JavaScript examples work.

✔ **Lesson 7: Exploring the Canvas and Animation:** This lesson, covered mostly in the book, gives you a taste of more advanced HTML5, CSS3, and JavaScript. The <canvas> element, new in HTML5, can hold JavaScript that draws images on screen. The book provides example code and pointers to sample files that enable you to start working with this powerful new feature. CSS3 animation is another new feature gaining broader support among browsers. The sample applications you find in the book provide very simple examples you can use as a starting point for further exploration of these exciting developments in CSS3.

✔ **About the CD appendix:** The appendix briefly outlines what the CD that accompanies this book contains and what you'll find in the online course, which is available here:

www.dummieselearning.com

The appendix also contains a few technical details about using the CD and troubleshooting tips, should you need them.

✔ **About the companion website:** The companion website holds sample files you can use to experiment with the code you find in the book. You can download these sample files at:

www.dummies.com/go/html5elearningkit

How This Book Works with the Electronic Lessons

HTML5 eLearning Kit For Dummies merges a tutorial-based *For Dummies* book with eLearning instruction contained on the CD and an online course. The lessons you find in this book mirror the lessons in the course, and you can use the two together or separately. (If you borrowed this book from a library, you can access the course via the CD only. See the appendix for details.) Both the book and the course feature self-assessment questions, skill-building exercises, illustrations, and additional resources.

In each lesson in the book, you'll find these elements:

✔ **Lesson opener questions:** The questions quiz you on particular points of interest. A page number heads you in the right direction to find the answer.

✔ **Summing Up:** This section recaps the content you just learned.

✔ **Try-it-yourself lab:** Look to this section at the end of the lessons for ideas that help you further hone your skills by applying what you've learned in a practical exercise. You will need to consider several concepts you've learned in a section to complete a lab.

✔ **Know this tech talk:** Each lesson contains a brief glossary.

Foolish Assumptions

I assume you know what eLearning is and want to learn how to work with the code that makes websites tick, using the most up-to-date features in HTML5, CSS3, and JavaScript. Although you may have used website-creation software, such as Dreamweaver or other free simple tools to create a website or a blog, I don't assume you have much, if any, experience with HTML, CSS, or scripting languages. I also assume you want to learn the fun and easy way, using the online course and book together to support your learning.

What Do You Need to Write Your Own Code?

You will of course need a computer with a keyboard to author HTML documents. Any operating system will suffice; you just need to be easily able to save files in a folder.

I do suggest that you create a separate folder for this course, and create subfolders for the examples and exercises you do in each lesson.

You also need a text editor and a web browser that supports HTML5 (or better yet, several browsers). Both are easy to come by, as the following bullets explain:

- **Text editor:** On the Windows operating system, Notepad is the good old standby. However, several other editors offer color coding that helps you read the code. Textpad and Editpad are highly recommended. Both have automatic indenting and color coding. Both have a free trial version, but if you like them, do the decent thing and pay the small, very reasonable license fee.

  On a Mac, know that the default text editor, TextEdit, adds all kinds of 'bling' to your code that can create problems when you display it in a browser. To avoid this problem, choose Format⇨Make Plain Text before saving your file.

- **Browsers:** Having a variety of browsers enables you to test your pages. For this course, I recommend you get (or check that you have) the most current version of each of the following browsers: IE (the default browser in Windows), Firefox, Chrome, Safari (the default on the Mac), and Opera.

To check out certain mobile features and layouts in this course, you'll find that access to at least one web-capable mobile device is helpful. When you start programming actual websites for mobile platforms, try to beg, borrow, or steal as many devices as possible for testing your pages!

Conventions Used in This Book

A few style conventions will help you navigate the book piece of this kit:

- Terms I truly want to emphasize are defined in Lingo sections.
- Website addresses, or URLs, are shown like this: `www.dummies.com`.
- Numbered steps that you need to follow, and characters you need to type (like a user ID or a password), are set in **bold**.

Icons Used in This Kit

The familiar and helpful *For Dummies* icons guide you throughout *HTML5 eLearning Kit For Dummies,* in the book and in the electronic lessons, too.

The Tip icon points out helpful information that's likely to make your job easier.

This icon marks an interesting and useful fact — something you probably want to remember for later use.

The Warning icon highlights lurking danger. When you see this icon, you know to pay attention and proceed with caution.

The Practice icon highlights where I've provided you with a short exercise to perform.

In addition to the icons, you also find these friendly study aids in the book that bring your attention to certain pieces of information:

- ✔ **Extra Info:** This box highlights something to pay close attention to in a figure or points out other useful information related to the discussion at hand.

- ✔ **Go Online:** This box sends you online to view web resources, complete activities, or find examples.

- ✔ **Lingo:** When you see the Lingo box, look for a definition of a key term or concept.

Class Is In

Now that you're primed and ready, it's time to begin. If you're altogether new to using HTML5, CSS3, and JavaScript, this course starts at the beginning (see Lesson 1) and helps you lay the groundwork for using each type of coding as you go. You can also jump right to a topic that interests you. Whichever path you choose, you can use the book in tandem with the CD and the online course — the content of each reinforces the other.

Lesson 1
Getting Started with HTML5

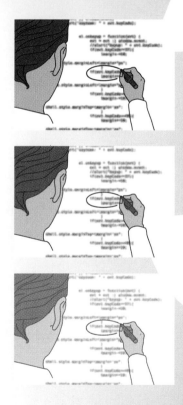

- ✔ The *W3C and WHATWG work together* to keep the development of the HTML5 specification moving forward.

- ✔ HTML5 offers *new features for editable content, inserting audio and video, and more.*

- ✔ HTML documents include a *DOCTYPE, root element, head, and body.*

- ✔ The *HTML document tree* sees each element in an HTML document kind of like a node on a family tree.

- ✔ Different web *browsers support and display HTML5 features differently.*

*I*n this lesson, you start writing your own web code right away. Well, almost. I walk you through a little history of where HTML5 comes from and why it's still evolving — essential points to understand before you start creating your own web pages. After that though, you jump right into creating a framework for a web page, using a simple example page called Hello HTML as a reference point. You learn basic concepts about HTML elements, too. After you get started, you discover how easy writing your own HTML can be.

Introducing HTML5

HTML5 is stepping up to the many challenges that the modern web user presents. At the time of this writing, HTML5 is not yet standard — the W3C is working on the specification. However, many web browsers are already being updated to conform to the HTML5 specification.

Although HTML5 has many new additions and features, it still includes features from previous versions of HTML. (Otherwise you'd have to rebuild all your existing sites!) The following sections introduce you to what still works and what exciting new features HTML5 has to offer.

Understanding the evolution of HTML

With HTML5, HTML has come of age.

Tim Berners-Lee invented HTML ostensibly for the exchange of scientific and technical documents. Although 1993 is credited as the official invention date, he had, in fact, been tinkering with it since the 1980s. His inspired stroke of genius was to envision an interconnected web of self-descriptive documents connected by hyperlinks, and his energy and dedication made this idea a reality. Because HTML grew rapidly, going through three versions in a short period of time, it became quite unruly and littered with styling tags and attributes. Browsers didn't help, tolerating all kinds of markup and doing their best to interpret *illegal documents* (that is, documents that didn't conform to the rules of HTML). To help curb this unruliness, HTML was passed off to the sterner tutelage of XML, producing XHTML.

In XHMTL, all style tags were *deprecated* (or phased out), and the newly created Cascading Styling Sheets (CSS) was used instead for styling. This certainly got things under control, and authors gradually moved over to the new paradigm and started creating legal documents. However, the XML definitions were somewhat constricting and, to a certain extent, curtailed development. For this reason, the Web Hypertext Application Technology Working Group (WHATWG) group was founded; it freed HTML from the constraints of the XML Document Type Definition (DTD) and allowed continuous development of HTML. The World Wide Web Consortium (W3C) soon fell into line with HTML5, and the two groups have worked almost in lockstep, as you discover later in this lesson. Not to push an analogy too far, but HTML is now officially free of its parents and faces a bright and almost limitless future.

In HTML5, you find the following changes and innovations:

- ✔ Style attributes and style tags are obsolete.

- ✔ Numerous new semantic tags enable designers and developers to fine-tune how web page content is marked up.

- ✔ Closer integration with scripting languages provides several new events and has eased the integration of scripts with markup.

- ✔ Improper markup is handled in an improved, and standardized, way.

- ✔ Better control over multimedia helps website visitors viewing media on mobile devices.

LINGO

A **semantic** tag is a tag whose name describes the type of content it contains. So, for example, heading tags contain headings.

Introducing W3C and WHATWG

W3C and WHATWG have the most influence on what's happening with web languages. Although these organizations work together, they approach the changes in HTML a bit differently.

Throughout this book, I refer to W3C and WHATWG documentation, which — according to the Ian Hickson, the editor of HTML5 — originate from the same source documents. They're the Rosetta Stone, if you will, for all things web and are the places you go if you want to read the actual working recommendations for HTML5 and follow their progress. Interpreting them, however, may be another matter altogether.

W3C

The W3C is the international body that develops the standards driving the web. Tim Berners-Lee, the guy who invented the original web, is the director of the W3C — a pretty logical relationship! This group — which comprises designers, web browser developers, and executives — publishes the recommendations and specifications that become the basis for how web browser developers support standards.

The W3C works on a number of different things and — most importantly to anyone interested in designing a site based on HTML5 — helps drive the development of the HTML5 and CSS3 standards, along with all the (many!) components that go into them.

GO ONLINE

The W3C's home on the web is www.w3c.org. Here you find all the working drafts and current specifications for HTML5, CSS3, and their predecessors, as well as countless discussions around changes and new ideas. The W3C's work on web standards is done in years-long cycles of development, analysis, and ultimately consensus (though often controversial) among its members.

The W3C is not just about the web as you typically know it through the major browsers, either. Every year, the W3C focuses on different aspects of web technology to address current and future needs. As this book goes to press, the W3C has five major areas of focus:

- **Web applications:** Combining video, graphics, style, fonts, geolocation, 3D, and other technologies (both locally and across networks) to create new forms of entertainment, games, education, governance, social networking, and so on.

- **Data and service integrations:** As the web grows in size and scope, more and more data is available to use and analyze for countless purposes. The W3C explores ways to integrate and share data across applications.

- **Web of trust:** Trust and data security is an ongoing issue across the web. The W3C explores better ways to secure data even (and especially) while finding ways to share it.

- **Television, mobile, and the web of devices:** The web is no longer limited to a browser on a computer. Televisions, game devices, mobile phones, medical equipment, and more all access the web. The W3C tries to make the specification so open that it's completely device-independent, with a particular focus on bringing the web and TV closer together.

- **One web for all:** Web accessibility is an important goal for the W3C, and it's working to ensure that the specification permits equal access to the web independent of device, network, bandwidth, language, or disability.

WHATWG

WHATWG (Web Hypertext Application Technology Working Group) is, as its name suggests, the group of folks who focus on the specification process. WHATWG is responsible for the HTML5 specification's progress along the W3C recommendation track, which is a long and arduous process.

WHATWG is founded on open-source community principles: Unlike the W3C, anyone with an interest in the process can contribute at no cost. The contributions are moderated by a core group who research the various ideas, suggestions, and designs and then incorporate the good and workable ones into the development effort. The other major difference from W3C is that the WHATWG group does not version and instead looks at development as a continuous process. At some point, the W3C will stop the ongoing development of HTML5 and version an HTML5 specification as a recommendation, which means that development is done. Then, the W3C will start on HTML6! The advantage of versioning is that web developers don't have to aim at a moving target; however, the advantages of a living standard is that developing new ideas is much easier, although the rigor that goes with standards creation is absent.

Partly because WHATWG has an open model, a critical difference exists between the W3C and WHATWG, in addition to (or perhaps because of) their underlying organizational structures. WHATWG refers only to HTML, rather than HTML5 as W3C does. Instead of working toward a single standard or version that gets locked down after a certain scheduled date (which in both organizations has slipped by *years*), WHATWG continuously maintains HTML as a *living standard* — it recognizes that external conditions constantly change (just as spoken language does), and HTML should be flexible enough to shift with those conditions.

GO ONLINE

WHATWG (`www.whatwg.org`) has major categories of effort: HTML, for people who want to read the full spec, usually for developers of browsers, readers, and so on; the Web Dev Edition, for humble web developers; Web Apps 1.0, for developers who build apps and APIs; as well as the various conversation platforms available to people interested in following or contributing.

As a web designer and developer, Web Dev Edition can tell you things you want and need to know about the most current elements, attributes, and properties in HTML, including changes from previous versions, while leaving out the *really* technical language that applies only to actual web browser developers.

EXTRA INFO

WHATWG lists the differences between its handling of the HTML specification and that of the W3C. Read the list here: `www.whatwg.org/specs/web-apps/current-work/multipage/introduction.html#how-do-the-whatwg-and-w3c-specifications-differ.`

Handling deprecated and obsolete features

You often hear designers and coders talking about deprecated and obsolete features. They're nearly the same thing, but here you find out how they're different and why it's important to understand the difference.

As the web evolves, new and improved features are developed, and others grow old:

- ✔ **Obsolete:** An obsolete feature is altogether gone and is no longer supported in the current version of the HTML specification.

- ✔ **Deprecated:** On the other hand, a deprecated feature is still supported, but is being phased out with a new method.

For example, *presentational markup,* such as `<font color="#ff0000">`, has been deprecated since HTML 3.2 and is now obsolete.

HTML5 supports pages that include deprecated attributes and features, but if you're writing new pages, your best bet is to avoid the deprecated features and conform to their replacement features instead. In a few cases, a web browser or browsers may support obsolete features, but if you use a conformance checker, such as the W3C's found at `http://validator.w3.org`, you see alarms. You can find details about testing your pages in Lesson 2.

Exploring what's new in HTML5

HTML5 is being developed to do new things and to improve upon things that HTML has been doing well for more than 20 years.

The following sections introduce you to the new and improved features in HTML5 so that you can identify what parts of an existing site you might improve with an update to HTML5 or how you might go about designing new sites differently. In later lessons, you discover the code needed to make these new features work in your web designs.

Text and layout

In HTML5, you can take advantage of the following updates to text and layout options:

- ✔ **Define editable page content and edit page content on the fly** (what you see is what you get-style). See Lesson 2 for details.

- ✔ **Choose from tons more fonts than in previous versions.** And you can embed fonts so that your visitors don't need to load fonts on their own computers to see whatever fonts the design uses. See Lesson 5.

- ✔ **Create actual columns (great for newspaper/newsletter layout, for example) instead of hacking together content using tables and scripts.** You don't find much about the columns feature in this book because the feature is still under development, but keep an eye out for updates. This feature will be handy if development of the specification and browser support live up to current expectations.

Multimedia and games

Although the majority of the web still deals with traditional web pages, the web is fast becoming the primary source of entertainment for many people. HTML5 reflects the growing need for websites to support multimedia and games by offering the following features:

- ✔ **Native audio and video:** Browsers supporting HTML5 no longer require the Flash plugin or workarounds for mobile devices. Find out how the new `<audio>` and `<video>` tags work in Lesson 2.

- ✔ **Streamlined commands and styles:** Whereas previous HTML versions required a combination of tags and styles, HTML5 requires only one. Throughout this book, you learn about many of those consolidated commands. For example, Lesson 5 explains the new way to add images to a web page and how HTML5 handles *scalable vector graphics,* an exciting and very flexible image format also know as SVG. Lesson 2 introduces SVG.

> **LINGO**
>
> **Native media support** means that HTML5 is built to display images, play sounds, and show video content, all without the need for an external plugin, such as a Flash or an MP3 player.

Mobile devices

Because the bandwidth for mobile devices is a lot narrower than the broadband connections found in many homes and offices, web pages designed for mobile devices have to be simpler, leaner, and cleaner.

Updates to HTML5 respond to demands of mobile web surfing. The improvements HTML5 delivers for mobile sites include the following:

- **Native video support and improved video compression:** Older video formats, such as Flash, can do great stuff, but even short Flash animations tend to be big files, which take forever to load onto a mobile device.

  To address the greater demand for video at smaller file sizes, HTML5 offers native support for embedded video content. This means your visitors don't need a plugin player installed with their browser to play the video. And because the new video formats are better compressed, the video files are smaller and download faster.

- **Improved image embedding and support for new graphics formats:** The `.png` and `.svg` graphics formats, which have developed over the past few years, can save images in smaller-but-better files, and HTML5 has come up with some better ways of embedding images in a page. Most browsers support `.png` and `.svg`, though support is a little uneven.

- **Location-based features:** Because many mobile devices can report location (with your approval, of course) via nearby mobile towers, GPS location, or a combination, web designers can deliver content based on the user's location by combining JavaScript and HTML5. When used appropriately and correctly, you can design sites that enable your visitors to find nearby restaurants, public transportation, or even clean bathrooms! Lesson 6 introduces you to geolocation.

LINGO

Bandwidth is the amount of data that can come through a connection at one time. Think of bandwidth as plumbing: Big, fat pipes let a lot of data pass through at one time, and narrow pipes only let a little bit through. Bandwidth is the size of the pipe, and connection speed (usually expressed as *Kbps, kilobytes per second,* or *Mbps, megabytes per second*) is the speed at which data can pass through a connection. Any kind of data connection involves an optimum combination of bandwidth, connection speed, and some pretty complex traffic control to work well.

LINGO

Geolocation is the ability to find your device (with your permission) based on its geographical location, either by locating it in relation to nearby mobile service towers or GPS. Geolocation also serves custom content to a mobile device based on that location.

Accessibility

In addition to what many standard browsers use, designers also need to take into account assistive technologies, such as tools that help blind, deaf, or otherwise disabled users browse and use the web.

Under certain circumstances, accessibility is required by law. The U.S. government, for example, requires federal agencies to make their electronic and information technology fully accessible to so-called standard users and those needing assistive technologies, under Section 508 accessibility compliance requirements (`www.section508.gov`).

The designers of the Section508.gov site designed to their own standards. So, for example, in Figure 1-1, the Laws menu expands and collapses for standard browsers, while screen readers look at the underlying code and say, "Open the Laws menu" to a visually impaired user. That's because a screen reader can look for the `title` attribute in the underlying code and say the title to the user. The code for that single element looks like this:

```
<div class="AccordionPanelTab1" role="application"><a
          href="#" title="Open the Laws menu">Laws</a>
          </div>
```

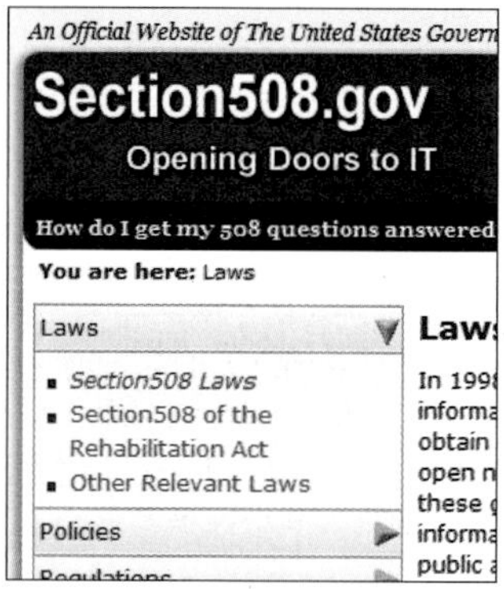

Figure 1-1

> **EXTRA INFO**
>
> Despite the increasingly strict legal requirements, many companies ignore accessibility standards for a number of reasons. The extra complexity of designing to accessibility standards is often daunting for designers. Although HTML5 isn't perfect, it has moved further along in creating a fully accessible web. However, addressing the needs of special users still requires extra work and good judgment.

Features in HTML5 that help designers create more accessible websites include the following:

- Ways to describe an element, such as a menu, tree item, slider, and progress meter, in the page code
- Ways to describe the structure of your page, such as headings, regions, sections, and tables, or grids (see Lesson 2)
- Attributes to describe the state of an element, such as `checked` for a check box (see Lesson 3)
- Keyboard navigation for the web objects and events, which is helpful for people who can't use a mouse or a graphical browser

The preceding examples introduce just some of the simpler features that help with website accessibility.

Building accessibility into your design plans offers some major advantages: In addition to being the right thing to do, it can expand your web audience by a significant proportion. Also, because accessibility standards require a kind of design simplicity, accessible websites are often clean, intuitive to use, and easy to navigate. And search engines love them!

GO ONLINE

The W3C site on accessibility contains a wealth of information. For a quick overview, go to www.w3.org/WAI/users/ overview.html. Specific guidelines for website authors can be found at www.w3.org/ TR/wai-aria-practices.

Creating the Framework for an HTML Document

This section walks you through the basics of setting up a web page. In keeping with programming-book tradition, you start with an absolutely basic HTML document called HelloHTML.htm. This file is a prop on which to hang a few discussion points. The following sections explain the role each part of this document plays in displaying a web page. You can see the code in Listing 1-1 or check out the sample file ch1_01.htm, which you can download from this book's companion site (see the Introduction for details).

Listing 1-1: HelloHTML.htm

```
<!DOCTYPE html >
<html lang="en">
<head>
    <title>Hello World Example</title>
    <link rel=" " type=" " href=" "
    <meta http-equiv="content-type" content="text/
        html;charset=utf-8" />
</head>
<body>
    <h1 id='h1'>Hello HTML!</h1>
    <p id='p1'><strong>HTML</strong> was invented by
        <em>Tim Berners-Lee</em> in 1993. All markup
        was considered <b>semantic.</b></p>
</body>
</html>
```

Figure 1-2 shows what you see when you run and view the preceding code in the Chrome browser.

Figure 1-2

You can run HTML files from your local folders. Double-clicking an HTML file displays it in your default browser. To see a web page in another browser, right-click it and then choose your desired browser from the context menu that appears.

HTML5 is actually quite relaxed about what's needed for a legal document. I urge you, however, to use the somewhat stricter XHTML rules. Doing so will make your site backward-compatible with older browsers that don't support HTML5 and make your code easier to read. The examples you see throughout this book show XHTML markup.

Starting with the DOCTYPE

An HTML document starts with a Document Type Declaration (also known as a DOCTYPE or DTD). In HTML5, the DOCTYPE is `<!DOCTYPE html >`. A DOCTYPE enables a *user agent* (also known as a browser) to see what kind of document it must handle. You can see the DOCTYPE for the `HelloHTML.htm` file at the top (refer to Listing 1-1).

Although the DOCTYPE has angle brackets like an HTML tag, it isn't a tag. You know this because it begins with an exclamation mark (!).

EXTRA INFO

Previous version of HTML and XHTML had much more complicated DTDs. For example, here is one of the possible DTDs for an XHTML document (there are actually several options):

```
<!DOCTYPE html PUBLIC "-//W3C//DTD XHTML 1.0 Strict//EN" "http://www.
   w3.org/TR/xhtml1/DTD/xhtml1-strict.dtd">
```

It contains, as well as the type of the document — HTML — a public declaration, and a site where the user agent can find another document to validate this one. That last sentence was probably a lot of gibberish to you. It's all about XML! If you want to find out more (and you don't need to for this book), see *XML For Dummies,* 4th Edition by Lucinda Dykes and Ed Tittel.

One of the beautiful things about HTML5 is that it doesn't require you to spell out all the gibberish; it just assumes that if you say that it's an HTML document, you mean that it's the most recent version, or HTML5. Makes sense, right?

Setting up the root element

In XHTML, all well-formed documents must have a root element that encloses the whole document. In Listing 1-1, you see the opening tag for the root element under the DOCTYPE:

```
<html lang="en">
```

The closing tag of the root element, `</html>`, appears at the end of the document. You may find it interesting that the DOCTYPE's name is always the same as the root element.

The root element is also a good place to tell the user agent what language the document uses with the `lang` attribute. The attribute's `"en"` value tells the browser that the web page is in English.

In XHTML, all attribute values must be in quotations. (This is not necessary in HTML5, but is a good practice.) In general, you can use single or double quotations. The important thing is that the quotations are present.

EXTRA INFO

In another document, you may find a root element that looks something like this:

```
<html xmlns="http://
   www.w3.org/1999/
   xhtml" >
```

The `xmlns` attribute is a namespace attribute. *Namespaces,* which are beyond the scope of this book, enable you to include mark up from other document type languages such as `'mathml'` and `'musicml'`. Again see *XML For Dummies,* 4th Edition by Lucinda Dykes and Ed Tittel for further information.

Filling up the head

The head of an HTML document is enclosed in `<head>` tags. Elements in this section aren't meant to be viewed but contain a lot of information that enables a browser to display your web page. The following sections introduce you to the most important elements you insert between the `<head>` tags. In the example page, `HelloHTML.htm`, the head of the document looks like this:

```
<head>
    <title>Hello World Example</title>
    <meta http-equiv="content-type" content="text/
        html;charset=utf-8" />
</head>
```

The important tags are highlighted so you can easily see them.

The <title> element

The HTML specification requires HTML documents to include a `<title>` element. The text it contains doesn't appear in the browser window, but does display the page title in the browser title bar, an important job. Also search engines, such as Google and Yahoo!, give a high rating to the information in the title, so try and make the title short and informative. You can see that the title for `HelloHTML.htm` looks like this:

```
<title>Hello World Example</title>
```

In the browser, Hello World Example appears in the browser's title bar.

The <link> element

The `link` element is used for linking to other files. The most important use is for linking to a file containing a CSS code, which contains the formatting and positioning instructions for your web page content. You find details about creating CSS in Lessons 4 and 5, and Lesson 5 has specifics about linking a CSS file to an HTML file.

For now, notice that the `<link>` element contains three attributes, which are *empty* (don't contain any values yet) in `HelloHTML.htm`:

```
<link rel=" " type=" " href=" "
```

Here's a brief introduction to what each attribute does:

  ✔ **rel** tells the user agent that it's dealing with a link to a style sheet.

  ✔ **type** gives the media type of the style sheet.

  ✔ **href** tells the agent where to find the style sheet file.

The *<meta>* element

Meta tags are mainly for providing information about your page, but have some other nifty uses. Search engines use them to categorize and rank your pages. The basic syntax is

```
<meta name="value" content="value"/>
```

name usually takes the value of keywords, description, or summary.

Here are a couple examples from a page about knee ligament repair:

```
<meta name='description' content='A
          paper describing the
          various techniques for
          repairing Anterior Cruciate Ligaments; their
          short and long term results' />
```

```
<meta name='keywords' content='Knee; Orthopedic Surgery;
          Sports Medicine; ACL; Anterior Cruciate
          Ligament; surgical outcomes;' />
```

Here is a meta tag with the http-equiv attribute, which you see in Listing 1-1. This meta tag is designed to complement information found in the HTTP header. One possible value of the http-equiv attribute is content-type. A content-type meta tag tells the browser what set of characters the web pages uses. For example, a web page written in Japanese might use EUC-JP or SHIFT_JS. One of the most commonly used character set values is UTF-8.

```
<meta http-equiv="content-
          type" content="text/
          html;charset=utf-8" />
```

> **LINGO**
>
> A **media type,** formerly known as a **mime type,** tells the web browser how to handle a linked file. Media types are usually two-part identifiers that give a broad description of the file, followed by a slash (/), followed by a more specific description. For example, the media type for an HTML document is "text/html", and the media type for a CSS style sheet is "text/css".

> **EXTRA INFO**
>
> You may also find a <base> element in the <head> of a web page. The <base> element tells the user agent what the base element is for the page. Include the <base> element if you think you'll be manually moving the page around a lot. Otherwise, this element is rarely used. Modern site maintenance software automatically changes relative href and src values.

Adding the document body

The <body> section is where you put all the text, images, links, tables, and anything else you want people to see when they visit the page. In other words, you build your HTML page here. Lesson 2 is devoted to specifics about filling the `<body>` element with content, but you can see examples of elements within the body in the example `HelloHTML.htm` file:

```
<body>
        <h1 id='h1'>Hello HTML!</h1>
        <p id='p1'><strong>HTML</strong> was invented by
             <em>Tim Berners-Lee</em> in 1993. All markup
             was considered <b>semantic.</b></p>
</body>
```

Before you start building web pages in HTML, knowing the following quirks about how HTML elements work will help you code pages that look the way you intend them to:

- ✔ **Block versus inline elements:** *Block elements,* as their name suggests, are blocks of text. When a user agent sees a block element, it adds a line break before and after the element. *Inline elements* are contained in block elements, and do not have line breaks before or after them.

  The `<body>` in `HelloHTML.htm` contains two block and three inline elements. In the preceding code, the block elements, shown in green, are the heading `<h1>` and the paragraph `<p>`. The inline elements, shown in maroon, are the `<strong>`, `<em>`, and `<b>` elements. Both `<strong>` and `<b>` apply bold to the text; `<em>`, which stands for *emphasis,* applies italics.

TIP

How do you know whether an element is a block or an inline element? Well, most elements are block elements. Throughout this book, I typically mention when an element is inline. Or, if an element isn't adding a line when you display a page in the browser, you're dealing with an inline element. Also good to know: You can change a block element into an inline element or vice versa, using CSS. Find out how in Lessons 4 and 5.

- ✔ **Semantic versus style elements:** *Semantic* HTML elements are names that are meaningful in English; the element describes the type of content it surrounds. The user agent decides how to present the HTML element, and most browsers use a similar presentation method. However, because the elements have a semantic meaning, an aural or a Braille browser can present your document in a suitable manner. *Styling* refers to such matters as color, indentation, and letter and word spacing — in short, how your plain text and other items should appear in the browser.

  You might argue that the `<b>` tag is a styling tag. Yes and no. The meaning of bold is so well known that it has taken on a semantic meaning.

Giving each block element an ID

In the `HelloHTML.htm` example earlier in this lesson, each block element has an ID. For example, `<h1 id='h1'>` gives the `<h1>` tag an ID of h1. An element ID takes a value that must be unique throughout the document. For example, if you had several `<h1>` elements, each one would need a unique ID.

Certain rules govern an ID's value. The ID name must start with either an underscore or an alphabetic character, and contain nothing but alphanumeric characters.

Routinely give all your block elements IDs for the following reasons:

- ✔ An ID provides an easy way to apply CSS style to only one element in your document (For example, you might want to make just one `<h1>` red, and all the others blue.) Find out more in Lessons 4 and 5.

- ✔ An ID allows outside documents to link to a specific place in your document. Lesson 2 explains how.

- ✔ An ID gives scripting languages an easy way to create a scripting object of your element via the Document Object Model (DOM). A *scripting object* is a JavaScript object that refers to an element. Lesson 6 offers an introduction to scripting.

Understanding the Document Tree

The HTML document tree is also called the *Document Object Model,* or *DOM.* Basically, the DOM is a concept that considers every element in an HTML document an object, organized into a tree. In programming, a *tree* is a system of organizing elements similar to a family tree, where each element in the document can be a parent with children that branch off. In HTML, the only element that doesn't have a parent is the root element, or the `<html> </html>` tag pair.

LINGO

The **Document Object Model (DOM)** considers every element in an HTML document as an object, organized into a tree.

To understand the DOM, you need to understand the concept of an *object.* Basically, everything is an object. Any object is composed of many smaller objects. For instance, human objects are made up of anatomical objects, or organs, which are made up of different types of cell objects, which are made up of organelle objects . . . you get the picture. Objects also have properties and attributes that describe them. For instance, your eyes may have a brown property, your hair may have a black (or if you're like me, gray) property, and so on. Some objects also have methods. For instance, your brain has a thinking method, your hand has a grasping method, and so on.

An HTML document is also made up of objects. Consider the following:

- ✔ Each HTML element is an object and has its own attributes.

- ✔ Elements are also made up of other objects; for example, every presentational element has a style object embedded in it.

- ✔ The DOM (which is central to HTML5) describes the object structure of the element. Take the <body> element object: It has several child objects. For example, in Listing 1-1, there are two child objects, the <h1> element object and the <p> element object. Each of these also has an id attribute. The <p> element object also has three child element objects, <strong>, <em>, and <b> objects. These objects, in turn, are composed of text objects that are composed of word objects that are composed of character objects, and so on.

Understanding how the DOM organizes elements into a hierarchy is important when you begin writing CSS code or if you want to add dynamic features with JavaScript. Lessons 4 and 5 introduce you to CSS, and Lesson 6 has an introduction to scripting.

Handling Browser Differences

Particularly because the HTML5 specification isn't done yet, not every web browser consistently supports every new feature of HTML5, but that's actually been true of previous versions of HTML, and HTML4 has been around for ten years! The good news is that every time a new browser version comes out, it supports more of the features in the newest version of HTML5.

Not all web browsers are created equal, however. Most of the major players have released versions that are largely compliant with the latest and greatest HTML standards, but no single browser complies with them all. Most browsers support a slightly different combination of the new features, and some browsers put their own unique spin on the interpretation of those features — or just march to a different tune altogether in some cases.

By no means universal yet (largely because the spec is still changing), HTML5 support has been gaining steady ground for a few years now. If you've been developing for the web for any length of time, you'll have encountered the webmaster's curse: browser compatibility. Alas, compatibility is still a problem even in HTML5, so your design plan needs to include contingencies for those differences. As this book went to press, here are the basics that web designers working in HTML5 need to know about browser support:

- ✔ **Each browser becomes increasingly compliant with HTML5.** For example, Internet Explorer 8 barely supported any HTML5 features, IE9 supports about half of the key HTML5 features, and the preview of IE10 promises to support even more.

- ✔ **Safari, Firefox, Opera, and Chrome browsers lead the pack in supporting HTML5 features,** but the other browsers are catching up quickly.

- ✔ **Each browser will nevertheless still have its own quirks with displaying HTML5 features,** so designers still need to test, test, and test their pages some more.

GO ONLINE

A useful online resource for testing which features your particular browser supports is found at `http://html5test.com`. Here you can check your browser version and code, and it reports how well your browser supports features in the latest HTML recommendations. Doing so gives you a good idea of whether your awesomely creative use of a new feature or attribute plays with different browsers (and of course, as designers and developers, it's always a good idea to test different browsers). I try and tell you what works and what doesn't work in various browsers throughout this book.

Summing Up

In this lesson, you found a little insight into the development of HTML and a quick review of the basics:

- ✔ HTML5 has evolved from earlier versions of HTML, and the W3C and WHATWG play its development. The W3C controls the many specifications that go into HTML5 and CSS3 as well as a number of other, related web technologies. The WHATWG moves HTML along the W3C's recommendation track.

- ✔ Deprecated features in HTML5 are supported but will go away in the future. Simple color attributes, border, and layer attributes are deprecated in HTML5.

- ✔ HTML5 has improved support for graphics, audio, and video. It also improves accessibility for users who must rely on assistive technology.

- ✔ The framework of an HTML5 document includes a DOCTYPE, root element, `<head>` element, and a body. The `<head>` element typically contains a `<title>`, `<link>`, and `<meta>` element.

✔ Web page content appears in the HTML file, and the formatting instructions appear in a related CSS file.

✔ The HTML DOM sees elements in an HTML document as objects with properties and attributes and with parent and child elements.

✔ Web browsers support different HTML5 features and may display them with somewhat different results. This makes testing web pages in different browsers important.

In Lesson 2, you learn about basic elements you add to the body of an HTML document, including text elements, images, links, tables, and multimedia.

Know This Tech Talk

accessibility: How available a website is to as many people as possible, regardless of how they access the Internet or any physical disabilities or special needs.

block element: An HTML element that spans the width of the space available to it and starts on a new line.

deprecated: Describes a feature that is still supported but discouraged, and possibly obsolete in future versions.

Document Object Model (DOM): A way of representing an HTML document for the purpose of manipulating it with CSS or JavaScript.

Document Type Declaration (DTD): A statement that associates a document with a formal definition of the document's language (such as XML, XHTML, or HTML).

geolocation: The use of mobile service towers, GPS, or both to locate a device and serve custom content based on location (this requires permission of the mobile user).

inline element: Elements that do not begin on a new line.

native media support: Support for images, audio, and video without the need for extra software or plugins.

obsolete: Describes a feature that is no longer supported.

presentational markup: Inline HTML code that's used to create one-off changes to style or layout. Discouraged in current HTML sites, some presentational markup is not supported at all.

root element: The element in a markup document that contains all the other elements. In HTML, the root element is `<html>`.

Section 508: The set of U.S. government requirements for making technology accessible to all users, regardless of physical or mental disability.

semantic markup: Markup that enhances the meaning of the content of a web page, rather than just its presentation.

style sheet: A separate file with the extension `.css` that is used to set the style and layout for modern web pages.

validator: A program that checks the correctness of a markup document.

W3C: The World Wide Web Consortium manages web technology specifications and recommendations.

WHATWG: The Web Hypertext Application Technology Working Group moves HTML along the W3C's recommendation track.

Filling the Body with Text, Links, and Multimedia

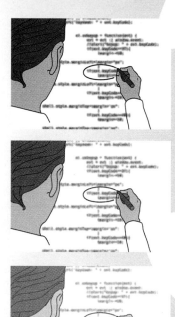

- HTML has *six levels of heading tags,* from `<h1>` to `<h6>`.

- The three types of HTML lists are *unordered, ordered, and definition.*

- The `contenteditable` attribute makes it possible for viewers to *edit text directly on a web page.*

- HTML entities help you *display special characters with HTML.*

- The `<table>` element *displays tabular data.*

- Use the `<img>` element to *insert images.*

- The `<a>` tag *creates hyperlinks within and between HTML documents.*

- Use `<iframe>` to *embed documents within documents.*

- HTML5's `<audio>`, `<video>`, and `<embed>` elements *place multimedia in your HTML documents.*

- The W3C validator can *check whether your code follows the rules in the HTML specification.*

*I*n this lesson, you learn about adding and marking up content. Content includes everything that users see, hear, or sometimes even feel (for Braille display) on your web page, including text, pictures, sounds, and animations. You learn how tags give meaning to content, and how attributes enhance that meaning.

Adding Text

Adding text to an HTML document is almost as simple as typing into a word processor. When you're creating an HTML document, you have the added step of surrounding text with tags that correspond to the way you want to display in a web browser, a concept you may already be familiar with. You probably also want to add an attribute or two because attributes not only enable you to give an element a unique ID, but also enable you do things like make content on the page editable and check the spelling.

In this section, you find an introduction to tags that are the mainstays of HTML as well as features new to HTML5.

Starting with the heading and paragraph tags

Almost any web page uses heading and paragraph tags. *Heading tags* surround titles or headings on a web page. By default, the browser displays text in a heading tag larger than the *body text,* or the text within a paragraph, or <p>, tag. You can use up to six levels of headings, with heading tags ranging from <h1> to <h6>. The <h1> tag indicates the highest level, and <h6> the lowest.

Both heading and paragraph tags work in pairs with an opening and closing tag. You can see them both at work in the following code snippet from this book's sample website, a fan site for the Scottish poet, Robert Burns:

```
<h1 class="body">The Life of
        Robert Burns</h1>

<p>Robert Burns was the firstborn
        of seven children
        and grew up on his
        father's farm in
        Scotland. His family
        was poor, and Burns
        worked hard on the
        farm and received
        little formal
        schooling. However,
he did receive an education at home and spent
some time studying in nearby schools. Burns'
interest in poetry began in earnest when he
was a young man and began writing songs and
poems.</p>
```

EXTRA INFO

The opening `<h1>` contains a `class` attribute, which you can use to organize elements into groups, based on how you want to style those elements using CSS. For example, you might divide headings into those for the body and a sidebar that appears on the right-hand column of the page, giving one group a `class` value of body and the other a `class` value of `sidebar`. You find out more about using the `class` attribute to style text in Lesson 4.

Making lists

In HTML5, you can create three types of lists:

- ✔ **Ordered:** This list type numbers the list items automatically.

- ✔ **Unordered:** Unordered list tags create a bulleted list. You can customize the look of the bullets using CSS. (I cover customizing bullets and numbering in Lesson 5.)

- ✔ **Definition:** A definition list is most often used to list terms and definitions. Web browsers format definition lists in a glossary style. This tag offers two child elements, one for a definition title and another for definition text. If you apply the definition of the definition list more loosely, they can also be handy for tying together items that have a direct relationship to each other.

To create an ordered list, you insert list items between an opening and closing `<ol>` tag, and use opening and closing `<li>` tags for each item in the list. Here's the syntax for an ordered list:

```
<ol>
    <li>Item 1</li>
    <li>Item 2</li>
    <li>Item 3</li>
 </ol>
```

An unordered list works much like an ordered list, except that you use the `<ul>` tag. The following code snippet shows an unordered list as well as how you nest one list inside another. The tags for the nested list are in maroon, so they stand out from the main list:

```
<ul>
    <li>Item 1</li>
    <li>Item 2</li>
        <ul>
            <li>Item A</li>
            <li>Item B</li>
        </ul>
    <li>Item 3</li>
</ul>
```

 Try creating your own lists and nested lists in a text editor.

You can do the following:

- ✔ Nest an ordered list in an ordered list.
- ✔ Nest an unordered list in an ordered list.
- ✔ Try doing three levels of nesting. (You may need to do this in a text-book's Table of Contents.)

A definition list lets you list items and give a brief description of each item. Here's the syntax:

```
<dl>
    <dt>Title 1</dt>
    <dd>Some descriptive text</dd>
    <dt>Title 2</dt>
    <dd>Some descriptive text</dd>
    <dt>Title 3</dt>
    <dd>Some descriptive text</dd>
</dl>
```

In the markup, `<dl>` marks the beginning of the definition list. For each list item, `<dt>` is where you place the definition title, and `<dd>` — which stands for *definition definition* — is a container for the actual definition.

Figure 2-1 shows how each type of list displays in a browser.

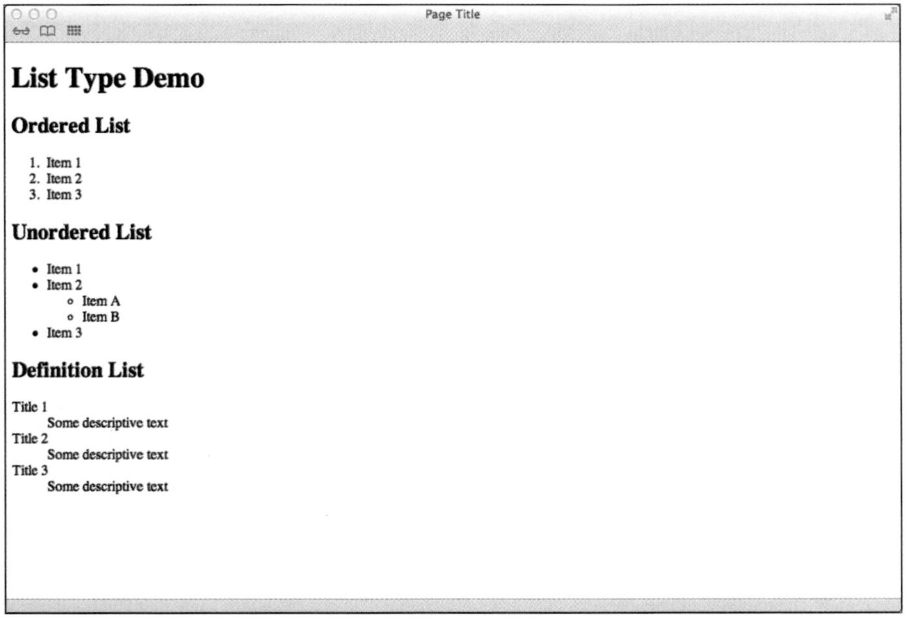

Figure 2-1

Making text editable

Consider the following very common scenario: You have to download a PDF of a form; fill it in *legibly* by hand (and if your handwriting is anything like mine. . .); sign it; and then scan, fax, or snail mail it back to the correct address. Wouldn't it be nice if you could just fill it out on the website by keying directly on to the page? Wouldn't that be a timesaver?

Well, you can if the page has been created using the `contenteditable` attribute, which is new in HTML5. You might still need to print the form so you can add a signature, but you could at least fill in all the other information electronically first.

Using the `contenteditable` attribute on any element means that your user can actually edit the content. The attribute takes the value of either `true` or `false`, and child elements inherit the value.

The easiest way to introduce how `contenteditable` works is with a simple example:

```
<p contenteditable="true">The content of this paragraph is
        editable!</p>
<ul contenteditable="true">
    <li>This list item is editable ...</li>
    <li>... and so is this, because the item inherits the
        value from the <code>&lt;ul></code> element</
        li>
      <li contenteditable="false">But this content
        is <b>not</b> editable because the list
        item's <code>contenteditable</code> value is
        explicitly set to <code>false</code>.</li>
</ul>
<p>This paragraph is NOT editable; it is a normal
        paragraph.</p>
```

If you are using Safari, the resulting web page will look something like Figure 2-2.

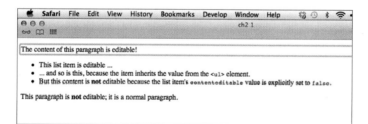

Figure 2-2

Here's a play-by-play of what's happening in the code:

- ✔ In the first paragraph, `contenteditable` is set to `true`, so it is editable. Any child nodes, such as inline `<i>` or `<b>` elements, would also inherit the value.

- ✔ The `<ul>` element has a `contenteditable` attribute that's set to `true`, so all the list items, by default, inherit the value.

- ✔ I explicitly set the third list item to `false`, so it does not inherit the `true` value of its parent, the `<ul>` element.

✔ Because the second paragraph has no `contenteditable` attribute set, it assumes the default value of `false`.

To practice adding the `contenteditable` attribute, fire up your favorite editor and type in the preceding example, along with the HTML document framework required to make the page display in a browser. Or, if you just want to play with the resulting page, open the `L2_01.htm` file that you can download from this book's companion site (see the Introduction for details) and run the file in a browser.

The following tasks can help you see how editable content works from a user's perspective:

✔ Type something in to one of the editable sections. It works!

✔ Save the web page to a local folder and then close the page. Reopen it, and your edits are still there!

✔ Print the web page to see how your edits carry over to the printout.

When an HTML element is editable, you can use the new HTML5 `spellcheck` attribute, too. To folks like me, who have bad spelling, it's the coolest thing since sliced bread. With this new attribute, the browser automatically spell checks the text as the user types it. Simply add `spellcheck="true"` to any editable element, and the browser checks spelling just like a word processor. Right-click a word the checker identifies as misspelled to see a list of alternative spellings. By default, all child elements of an element that is set to `spellcheck="true"` are also automatically spell checked.

EXTRA INFO

A lot goes on behind the scenes with any spell checker. In a typical spell-checker, the user agent (word-processor, publishing app, browser, and so on) has to monitor every key stroke. When it comes to a key stroke it recognizes as some kind of limitation to a word, such as white space or a punctuation mark, it reads off the word and compares it to a dictionary.

Each browser has its own built-in dictionary; other applications, especially in Linux, may share a dictionary. If no match is found, the browser will underline the word, or somehow indicate that there is a misspelling. If the user right-clicks the word, the spell-checker will use a complicated algorithm to search the dictionary for similar matches, and will display them in the familiar pop-up boxes.

There are numerous other details, but these are the essentials.

The great thing is that you can start using `spellcheck` right now. Nearly all modern browsers support the attribute, and if a user's browser doesn't, he's none the wiser.

In addition to elements that use the `contenteditable` attribute, editable elements include `<input>` and `<textarea>`. These are both form elements, which are introduced in Lesson 3.

Displaying special characters

Sometimes, you need to show characters such as < and &, which are illegal in HTML text. Other times, you need to show a character that can't be produced on a standard Western keyboard. In these cases, HTML entities and Unicode can help. Here's how each of these enables you to display special characters:

✔ **HTML entities:** You may have noticed that I have referred to a couple of these characters, such as the copyright character, as follows `&copy;` and the ampersand "&" character as `&amp;`. You may also wish to place a "<" in your text. You can't do this directly, so you'd have to use `&lt;`. These are known as HTML *named entities*.

> **GO ONLINE**
>
> You can find a full list of named entities at `http://dev.w3.org/html5/spec/Overview.html#named-character-references`.

✔ **Unicode:** You can also use any Unicode number to reference a character, and this means you can write any character that your browser supports using the following syntax:

```
&#unicode number;
```

So `&#65;` would produce an uppercase A.

Organizing Content into Tables

The `<table>` element is meant to be used to display tabular data, such as numbers or figures. In the old days, people used to also use tables to lay out images, links, text, and so on. This practice is strongly discouraged today because it emphasizes the presentation of data (layout) rather than the meaning of data (tabular). There are better ways to lay out text and images than with tables.

To illustrate how you add rows and columns to a table, here's the code to create a two-row, two-column table:

```
<table border="1">
    <tr><td>Row 1 Col 1</td><td>Row 1 Col 2</td></tr>
    <tr><td>Row 2 Col 1</td><td>Row 2 Col 2</td></tr>
</table>
```

Here's how the preceding example creates a table:

- ✔ The opening and closing `<table>` tags mark the beginning and end of the table. The `border` attribute on the `<table>` element is one of the few styling attributes that isn't obsolete in HTML5. This attribute determines whether lines appear around the table cells. If you don't want borders to appear, leave the value of the `border` attribute empty, like this:

  ```
  border=" "
  ```

- ✔ Each pair of `<tr>` tags marks the beginning and end of a table row.

- ✔ Within each pair of `<tr>` tags, you see a pair of `<td>` tags for every column in the table. Each pair of `<td>` tags holds the data that's displayed in the table.

If your table needs a title, you can add one using the `<caption>` element. You mark a column header with the `<th>` element. Here's how to add a caption and a header row to the earlier example table:

```
<table border="1">
<caption>Simple Table</caption>
    <tr><th>Head Col 1</th><th>Head Col2</th></tr>
    <tr><td>Row 1 Col 1</td><td>Row 1 Col 2</td></tr>
    <tr><td>Row 2 Col 1</td><td>Row 2 Col 2</td></tr>
</table>
```

You can combine table cells using the `colspan` and `rowspan` attributes. For example, the following cell spans two columns using the `colspan` attribute on the `<tr>` tag:

```
<tr colspan="2"><td>Spanning 2 Cols</td></tr>
```

Or a cell can span several rows using a `rowspan` attribute. Here's an example using a `<tr>` tag:

```
<tr rowspan="2"><td>Spanning 2 rows</td></tr>
```

Listing 2-1 uses all the options discussed in this section to organize a list of Robert Burns' popular poems. Check out the code and see how the code displays in a browser in Figure 2-3.

Listing 2-1: A Sample Table

```
<table border='1'>
    <caption>Robert Burns' Popular Poems</caption>
    <tr><th>Poem Title</th><th>First Line</th></tr>
    <tr><td>A Red, Red Rose</td><td>O my Luve is like a
        red, red rose</td></tr>
    <tr><td>To a Mountain Daisy</td><td>Wee, modest,
        crimson-tippèd flow'r,</td></tr>
    <tr><td colspan='2'>John Anderson My Jo, John  (First
        line same as title)</td></tr>
    <tr><td rowspan='2'>Last May a Braw Wooer (two
        different first lines)</td><td>Last May a braw
        wooer cam down the lang glen,</td></tr>
    <tr><td>Last May, a braw wooer cam doun the lang
        glen, </td></tr>
</table>
```

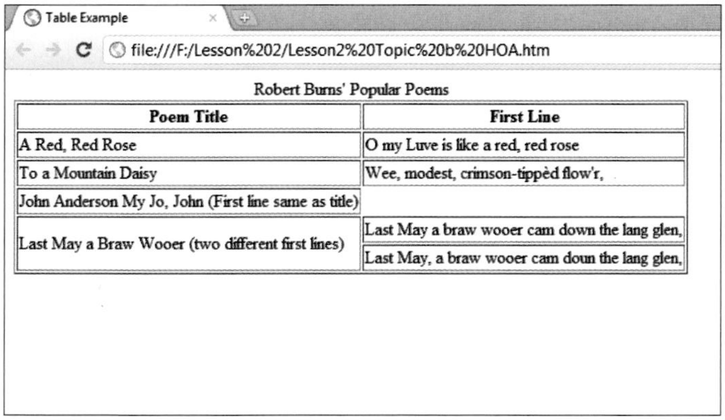

Figure 2-3

EXTRA INFO

As I mention nearby, designers have long used the `<table>` element not only to present information in a table format (the element's intended use), but also to lay out elements on a web page. Laying out web pages with tables used to be a necessity because there simply wasn't a better way.

With the introduction of CSS, and especially with HTML5 and CSS3, you can now lay out web pages without tables. The `<table>` element has been restored to its rightful place as the element to use when you want to display anything that you might put in a spreadsheet, such as a budget, a comparison of products and their features, or results from a series of experiments.

The upshot is that using tables for layout is strongly discouraged in the HTML5 specification. The reason is that assistive technologies have trouble knowing whether a table is showing data, as it's meant to, or is an invisible structure for layout purposes. Using tables for layout also makes your design less flexible, a concept addressed in detail in Lessons 4 and 5. All that said, if a table is the only way to create your desired layout, you can add the `role` attribute and set the value to `presentation`, like this `role="presentation"`, to indicate that assistive technologies can ignore a particular `<table>` element as they read content aloud to a user.

Inserting Images

To insert images, use the `<img />` element, an empty or void element that has no closing tag. To flesh out the tag with an image, you add the `src` attribute, which is required. Other important attributes are `alt`, `height`, and `width`, and in this section, you take a quick look at each one.

You can also insert SVG images, a vector graphic format that's an initiative of the W3C. You find a brief introduction to SVG images in this section, too.

Displaying image files with <img />

The `<img />` element's `src` attribute takes the network location (specified as a URL) as its value, which can be either relative or absolute:

- ✔ **A relative attribute** refers to a location in reference to the hosting page. In other words, a relative attribute refers to an image residing on the same site as the page displaying it. For example, many (most) sites keep their images in a separate folder, so if an image `myimage.png` was in a subfolder of the site called `myimages`, you could refer to the image file as follows:

  ```
  <img src="myimages/myimage.png"/>
  ```

  Although not strictly required in HTML5, you should *always* quote the value for reasons of backward-compatibility.

- ✔ **An absolute value** refers to a URL, which may or may not be on your site. If you're using an absolute URL, you *must* use the correct prefix `http://`. Here are two examples of absolute values. First a reference to your own site:

  ```
  <img src="http://mysite/myimages/myimage.png"/>
  ```

Now to someone else's site:

```
<img src="http://anothersite/theirimages/
         theirimage.jpg"/>
```

Another important attribute is `alt`, which holds alternate text for accessibility devices that read page contents aloud. *Alternate text* is a brief string of text describing the image, and you should always include an `alt` attribute (although it's not strictly required) to comply with accessibility guidelines. Alternate text is also handy in case the image does not display. The user may have images switched off, or the image may be in a format that the user agent (that is, the browser) does not support.

The `height` and `width` attribute control the display height and width of an image. Here's what you need to know about `height` and `width`:

- ✔ **The attribute values may be in pixels or a percentage.**

- ✔ **You can use these values to scale an image.** Proceed with caution, however: Pixel values greater than the actual image enlarge the image but can make it look pixelated, diminishing quality. Pixel values lower than the actual image shrink the display size, but the browser must still download the larger image, potentially forcing your user to use more bandwidth and wait longer for your page to load than necessary. Percentage values size the image relative to the container that holds it, a concept you explore in more detail in Lesson 4, which explains sizing elements with CSS.

  If you use an image twice, however, you don't have to worry about extra bandwidth and download time. Most browsers will cache your pages, scripts, and Images. This means that if you reuse your images, they don't have to be downloaded a second time. Thus using a scaled-down version of a large image can be quite efficient.

- ✔ **If just a single attribute is given, the other attribute value is scaled accordingly.** If both values don't match the image's aspect ratio, the image will look distorted.

- ✔ **If `height` and `width` are omitted, the image displays at the same size in which it was saved.** So, an image saved at a size of 120 pixels wide and 300 pixels tall will display that same size onscreen.

- ✔ **Omitting the `height` and `width` attributes can cause an annoying page jump when your image loads.** When your page downloads, first the HTML is downloaded and then the images. If the `height` and `width` values are given, a space is reserved for the image. If not, the page appears to jump when the image starts to download. Most users find this intensely annoying.

The following code snippet displays the same image twice on the page and uses all the attributes discussed in this section. Figure 2-4 shows the code displayed in a browser, where you can see that sizing the image as 50 percent makes the image width and height take up half the space of the browser window. (Again, you find about more about sizing in Lesson 4.)

```
<img src="images/babel.png" alt="Tower of Babel" />
<img src="images/babel.png" alt="Tower of Babel"
            height="50%" width="50%" />
```

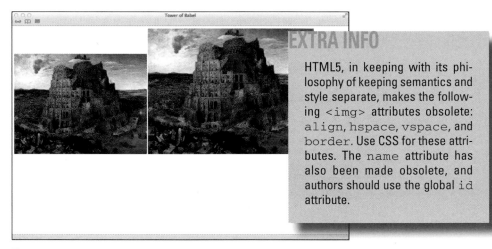

EXTRA INFO

HTML5, in keeping with its philosophy of keeping semantics and style separate, makes the following `<img>` attributes obsolete: `align`, `hspace`, `vspace`, and `border`. Use CSS for these attributes. The `name` attribute has also been made obsolete, and authors should use the global `id` attribute.

Figure 2-4

PRACTICE

You can use the sample image, `babel.png`, which is available via this book's companion site, with the following practice steps, or use an image of your own choosing.

In these steps, you practice working with the `<img />` tag:

1. **Create a folder for your HTML document and a subfolder called `images`, where you save the image file for this exercise.**

2. **Create the framework for an HTML document in your text editor and, within the `<body>` tag, add an `<img />` element that points to the image file.**

3. **Create a link to an off-site image, such as**

    ```
    http://media.wiley.com/spa_assets/site/wiley2/cvo/
            images/wiley-logo.gif
    ```

4. Create an `<img />` element with a bad `src` value, and give it an `alt` attribute.

5. Give your sample a `height` value much larger than its actual height.

6. Add a `width` value smaller than its actual width.

7. Save the HTML document as an `.htm` file and open it in your web browser.

Be sure to check out how the browser displays the different versions of the `<img />` element and the bad `src` value. Also check out the look of the `height` and `width` values.

Introducing SVG images

All modern browsers accept JPEG, GIF, and PNG image formats. These are *bitmap* graphics. Nearly all also accept the SVG (Scalable Vector Graphic) format, which is a *vector* graphic.

For simple drawings and diagrams, such as the one shown in Figure 2-5, a vector graphic is often much smaller than a bitmap, which is an advantage on the web. Vector images can also be blown up to almost any size without loss of resolution or an increase in file size. If you did the exercises in the preceding section, you know this is not the case with bitmap images. Vector images' chief disadvantage is that they don't show fine detail well and can't be used for photos.

LINGO

A **bitmap** graphic assigns a different color to each pixel that makes up the graphic. A **vector** graphic describes the graphic using a mathematical formula.

Vector graphics have been around for a long time, so what distinguishes the SVG vector format? SVG is

✔ **An initiative of the W3C.**

✔ **Designed to be readable.** In other words, by looking at the code that draws a vector graphic, a person can get an idea of what's going on with it. For example, the following code draws a simple line:

```
<line x1="0" y1="100" x2="100" y2="0" stroke-width="2"
      stroke="black" />
```

You just give the x- and y-coordinates near the beginning and end of a line, give the line a stroke-width in pixels, and give the stroke a color.

✔ **Increasingly used as a common medium for vector graphic programs** such as Inkscape, CoralDraw, and Adobe Illustrator.

SVG image

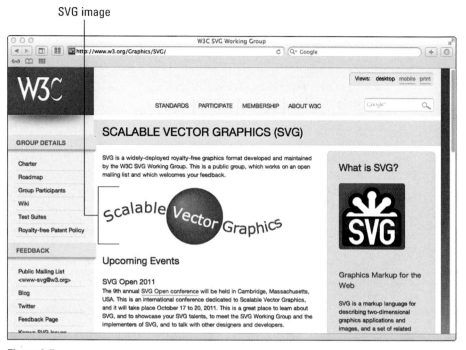

Figure 2-5

Although HTML5 enables you to write the code for SVG images from scratch using the `<svg>` element, most people simply produce SVG vector graphics in a vector-graphic program.

If you want to use raw code or see the code behind an SVG graphic, follow these general steps:

1. Create a vector graphic in your favorite graphics program and then save the graphic as an SVG format.

2. Open the folder containing the graphic, right-click the graphic, and open it in a browser.

3. Look at the view source, and then copy and paste it if necessary.

Although this section doesn't make you an expert, it does give you a solid grounding in the use of SVG. For more details, see the spec at `www.w3.org/graphics/svg`. Lesson 7 introduces ways to draw vectors with the new `<canvas>` element.

Linking from One Place to Another

Links are fundamental to what makes the web the web. You want your users to be able to click here and there, move wherever they want to go, and find what they're looking for — or what *you* want them to find, such as your product or service if a website is for business purposes. The following sections introduce you to the many ways you can insert links.

Creating text links

To link from one page to another, use the <a> element. The general syntax of a link element is as follows:

```
<a href="address">clickable
          area</a>
```

You replace *address* with the link's destination point and replace *clickable area* with the text that users click to visit the link. A link falls into one of three broad categories:

- **Cross-site:** This is a link to a page on a completely different website. The href value must be a full absolute URL, including the correct protocol — usually http://. Say your website is http://robertburnsbard.com and you want to link to another fan page about the poet, Robert Burns. You'd use a cross-site link that looks like this:

  ```
  <a href="http://www.poetrobertburns.com">Poet Robert
        Burns</a>
  ```

- **In-site:** This is a link to a document within your own site. In-site links are important navigational tools that enable your visitors to move around your site. You can use them to create navigation bars or point to useful pages in context of other content on your site.

EXTRA INFO

To keep your links organized, consider developing a linking policy for a website. Group similar types of links together, with no more than five links per group, so that your visitor isn't overwhelmed with places to go. If you have a larger group than five, create subcategories of links and divide them on the page. Also, place certain groups where visitors are most likely to look for them. For example, navigation links to main areas of a site often appear along the top of a web page, or along the left side. Links to resources outside a website often appear on the right-hand column of a page. Legal and copyright information typically appear at the bottom of a page. And of course, you always want to give users a way in and out of every page with organized links, usually with a link back to the home page and navigation bar. Find out more about grouping links in your HTML code in the "Creating Sections" section later in this lesson.

To create an in-site link, you can use an absolute or a relative address. If you want to link to a page called `life.htm` using an absolute address, it'd look like this:

```
<a href="http://www.robertburnsbard.com/life.htm">Find
     out more about Robert Burns' life.</a>
```

If all the files in your website are in the same folder, you can use a relative link, like this:

```
<a href="life.htm"> Find out more about Robert Burns'
     life.</a>
```

✔ **In-document:** An in-document link refers to a place within the same document and is often used on a long page, with lots of headings. At the top of a long page, you might link to each heading on the page so your visitors can jump to the section that interests them.

To add this type of link, the `href` value is a # and the `id` value of the page element. So if the seventh heading on a page has an `id` of s7, an in-document link to that heading looks like this:

```
<a href="#s7">Heading title</a>
```

You can use the same format to link to a specific point on another page. Simply combine the `id` technique used for in-document links with the absolute or relative value. In the following example, a relative link points to element with an `id` of s7 in the file `life.htm`:

```
<a href="life.htm#s7">Early
     years</a>
```

> **EXTRA INFO**
>
> In some legacy pages, you may see `< a name="somename">` used as an anchor instead of the `id` attribute. Don't even consider using this. It is obsolete!

Making images clickable

When you want images on your page to be clickable links, you can simply wrap them with an `<a>` element, like this:

```
<a href="mylink.html"><img src="images/babel.png"
          alt="Tower of Babel" width="200" height="200"
          /></a>
```

You can also make different areas of an image point to different destinations using an area map. These are rarely used now-a-days, but a classic example is an image of an actual map you can click to visit the web page pertaining to a specific location. To see how an area map works, check out the code snippet in Listing 2-2.

Listing 2-2:   Example Area Map

```
<body>
     <img src='scotland.jpg' usemap='#scot1'
          style='border:1px solid navy' alt=''/>
     <map name='scot1'>
          <area shape='circle' coords='250,360,20'
          href='#glasgow' alt='Glasgow'/>
          <area shape='circle' coords='330,360,20'
          href='#edin' alt='Edinburgh'/>
          <area shape='rect' coords='220,400,300,470'
          href='#ayr' alt='Ayrshire'/>
     </map>
     <div style='height:100px'>
     <h1 id='glasgow'>Glasgow</h1>
     <p>Ipsum Lorem...</p>
     </div>
     <div style='height:100px'>
     <h1  id='edin'>Edinburg</h1>
     <p>Ipsum Lorem...</p>
     </div>
     <div style='height:600px'>
     <h1 id='ayr'>Ayrshire</h1>
     <p>Ipsum Lorem...</p>
     </div>
</body>
```

Here's how the code in Listing 2-2 works to create an area map on the image shown in Figure 2-6

✔ I have given the image a usemap attribute, such as usemap='#scot1'. There goes the # sign again! The usemap attribute tells the browser to use an image map to create links in the image.

✔ The markup that begins with <map name='scot1'> and ends with </map> is the actual map; it uses coordinates and shapes within the image to create links.

✔ I have selected three areas, two circular areas and a rectangular area.

  • Circular areas take the x- and y-coordinates (in pixels from the top-left corner of the image) of the center and a radius in pixels.

  • Rectangles take two sets of x- and y-coordinates, the top-left and the bottom-right coordinates.

✔ The href attribute of the <area> element tells the browser what link to open when a user clicks within the region defined by the shape and coords attributes.

Figure 2-6

When you run your cursor over a designated area, a hand pointer appears, and if you click the map, you're linked to the correct place.

To experiment with area maps, try the following tasks with the `scotland.jpg` file, which you can download from this book's companion site. You may also discover why area maps are used so seldom now-a-days: They're very labor intensive!

Do the following:

- Make a circle link to Aberdeen City.
- Make a rectangular link to the Shetland isles.

Setting link targets

Take a quick look at the `target` element before moving on to the important topic of accessibility. The `target` attribute of the `<a>` element tells the browser where to load the page that the `href` attribute points to. By default, linked pages replace the current one in the same browser window. By using different values for `target`, you can change this default behavior.

For example, type the following:

```
<h1>Page 1</h1>
<p><a href='ch6_target1.htm'> Load this page by replacing
        this one</a></p>
<p><a href='ch6_target1.htm' target='newpage'> Load this
        page in a window named newpage</a></p>
<p><a href='ch6_target1.htm' target='myframe'> Load this
        page in an iframe named 'myframe'</a></p>
<iframe name='myframe'></iframe>
```

Click the various links and see where the page loads. In the second link, if you look carefully, you see that a new window has been created. No prizes for guessing where the page will be loaded in the third example!

Embedding Pages with the <iframe> Element

The <iframe> element enables you to embed a complete HTML document in a web page. For example, when a website needs to display banner ads from an ad server or an advertising network, such as Google AdSense, one way to place these ads on your site is by creating a window within your browser window (known as an *inline frame*) with the iframe element.

The basic syntax for the <iframe> element is simple:

```
<iframe src="http://www.someothersite.com/info.htm" />
```

Notice the slash before the closing > symbol in the iframe element. This slash indicates that the element is an empty element. You can also write an iframe element like this:

```
<iframe src="http://www.someothersite.com/info.htm"></
        iframe>
```

Both ways of writing an <iframe> element produce the same result. Which one you use is a matter of personal choice.

<iframe> takes the following global attributes:

✔ src is any relative or absolute URL.

✔ name allows easy referencing of the element using JavaScript.

✔ `width` and `height` are measured in pixels.

✔ `srcdoc`, `sandbox`, and `seamless` are attributes that can be used to increase security.

Creating Sections

When people create documents, they typically divide them into sections. For example, a letter might contain a header (with the address of the recipient and the address of the sender), the body (containing the real message of the letter), and a footer. For longer documents, you might have additional sections, such as chapters and parts.

You use all these sections to group related types of content to help the reader make sense of it. To facilitate the creation of sections in web pages, use *grouping elements,* which I explain in the next section.

Introducing new HTML5 elements

HTML5 offers a bundle of new grouping elements. Most important among those are the following:

✔ **<header>** groups elements that form the displayed header of the document. A website's header is often the same for several pages, and the header element creates a coherent, semantically descriptive group. For example, the following code creates a very simple header for a page about Robert Burns' life. You can see the header displayed in the browser in Figure 2-7. However, most headers, like the one shown in Figure 2-8, are more complex.

```
<header>
<h1>Robert Burns, Bard<br/>1759-1796</h1>
</header>
```

Header

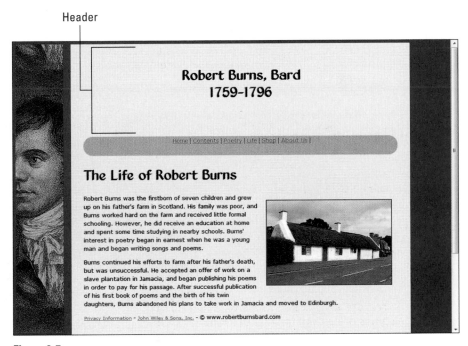

Figure 2-7

- ✔ **<hgroup>** groups headings. For example, it's common for articles to have a title followed by a subheading. By grouping the two headers with <hgroup>, you make it clear that the headers are closely related, as in this example from a future news site:

  ```
  <hgroup>
    <h1>Surviving the Zombie Apocalypse</h1>
    <h2>Be Prepared When the Undead Arrive</h2>
  </hgroup>
  ```

- ✔ **<article>** denotes content that works as a standalone article. The <section> element can be used to divide up the article.

- ✔ **<section>** defines a group of related content within a larger document that generally begins with a subheading that would be listed in an outline of the document. For example, terms and conditions and other long legal documents are often organized by sections.

- ✔ **<nav>** surrounds a *major* group of links, such as a linked Table of Contents or a navigation bar.

- ✔ **<footer>** groups the elements in a page footer.

Header

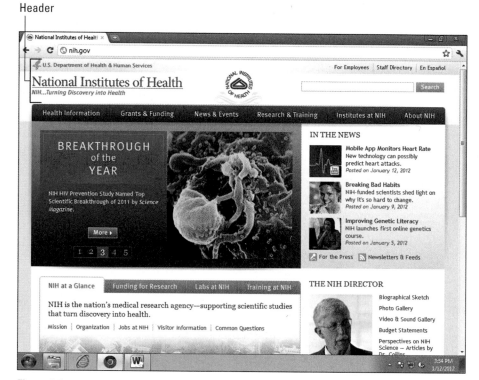

Figure 2-8

Figure 2-9 shows examples of an article, a major navigation element, and a footer, as they would display in a browser.

Article   Navigation   Footer

Figure 2-9

EXTRA INFO

A *server-side include* is, for the purposes of this lesson, a snippet of HTML that you intend to reuse throughout a website. Elements that appear on a website, such as the header, main navigation, and footer, are ideal candidates for server-side includes, which streamline website creation and updates. After you create an element that will repeat and insert it in the site's pages using server-side includes, you can edit just the include and not every page the element appears on. Any changes you make to that element appear everywhere in the site. Server-side includes are beyond the scope of this book, but I encourage you to find out more as you continue to explore web development.

Other new tags for layout include

✔ **<aside>** is for a block of text set off from, but related to, the main narrative. In typography, examples include a pull quote or a sidebar.

✔ **<figure>** defines a figure or illustration. Think about the figures in magazine articles to understand the purpose of this element. A figure is typically related to the content of the article, but not dependent upon being in any exact location in the article. So, if I were to say "Here is a picture of my puppy," you'd expect the picture to follow that sentence immediately. But if I were to say "See Figure 1-1 for a picture of my puppy," you'd expect the figure to be nearby, but not necessarily next in the flow of the page.

✔ **<figcaption>** is usually the child of a <figure> element and contains text that explains the figure.

GO ONLINE

The HTML5 spec, at the time of this writing has added 30 new elements, as well as numerous new attribute values. I cover the main new elements throughout this book. A good summary of the new elements can be found at www.w3schools.com/html5/html5_new_elements.asp.

Choosing a <div> or new semantic element

The <div> element is for marking off logical groups of content and giving it semantic meaning. In the past, the <div> element has been grossly overused and became a catch-all element. The new semantic HTML5 elements described in the preceding section now replace the main uses of <div>, but <div> still has uses within an HTML document.

REMEMBER

If your grouping seems to fall outside the new HTML5 elements or if you just need a general wrapper, use <div> to group elements in your code.

For example, refer to Figure 2-7, and you see a decorative image on the left side of the page. In the code, a `<div>` element keeps this decoration separate from the page content so that the image can tile down the page alongside the information about Robert Burns. The `<div>` element simply has an `id` attribute and no text or images; the image you see in Figure 2-7 is inserted as a background image using CSS:

```
<div id="burnsimage">
</div>
```

LINGO

In the context of HTML, **semantic** means that the name of the HTML element describes the purpose or role of the text that the element is meant to mark up. So header and footer, for example, are more semantic than a `<div>` with an `id` that may mean something to the developer, but not necessarily anyone else.

Adding Media Elements

The `<audio>` and `<video>` elements, new in HTML5, offer native media support for audio and video. Users don't need a plugin that can play the file type installed on their computers as they do with the `<embed>` element. All users do is click the file to play it.

Because the `<audio>` and `<video>` elements are new, however, you need to be aware of some current limitations and potential downsides to using these elements:

LINGO

Native support means that the HTML code can simply point to the media file that you want to play and then the browser plays the file.

- Your visitors must have an HTML5-capable browser that can work with the `<audio>` or `<video>` tag. Anyone using an older browser can't play the media.

- Among HTML5-capable browsers, support for different types of audio and video files is inconsistent. For example, an MP3 file plays in the Chrome, Internet Explorer 9, and Safari browsers, but not in the Firefox or Opera browsers.

- It's unclear whether the browser will download the file before determining that the file will play. Potentially, these elements could use bandwidth for a resource your website visitor can't access.

- When a browser can't play a file in an `<audio>` or `<video>` element, some browsers display a message for the visitors but others display nothing at all.

Because of these issues, it's important to provide an alternate way for users to view multimedia content. The most widely-supported of these is the <embed> element. So, in the following sections, I introduce you to the new elements and explain how to use the old standby, <embed>.

GO ONLINE

For up-to-date information about which media file types HTML5-capable browsers support, visit the following page from Mozilla: `https://developer.mozilla.org/En/Media_formats_supported_by_the_audio_and_video_elements`.

Knowing the attributes

The <video> and <audio> elements have a common set of attributes, in addition to the global attributes. The most commonly used attributes are

- **src** gives the address of the media resource.

- **autoplay** is a Boolean attribute, which means that it's either true or false. By default, autoplay is false. When the attribute is present, the audio or video will play as soon as it can. Unless you have a good reason to use autoplay, I recommend not using it so that mobile visitors don't use bandwidth for content unless they request to see it and so that other visitors aren't scrambling to mute the media if it plays unexpectedly in a quiet space.

  ```
  To set a Boolean attribute to true, you simply include
          the attribute in the element, as follows:
  <video src="myfile.mp3" autoplay>
  You may also see Boolean attributes with values, which
          is the more technically correct way to use
          them, but is less common:
  <video src="myfile.mp3" autoplay="autoplay">
  ```

- **loop** is another Boolean attribute. When set, the media plays in a loop, over and over and over and over again. Best practice is to *not* loop your audio.

- **muted** is a Boolean attribute that controls the default state of the audio output. When set, the audio is muted. This attribute may be helpful with a video that users didn't request, such as one embedded in a banner ad. By starting the video with the audio muted, you can then give the user control over whether he wants to hear the audio.

- **controls** is a Boolean attribute that indicates the author hasn't created a scripted controller and wants the user agent to provide its own set of controls.

- **width** enables you to set the media display width in pixels.

- **height** sets the media display height pixels.

Inserting media with new <audio> or <video> tags

The syntax for displaying an audio or video file can be as simple as the following:

```
<video src="videos/movie.ogg" controls></video>
```

The src attribute points to the movie.ogg file, which is saved in the videos subfolder of the website's root folder. The controls attribute tells the browser to display its default player for the site visitor to control playback.

Here's how the basic code for an audio file might look, just so you can see how similar the code for <audio> and <video> is:

```
<audio src="audio/sound.mp3" controls></audio>
```

If the src attribute of <audio> or <video> is absent, an element may take zero or more <source> elements. This element is handy because browsers don't all play all the different formats, and it enables you to give the browser a few file options. With the <source> element, you can put in multiple source files of different formats to make sure that the browser plays one of them. The <source> element is a child of the <audio> or <video> element, as depicted in the following example code:

```
<video width="320" height="240" controls="controls">
    <source src="movie.mp4" type="video/mp4" />
    <source src="movie.ogg" type="video/ogg" />
    Your browser does not support the video tag.
</video>
```

In this example, the width and height attributes set the dimensions for the player in pixels. You also see the controls attribute, and the text Your browser does not support the video tag.. When a browser follows the specification appropriately, a visitor to your site sees this text only if her browser can't play the file. Implementation of this feature is inconsistent at this time. Within each <source> element, an src attribute points to a video file, and the type attribute tells the browser what type of file the <source> element contains.

Embedding media the old-fashioned way

In 2000, I wrote, "There are two ways of embedding a multimedia file in an XHTML document: the official way of using the <object> element, and the way that works, the <embed> element!" Most browsers have supported the <embed> element for years, but it didn't become an officially supported element until HTML5.

The `<embed>` element has the following attributes in common with `<audio>` and `<video>`: `src`, `width`, and `height`, together with the global attributes. Most browsers also support an attribute that isn't official in them yet: `autoplay`. However, `autoplay` is official in the `<video>` and `<audio>` elements. (See the earlier section, "Knowing the attributes" for details.)

The syntax for `<embed>` is simple:

```
<embed src="slo-mo-3-hires.wmv"/>
```

The `<embed>` element plays multimedia content using a browser plugin. In the preceding example, `<embed>` looks for the correct plugin to use for a Windows Media Player (WMV) file. The website visitor still needs to have the correct plugins installed. Figure 2-10 shows what you see in Firefox if you don't. With other browsers, the behavior if you lack the correct plugin is patchy. Chrome tells you you're missing a plugin, but Safari shows nothing!

EXTRA INFO

Actually technically speaking, the `<embed>` element does allow the `autoplay` attribute. The element just considers the attribute to be an instruction to the plugin. The specification states, "unknown attributes are then passed as parameters to the plugin."

EXTRA INFO

Some of the most common plugins that people have installed are the Adobe Flash Player, Adobe PDF, Apple QuickTime, and Windows Media Player.

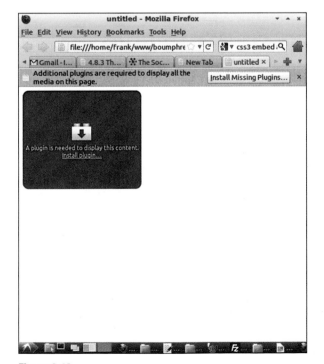

Figure 2-10

TIP

You also can use the `<a>` element to link to multimedia files:

```
<a href="slo-mo-3-hires.wmv">Bobby Jones Golf
          Swing</a>
```

Creating Accessible HTML

As you create your HTML code, you can do a few important things behind the scenes to ensure that a website is accessible to visitors with disabilities.

Blind people typically surf the web using either an aural or a Braille browser. An *aural browser* reads a page aloud to the user, and a *Braille browser* has a refreshable Braille display that raises dots in Braille to reflect what a screen reader captures from a web page. For these visitors, keep the following points in mind:

GO ONLINE

You can find a list of tools that test how accessible web pages are at `www.w3.org/wai/er/ tools/complete`.

✔ Tables do not display well on either type of browser, and the non-visual browsers usually render tables in list form, so bear this in mind when designing your site.

✔ Images should all have `alt` attributes describing the image succinctly. Also if the image is a graph or conveys information, make sure it has a descriptive caption spelling out its meaning. Find out how to add `alt` attributes in the section, "Inserting Images," earlier in this lesson.

✔ Use semantic markup, especially in headings and lists. A good test is to get rid of all styling and see whether your pages still convey a clear meaning.

✔ Almost 10 percent of users are red/green colorblind, and 3 percent are completely colorblind, so don't use color alone to convey differences of meaning. If you use colors, such as red and green, make sure they are different shades. This way a colorblind person can still distinguish between the two.

✔ People with poor sight often want to enlarge text. If you give your fonts an absolute size, this may create problems. Therefore, for font sizes, make sure that you use relative values, such as ems. Find out more about relative and absolute sizing in Lesson 4.

Accessibility also impacts people with motor impairments. For example, a user may not be able to use a mouse, so make sure that all elements, particularly form elements, are accessible via the keyboard.

Epilepsy is another consideration: Rapid flashing can trigger epileptic seizures, so don't have any rapidly flashing signs on your site, such as "You are a winner!" flashing over and over again. Most users find this intensely annoying anyway, and I suspect . . . no, I am sure the *only* reason flashing content is used is to try and trick the user to click it to get rid of the flashing!

Generally speaking, the following guidelines are just good web design fundamentals that also make for accessible websites:

- ✔ **Navigation:** Make navigation elements clear and predictable and give the links meaningful labels. Follow the guidelines I give earlier in the section, "Linking from One Place to Another.".

- ✔ **Readability:** Make your prose clear and precise.

- ✔ **Color:** Look at your page in black and white. To do this, you may have to take a screenshot of your page and import it into an imaging program that can convert your screenshot to a grayscale image. Check whether all the web page elements are still clear and readable.

GO ONLINE

The basic principles of designing accessible websites are straightforward enough, and if you just concentrate on good page design, you meet most of the accessibility requirements. Conversely, if you meet good accessibility guidelines, you have designed a good page.

Indeed the requirements for the mobile web and for people with disabilities are so similar that the W3C has devoted an entire section to it! You can find it at `www.w3.org/wai/mobile`.

For more details about accessibility and creating accessible sites, check out the W3C working group devoted to the accessibility guidelines at `www.w3.org/wai/policy`.

Saving and Validating an HTML Document

All good authors want to make sure that their documents are valid. A *valid document* is one that obeys the rules of the HTML version in which it was written. Luckily, validating a document is quite easy to do. Several validators are available, but the first and probably best, is the W3C validator (see Figure 2-11), which you can find at `http://validator.w3.org`.

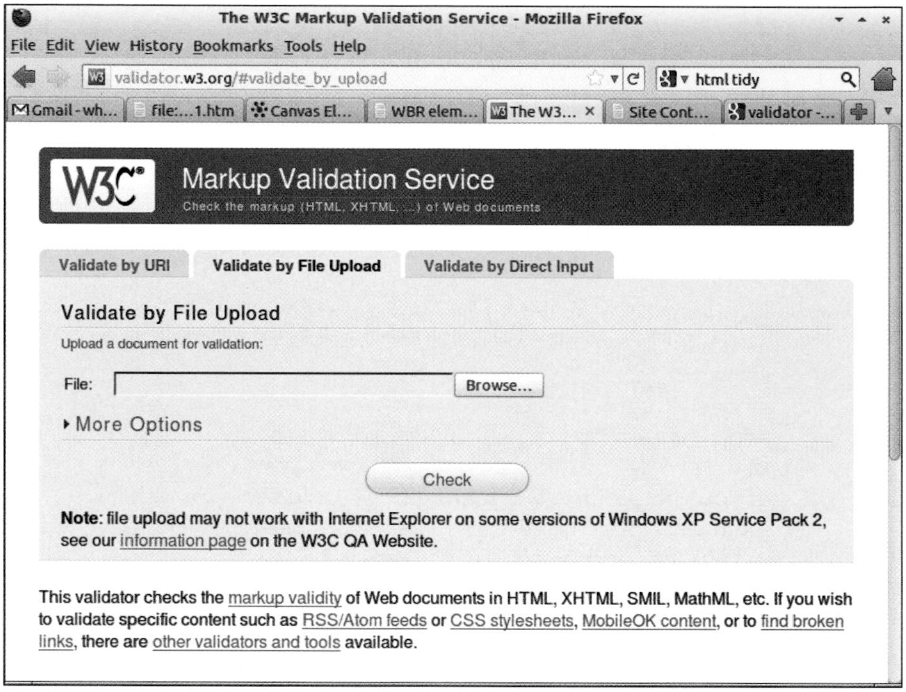

Figure 2-11

As you can see, the W3C validator offers three ways to validate an HTML file:

- ✔ If the file is already online, point the validator to the file's URL on the Validate by URI tab.
- ✔ Upload the file via the Validate by File Upload tab.
- ✔ Paste your document into a text box on the Validate by Direct Input tab.

This validator looks at the DOCTYPE of your file and validates it accordingly.

Listing 2-3 is a skeleton XHTML file for validation. The file contains a couple obvious errors and some not so obvious. See whether you can spot them.

Listing 2-3:   Sample File for Validation

```
<!DOCTYPE html PUBLIC "-//W3C//DTD XHTML 1.0 Strict//EN"
      "http://www.w3.org/TR/xhtml1/DTD/xhtml1-strict.dtd">
<html xmlns="http://www.w3.org/1999/xhtml" xml:lang="en"
          lang="en">
<head>
```

```
        <title>Validate</title>
        <meta http-equiv="content-type" content="text/
            html;charset=utf-8" />
        <meta name="generator" content="Geany 0.20" />
  </head>
  <body>
        <header><h1>Robert Burns</h1      </header>
        <h2>Life & Times</h2>
        <div class='body'>
            <p id='1'>"Lorem ipsum dolor sit amet, ...
            ...anim id est laborum."
            <p id='2'>"Lorem ipsum dolor sit amet, ...
            ...anim id est laborum."</p>
        </div>
        <footer><p>&copy Wiley</p></footer>
  </body>
  </html>
```

If you want to practice writing HTML, you can type this code into a text editor and save this file as L2_02.htm. Generally speaking, you can name an HTML file anything you like, with a few rules:

✔ The filename must start with a letter or number.

✔ The filename can't contain spaces, quotation marks, or certain disallowed characters ($ &+,/:;=?@<>#%{}|\^~[]`).

✔ The file must have the .htm file extension.

    If you want a file to display when someone visits your website address without entering a specific web page to display (such as when someone types **www.example.com**), name your file index.htm.

If you just want to practice validating the file, use the file L2_02.htm, which you can download from this book's companion website. (See the Introduction for details about the website.)

Now, you can validate the code in Listing 2-3 in the W3C validator. The following steps walk you through a couple trial file validations:

1. **Click the Check button when the file is ready to validate, using whichever method you prefer.**

    Here's what you should see in the results that the validator generates:

    • You already know that the header and the footer elements are new to HTML5, which is why the validator marks these as an error in XHTML.

    • The closing <h1 tag is not completed.

- The ampersand (&) should be made into an entity — `&amp;` — which you learn about in Lesson 2.

- The missing `</p>` tag was noted.

- The `id` attributes have illegal values, `<p id='1'>`. In XHTML, `id` values must start with an underscore or an alphabet letter.

- The `&copy` does not have a closing semicolon. The code should be `&copy;`.

2. **Change the file to a HTML5 DOCTYPE and save it as** `L2_03.htm`.

   Remember that the HTML5 DOCTYPE looks like `<!DOCTYPE html >`.

3. **Fix the closing `</h1>` tag.**

4. **Run `L2_03.htm` through the W3C validator.**

   Because you changed the DOCTYPE, the validator will see the document as an HTML5 document and thus finds only one error! Of course HTML5 accepts the `<header>` and `<footer>` elements. HTML5 also accepts the bare ampersand, the missing `<p>` tag, and the ID values. The validator only notes the missing semicolon in the `&copy` entity.

HTML5 is much laxer than XHTML in its markup requirements. Having noted that, for reasons of backward-compatibility, I still urge you to write to the stricter standards of XHTML. Validate your documents as XHTML and ignore the unsupported element error messages.

Summing Up

In this lesson, you learned the following basics about HTML5:

- ✔ Among the most often used elements for adding text are heading and paragraph elements. Headings can be structured in up to six levels. Other frequently used elements that contain text are ordered lists, unordered lists, and definition lists.

- ✔ You can make text editable in the browser by adding the new `contenteditable` attribute.

- ✔ Entities or Unicode characters in HTML code enable you to display special characters. Examples include symbols that aren't available on the keyboard, such as the copyright symbol, and characters that have a special meaning in HTML, such as the < character.

- ✔ Tables can organize data on a web page. Use the `<table>` element to set up the table, and the `<tr>`, `<th>`, and `<td>` tags to organize the data into rows and columns.

✔ To insert images, use the `<img />` tag with an `src` attribute to point to the file. The `src` attribute value can be absolute or relative.

✔ Text and images can turn into clickable links with the `<a>` element. You can set links to a point within the same page, a different page in a website, or another website.

✔ The `<iframe>` element can be used to embed external documents into your current web page.

✔ Grouping elements, such as `<header>`, `<article>`, and `<footer>`, help you organize web page content into semantic sections.

✔ The new `<audio>` and `<video>` tags offer native support for audio and video files, although browser support for these elements was unreliable as this book went to press. You can also insert multimedia files with the `<embed>` element, which is more broadly supported in browsers.

✔ Accessible web pages organize information clearly, use semantic tags, and otherwise follow design practices that make web pages easy to use for everyone, including those with visual, motor, or other disabilities.

✔ Running an HTML document through the W3C validator enables you to see how well your document conforms to the HTML version specified in your DOCTYPE.

Try-it-yourself lab

To experiment with some of the elements you learned in this lesson, follow these steps:

1. **Open a blank document in any text editor, such as Notepad (Windows) or TextEdit (Mac), and then save it as `test.htm`.**

2. **Insert the basic HTML5 page template markup.**

   Every HTML5 document that you create has certain basic elements. You can use the following markup as a template for every page you write:

   ```
   <!DOCTYPE html>
   <html>
   <head>
       <title>Page Title</title>
   </head>

   <body>

   </body>
   </html>
   ```

3. **Create some sections within the `<body>` element.**

   For example, start your page with an `<article>` element and then create an outline inside it using `<section>`, `<hgroup>`, and different levels of `<header>` elements.

4. Add content inside the article sections.

Any content will do. If you don't feel like writing actual words, go to www.lipsum.com to generate paragraphs of nonsense filler text. Make sure to wrap your paragraphs with <p> elements.

5. Save your document and then use the Open feature in your favorite browser to locate and open the web page.

Know this tech talk

The important terms used in this lesson are as follows:

absolute value: An src or href attribute value that uses a file's full locator, including the http:// and the website domain to locate a file.

area map: An image divided into different clickable areas that link to different destinations on the web.

bitmap image: An image made of pixels, which means sizing it up causes the image to lose resolution.

cross-site link: A link that points to a different website.

HTML entities: Code that a browser can convert into special characters, such as the copyright symbol.

in-document link: A link that points to a location on the same page as the link, using an HTML element's id attribute value and the # symbol in the <a> element's href attribute value.

in-site link: A link that points to a different page within the same website. This link may use a relative or absolute URL to point to the link destination.

relative value: An src or href attribute value that assumes files are all located in the same site root folder.

semantic markup: Markup that describes the meaning or purpose of content.

SVG: Scalable Vector Graphic; a web graphics format that describes shapes and lines using markup.

Unicode: A set of numbers representing characters developed by the Unicode consortium. See http://unicode.org.

vector image: An image that uses a mathematical algorithm to create a two-dimensional image. Changing the size of a vector image doesn't change its resolution.

Here's a quick reference of the HTML tags you learned about in this lesson.

Tag	Description	Tag	Description
`<a>`	Creates a link.	`<hgroup>`	Used to create a group of headings that are closely related.
`<article>`	Sets off a complete article.	`<iframe>`	Inline frame. Used to embed a document within another web page.
`<aside>`	Marks related but separate material, such as a sidebar.	`<img />`	Points to an image file and displays it on the page. Has no end tag but ends with `/>`.
`<audio>`	Inserts an audio file with native browser support for playback.	`<li>`	Creates a list item. Child of the `<ol>` or `<ul>` tags.
`<caption>`	Adds a caption to a table. Child of the `<table>` element.	`<nav>`	Denotes a major group of navigation links.
`<dd>`	Holds text of a definition. Child of the `<dl>` element.	`<ol>`	Creates an ordered list that automatically numbers list items.
`<div>`	Creates a wrapper when content needs to be grouped with a `class` or `id` attribute and a semantic tag isn't available.	`<section>`	A grouping element for defining subsections inside a document. Each typically has a subheading.
`<dl>`	Creates a definition list.	`<source>`	Child of the `<audio>` or `<video>` element. Used to specify multiple file formats for the content.
`<dt>`	Holds the word defined in a definition list. Child of the `<dl>` element.	`<table>`	Creates a table. May have a `border` attribute with a value of 1 or an empty string.
`<embed>`	Inserts multimedia (such as audio or video) but without native support for playback. User needs a plugin.	`<td>`	Holds table data, or the contents of a table cell. Child of the `<tr>` element.
`<figcaption>`	Holds text for an image caption. Child of the `<figure>` element.	`<th>`	Marks a column heading in a table. Child of the `<tr>` element.
`<figure>`	Hold illustrations or figures that don't need to be placed precisely in a document.	`<tr>`	Creates a row in a table. Child of the `<table>` element.

continued

Tag	Description	Tag	Description
`<footer>`	Marks up the content that holds footer content, such as copyright and administrative information, on a web page.	`<ul>`	Creates an unordered list, which automatically adds a bullet point to each list item.
`<h1>`...`<h6>`	Marks headings on a page and organizes them into levels.	`<video>`	Inserts a video into a web page and offers native browser support for playback.
`<header>`	Indicates the header content that typically appears at the top of a website's pages.		

Lesson 3

Creating Forms

- ✔ Use form and input elements to *create a framework for a form.*

- ✔ Create text boxes so that *users can fill in information to a form.*

- ✔ *Let visitors choose from a set of options* with check boxes, radio buttons, drop-down lists, and attributes.

- ✔ Add a button to *control the form.*

orms allow a user to communicate either with the page he's perusing, or to pass on information to a server. Every time you do a search in Google or Yahoo!, you use a form. Every time you shop online, you use several forms. Every time you log in to an account, you use a form. I'm not exaggerating when I say that forms are the engine powering modern commerce!

In this lesson, you learn how to set up your forms in an HTML document, combining form elements that have weathered the test of time with elements that are new in HTML5.

What you don't learn in this lesson is how to connect your form with a server so that data that site visitors enter is passed to a server. This lesson focuses on the HTML. Lesson 6 offers an introduction to scripting and explains how to make your form functional.

Setting Up the Form Structure

Setting up the structure of a form not only keeps your form organized so that users can navigate through the options easily, but also enables the browser to read all your form elements accurately. This topic starts with the <form> element that frames every form and goes on to show you how to organize form elements into sections with <fieldset>, label those sections with the semantic <legend> element, and group each form input with its corresponding label.

Starting with the <form> element

You show a form using the <form> element, which can take all the global attributes, plus the following:

✔ **action:** The address where information on the form is sent.

✔ **name:** This attribute gives the form a unique name, which then enables the script to access the form by name.

✔ **method:** The method value indicates what method is used to send the information on the form: GET or POST. The default is GET.

An empty form element and attribute values look like this:

```
<form action=" " name=" " method=" ">
</form>
```

You find out how the values for these attributes enable your form to work in Lesson 6. For now, just know that these are the <form> attributes you use most often.

Within a form element, you can add most any element that appears within the body of an HTML document. For example, you can insert headings, paragraphs, images, and so on. The <form> element can also take several child elements that are specific to <form>, including the following:

✔ **<input>:** This is the workhorse of a form. I explain this element in detail throughout this lesson.

✔ **<textarea>:** When you want the user to be able to input large amounts of text, this is the form element to use. See "Letting visitors add lots of text" later in this lesson for details.

✔ **<select>:** You use <select> to create a drop-down list. Add an <option> element for each option on the drop-down list. See "Enabling Visitors to Choose Options" later in this lesson for details.

✔ **<button>:** This element, rarely used now-a-days, produces a button with an image on it. Most forms create buttons using an <input> element, as you discover in "Adding Buttons to Control the Form" near the end of this lesson.

✔ **<datalist>:** The <datalist> element, new to HTML5 and not yet supported by every browser, provides a list of predefined options for a standard text input field. The browser can use this list to provide an autocomplete feature for text inputs.

✔ **<keygen>:** Also new to HTML5, the <keygen> element is designed to be used in logging in a user to a server. The problem, however, is that it's supported by every browser except for Internet Explorer — and Internet Explorer has no plans to support it. So, for now, this element isn't really practical.

✔ **<output>:** The final new form element in HTML5, the <output> element, can be used to display the result of a calculation involving several <input> elements. For example, if you asked users for two numbers, the <output> element could display the result of adding those numbers together.

Organizing a form into sections

On a longer form, dividing the form into smaller sections can help visitors fill out the form.

To create sections in the form, you can use the <fieldset> element to form groups and the <legend> element to label the groups.

Each section you want to create needs an opening and closing <fieldset> tag. Within the <fieldset> tags, you insert a pair of opening and closing <legend> tags. In each tag, add the name of the section. For this form, I created three sections: Contact Information, Robert Burns Preferences, and Comments. Check out the sections in Figure 3-1.

```
<form action=" " name=" " method=" ">

<fieldset>
     <legend>Contact Information</legend>
</fieldset>

<fieldset>
     <legend>Robert Burns Preferences</legend>
</fieldset>

<fieldset>
     <legend>Comments</legend>
</fieldset>

</form>
```

Legend for each section of the form

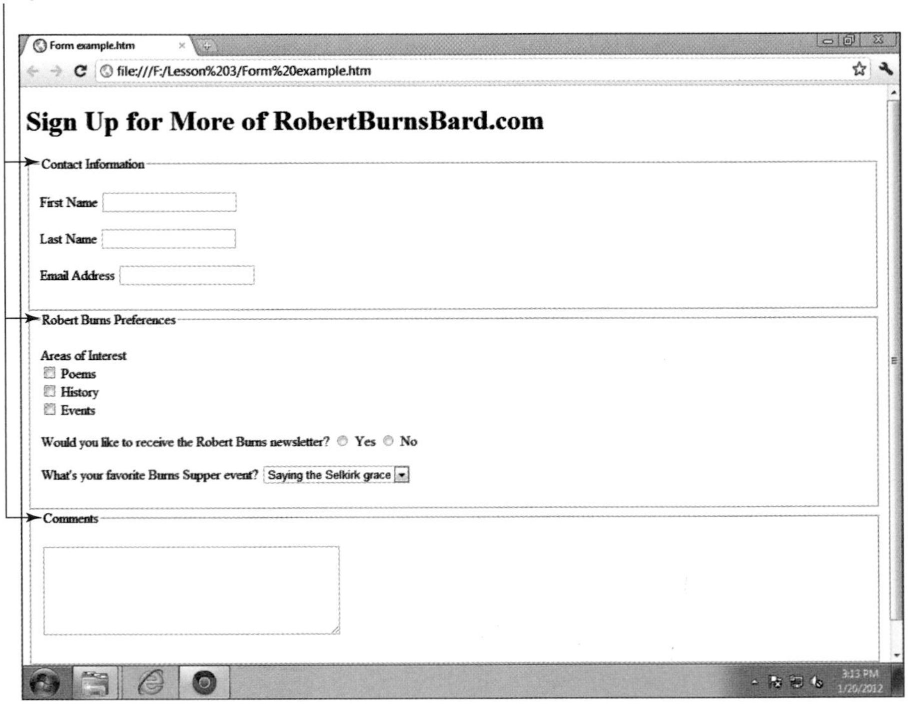

Figure 3-1

Labeling <input> elements

The `<input>` element is the workhorse of a form. For most elements that enable visitors to fill out a form, use the `<input>` element's `type` attribute to tell the browser what type of form element you want to show. Each input also needs a label, which tells visitors what information to provide or select.

To group each label with its corresponding input, you can surround each input with a paragraph tag, like this:

```
<p>
    <label>First Name</label>
    <input type=" " />
</p>
```

To plot where visitors supply information in the example form, you can insert the paragraph tags for each label and input. Then add the <label> and <input> elements with empty type values:

```
<form action=" " name=" " method=" ">

<fieldset>
     <legend>Contact Information</legend>
     <p>
          <label>First Name</label>
          <input type=" " />
     </p>

     <p>
          <label>Last Name</label>
          <input type=" " />
     </p>

     <p>
          <label>Email Address</label>
          <input type=" " />
     </p>
</fieldset>

</form>
```

The next section, "Making Different Types of Input Boxes," introduces different values you can use for the type attribute, depending on the kind of information you want the <input> element to collect.

PRACTICE

Imagine you need to create a form for a real estate agent's website. On the inquiry page, the agent wants the form to ask website visitors for the following information: name, e-mail address, and what type of work the visitor is interested in (selling a home, buying a home, staging a home, renting a home, or something else). The form also needs to include a brief description of the property the visitor is selling or looking for, the neighborhood, and the price range. The agent also wants the form to ask what's the best way to contact the visitors. Using all this information, create a framework for the form as follows:

1. **Decide how you'd organize the data into groups of information.**

2. **Create <fieldset> elements and a <legend> element for each group.**

3. **Set up a <label> and an <input> element for each box or other form element the visitor will need to fill out.**

Making Different Types of Input Boxes

A box where visitors input text is a basic form element. You can make text boxes more specialized — and get better information from website visitors — by selecting a `type` attribute that corresponds to the type of data the form requests. For example, if you want an e-mail address, you can use a special `type` attribute called `email` that will check whether the data follows the format of an e-mail address when the user submits the form. This process of checking data is *validation*.

The `type` you use is important when it comes time to validate the form, as you discover in Lesson 6. In this lesson, you focus on setting up the HTML in the form so the data is validated in the browser. HTML5 adds several new `type` values that enable you to make greater use of browser validation features.

In this section, you start by creating a basic text entry box. Then, you discover how to create specialized types of text boxes using `type` values that are new in HTML5. Also, you find out how to use the `<textarea>` element, which creates another special type of text box that's new in HTML5.

Creating a basic text entry box

The example form shown earlier, in Figure 3-1, has a basic text entry box for the visitor's first name and last name.

To create a basic text entry box, use an `<input>` element with a `type` attribute of `text`. This tells the browser that visitors can input any sort of text into the box. Basic text boxes are generally used for input that's expected to be relatively short, such as a name or phone number. Although you can allow users to enter millions or characters into a text box or paste in a whole document, it's not practical because text boxes display on only one line.

You also add a `name` attribute so that the form can send whatever the user types as a name/value pair, in which the *name* is whatever you enter as the `name` attribute and the *value* is the text that your visitor enters into the form. Here are the two input elements for First Name and Last Name:

```html
<input type="text" name="firstname" />

<input type="text" name="lastname" />
```

After I add labels to each input, the code looks like this:

```
<p>
    <label>First Name</label>
    <input type="text"
        name="firstname" />
</p>

<p>
    <label>Last Name</label>
    <input type="text"
        name="lastname" />
</p>
```

Figure 3-2 shows how these elements display in the browser, along with an e-mail text box that I explain in the next section.

If you want whatever a user types into a box to be hidden from view, you can use the `password` type value, instead of `text`. When you use this value, the browser displays dots or a similar character to hide a user's typing, a practice you're likely very familiar with. Here's what the code looks like:

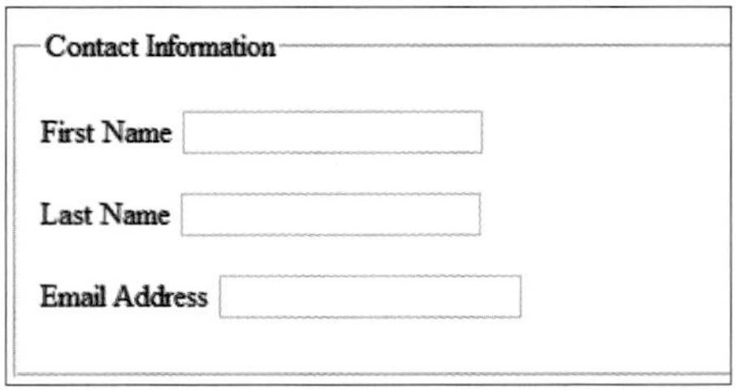

Figure 3-2

```
<input type="password"
        name="pwd" />
```

Exploring new HTML5 input types

HTML5 adds several new input types that enable you to designate a special purpose for a text box. The following list introduces you to the more popular ones:

- ✔ **email:** If you create an `<input>` element with a `type` attribute value of `email` (and the browser supports this input type), the browser will accept only a valid e-mail address in that text box from the user filling out the form. The browser determines the address is valid by checking the input to make sure that it matches the standard format for an e-mail address: name@something. something. In other words, if you typed joe@testing.com, the browser would accept that as a valid e-mail address. But, if you typed this is my email address into an <input> element with a type attribute value of email, the browser would reject it.

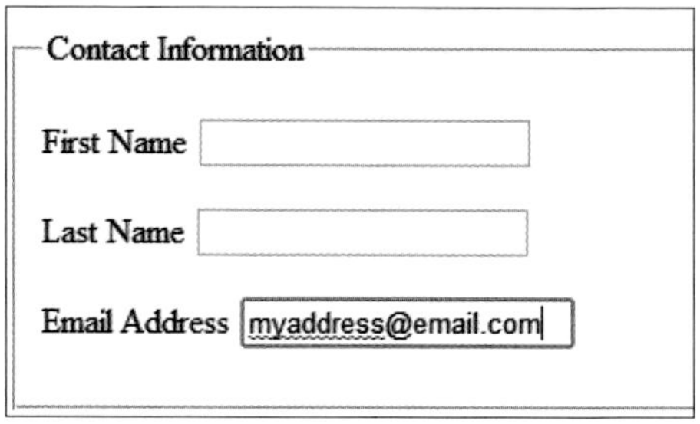

Here's an example of the code behind the Email Address text box in Figure 3-3:

```
<input type="email" name="email" />
```

> Contact Information
>
> First Name [   ]
>
> Last Name [   ]
>
> Email Address [myaddress@email.com]

Figure 3-3

✔ **url:** When you want users to enter a website address, use the url value. The browser checks for a standard URL format, such as http:// www.test.com or http://website.test.net. Here's an example:

```
<input type="url" name="addnamehere" />
```

✔ **number:** The number value tells the browser to check whether the characters entered are all numbers. You can also set an upper and lower limit on the number with the min and max attributes. The min value of 1 means the number entered must be no less than 1. The max value of 100 means the number entered can't be greater than 100. When you set limits, a scroll box enables visitors to choose a number within the limits you set.

```
<input type="number" name="addnamehere" min="1"
       max="100" />
```

✔ **range:** This value, too, limits what users can enter, but to select a number within a specified range, site visitors must use a slider instead. Set the range using the min and max attributes.

```
<input type="range" name="addnamehere" min="1"
       max="100" />
```

✔ **search:** The user enters a search term. The box behaves like a regular text box, but the search value makes the code semantic.

```
<input type="search" name="addnamehere" />
```

In Figure 3-4, you can see how the different `<input>` type attributes appear in a browser.

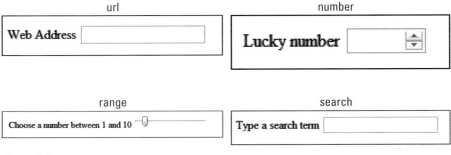

Figure 3-4

Letting visitors add lots of text

When you want to provide users with a multiline text box suitable for entering large amounts of text, use the `<textarea>` element. Like `<input>`, `<textarea>` has angle brackets and is a child of the `<form>` element. Unlike `<input>`, `<textarea>` has both an opening and closing tag.

To control the size of the text box that `<textarea>` creates, use the `rows` and `cols` attributes or, preferably, use CSS to specify a height and width. You must also give `<textarea>` a name value. Here's an example of code for a `<textarea>` element, and you can see how it appears in a browser in Figure 3-5:

Figure 3-5

```
<textarea rows="6" cols="40" name="addnamehere">
          </textarea>
```

You can practice working with different types of input boxes by continuing to work on the imaginary form for a real estate agent. (See the Practice icon at the end of "Labeling <input> elements" earlier in this lesson if you need a refresher on this example.) Within the organization that you created for the form, do the following:

1. Use an `<input>` element with a `type` value of `text` for the text box where users enter a name.

2. Use an `<input>` element that checks for an e-mail address where the form requests it.

3. Set up a text box that checks whether users entered only numbers for a phone number.

4. Use the `<textarea>` element to create a place where users can enter a longer property description.

5. Create a slider that users can adjust to indicate their price range.

Enabling Visitors to Choose Options

Forms often limit what options users can choose through elements like drop-down lists, list boxes, check boxes, and radio buttons. Some options enable users to choose only one option, and others enable users to choose as many as they like. Either way, form elements that limit users' options enable you to receive more consistent answers via your form.

The following sections explain how you can give users a list of options to choose from. You also learn how HTML5 adds new `type` attribute values for dates, times, and more.

Offering multiple options with check boxes

Use the `checkbox` input type when visitors need the ability to make multiple selections from a list of options. The following steps walk you through the setup of a set of check boxes:

1. **Add a paragraph element and label to group the options together within the form and provide instructions about how the user fills out the form element:**

```
<form action=" " name=" " method=" ">
<p>
<label>Does the item contain any of the following
        colors?</label><br />
</p>
</form>
```

2. **Add an `<input>` element for each check box you want to appear on the form:**

```
<form action=" " name=" " method=" ">
<p>
<label>Does the item contain any of the following
        colors?</label><br />
    <input type=" " name=" " />
    <input type=" " name=" " />
    <input type=" " name=" " />
    <input type=" " name=" " />
    <input type=" " name=" " />
</p>
</form>
```

3. **Set the `type` attribute to `checkbox` and give each `<input>` element a unique `name` attribute:**

```
<form action=" " name=" " method=" ">
<p>
<label>Does the item contain any of the following
        colors?</label><br />
    <input type="checkbox" name="red" />
    <input type="checkbox" name="white" />
    <input type="checkbox" name="blue" />
    <input type="checkbox" name="orange" />
    <input type="checkbox" name="yellow" />
</p>
</form>
```

4. **Add text after the `<input>` element that tells the user what option the check box stands for.**

   The text for the example form is colored green in the following code. You can also use the `<br />` tag to add a line break so that each check box appears on a separate line.

```
<form action=" " name=" " method=" ">
<p>
<label>Does the item contain any of the following
        colors?</label><br />
  <input type="checkbox" name="red" /> Red <br />
  <input type="checkbox" name="white" /> White <br />
  <input type="checkbox" name="blue" /> Blue <br />
  <input type="checkbox" name="orange" /> Orange
        4<br />
  <input type="checkbox" name="yellow" /> Yellow
</p>
</form>
```

The boxes that a user checks will return an on value after you make the form function by adding scripting, the topic of Lesson 6. Figure 3-6 shows how this group of check boxes appears in a browser.

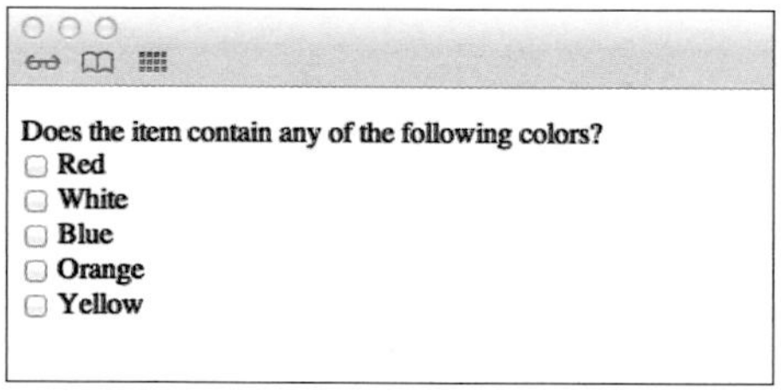

Does the item contain any of the following colors?
☐ Red
☐ White
☐ Blue
☐ Orange
☐ Yellow

Figure 3-6

REMEMBER

Giving each <input> element a different name value is what enables visitors to check more than one check box.

Selecting only one option with radio buttons

Radio buttons limit users' choice on a form to only one of the options provided. The following steps walk you through the creation of a group of radio buttons:

1. **Add a paragraph element and label to group the options together within the form and provide instructions about how the user fills out the form element:**

   ```
   <p>
   <label>Is it animal, vegetable, or mineral? </label>
   </p>
   ```

2. **Add an <input> element for each radio button you want to appear on the form:**

   ```
   <p>
   <label>Is it animal, vegetable, or mineral? </label>
   <input type=" " />
   <input type=" " />
   <input type=" " />
   </p>
   ```

3. **Set the type attribute to radio and give each <input> element the same name attribute:**

   ```
   <p>
   <label>Is it animal, vegetable, or mineral? </label>
   <input type="radio" name="composition" />
   <input type="radio" name="composition" />
   <input type="radio" name="composition" />
   </p>
   ```

By giving several radio buttons the same name, you limit the choice to one of the options.

4. **Add a unique `value` attribute for each radio button so that the script (which you add later) can determine what option the user selected:**

```
<p>
<label>Is it animal, vegetable, or mineral? </label>
<input type="radio" name="composition"
       value="animal"/>
<input type="radio" name="composition"
       value="vegetable"/>
<input type="radio" name="composition"
       value="mineral"/>
</p>
```

5. **Add text that follows each `<input>` element and tells the user what option the radio button stands for.**

```
<p>
<label>Is it animal, vegetable, or mineral? </label>
<input type="radio" name="composition"
       value="animal"/> Animal
<input type="radio" name="composition"
       value="vegetable"/> Vegetable
<input type="radio" name="composition"
       value="mineral"/> Mineral
</p>
```

Figure 3-7 shows how this example would appear in a browser.

| Is it animal, vegetable, or mineral? ○ Animal ○ Vegetable ○ Mineral |

Figure 3-7

Creating a drop-down list of options

When you want a form to present a list of options as either a drop-down list or a list box, use the `<select>` element in conjunction with the `<option>` element.

The `<select>` element, like `<input>` and `<textarea>`, is a unique child element of `<form>`.

This example drop-down list appears within a set of paragraph tags and has a label, just like preceding examples in this lesson. The following steps walk you through how I created the rest of the drop-down list:

1. **Add a `name` attribute to the `<select>` element so that whatever option the user chooses from the drop-down list can be sent to the server as a name/value pair:**

```
<form action=" " name=" " method=" ">

<p>
<label>What is your favorite Burns Supper event?
     </label>
   <select name="supperevent">
   </select>
</p>

</form>
```

2. **Add an `<option>` element for each option that needs to appear in the drop-down list:**

```
<form action=" " name=" " method=" ">

<p>
<label>What is your favorite Burns Supper event?
     </label>
   <select name="supperevent">
        <option > </option>
        <option > </option>
        <option > </option>
        <option > </option>
   </select>
</p>

</form>
```

A `<select>` element can have any number of `<option>` child elements. Each `<option>` element corresponds to an item that users can choose from the drop-down list.

3. **Give each `<option>` element a `value` attribute and text that will display in the browser so that users know what option they're choosing:**

```
<form action=" " name=" " method=" ">

<p>
<label>What is your favorite Burns Supper event?
     </label>
```

```
<select name="supperevent">
    <option value="grace">Saying the Selkirk
grace</option>
    <option value="piping">Piping</option>
    <option value="haggis">Cutting the haggis
</option>
    <option value="auld">Singing <em>Auld Lang
Syne</em></option>
</select>
</p>

</form>
```

TIP

If you want to create a list box instead of a drop-down list, use the `<select>` element's `size` attribute. If set to a value greater than 1, a list box displaying the number of options indicated in the `size` attribute appears instead of the drop-down list. For example, if the `<select>` element has four options, set the `size` attribute to 4 so that users could see all the options in the list box. Here's what the code for a list box looks like, and you can see this element displayed as a drop-down list and a list box in Figure 3-8.

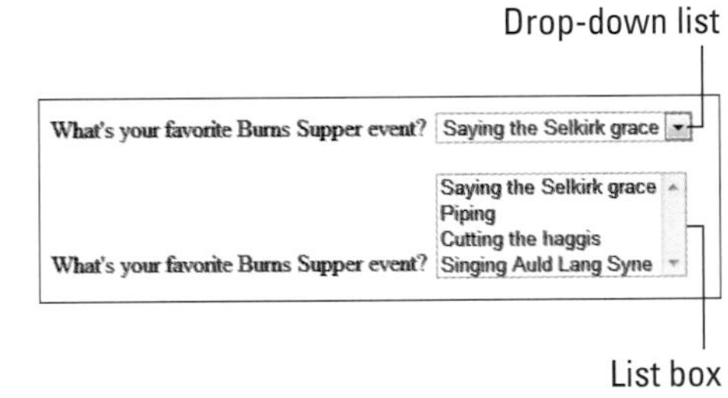

Drop-down list

List box

Figure 3-8

```
<form action=" " name=" " method=" ">

<p>
<label>What is your favorite Burns Supper event? </label>
    <select name="supperevent" size="4">
        <option value="grace">Saying the Selkirk grace
        </option>
        <option value="piping">Piping</option>
        <option value="haggis">Cutting the haggis
        </option>
        <option value="auld">Singing <em>Auld Lang
        Syne</em></option>
    </select>
</p>

</form>
```

Adding attributes for selecting time and date

The following time and date input type values are new in HTML5:

✔ `<input type="time" name="addnamehere" />`: Allows the user to select a time, without a time zone

✔ `<input type="date" name="addnamehere" />`: Allows the user to select a date

✔ `<input type="datetime" name="addnamehere" />`: Allows the user to select a date and time, with a time zone

✔ `<input type="datetime-local" name="addnamehere" />`: Allows the user to select a date and time, without a time zone

✔ `<input type="week" name="addnamehere" />`: Allows the user to select a week and year

✔ `<input type="month" name="addnamehere" />`: Allows the user to select a month and a year

When these new date types are supported by browsers, a date picker opens, as shown in Figure 3-9, and you can select the appropriate data. Today, however, these date input types are fully supported only by the Opera browser.

Figure 3-9

PRACTICE

To practice creating check boxes, radio buttons, and drop-down lists, return to the imaginary form for a real estate agent. (See the Practice icon at the end of "Labeling <input> elements" earlier in this lesson if you need a refresher on this example. Note that this earlier Practice was built upon the section "Letting visitors add lots of text.") Within the organization that you created for the form, do the following:

1. **Add check boxes that enable visitors to select each service a visitor might need.**

   So, if the agent offers services for anyone selling a home, buying a home, staging a home, or renting a home, add a check box for each of these.

2. **Create a drop-down list that enables visitors to select the neighborhood or zip code that most interests them.**

   You can make up neighborhood names or use names from your own area. This form is just for practice, after all.

3. **Add radio buttons that enable visitors to select their preferred method of contact.**

   For example, visitors might be able to select E-Mail, Phone, or Text Message.

Adding Buttons to Control the Form

When users are done filling out a form, they expect to see a button that whisks their information off to the right server.

In the HTML part of a form, you just make the button appear on the page and assign it a basic function: a blank button, a reset button, or a submit button. The blank buttons don't do much until you add scripting that can respond to a user's button click.

To create the HTML part of a button, start with a basic <input> element. Use the type attribute to indicate what the button's function will be. You can also set the type attribute to button, reset, or submit, as follows:

```
type="button"
type="reset"
type="submit"
```

When you use an <input> element to create a button, you typically add a value attribute as well. The value attribute enables you to choose what text appears on the button. If you don't add your own button text, the default button text appears. Table 3-1 outlines what you need to know for each type of button. Figure 3-10 shows how example buttons from Table 3-1 appear in a browser.

Table 3-1   **What You Need to Know for Each Button**

Button Type	Example Code	Default Button Text	Without Scripting, the Button....	With Scripting, the Button....
Blank	`<input type="button" value="Click Me"/>`	No text appears on the button.	Does nothing at all. (Scripting adds all the magic for this button.)	An event handler captures a JavaScript event, which you learn all about in Lesson 6.
Reset	`<input type="reset" value= "Clear Form Entries"/>`	Reset	Resets all the form elements, which means they revert to their default values.	Scripting is rarely used on this button.
Submit	`<input type="submit" value=" Submit Form"/>`	Submit Query	Sends the name/value pairs on the form to the server, based on the address in the form's `action` attribute. Things must be set up on the server-side to accept the data, a concept beyond the scope of this book.	Scripting is often used to check the validity of the fields before the form is submitted. When the code contains new HTML5 input types, such as `type= "date"`, the browser checks without additional scripting. See Lesson 6.

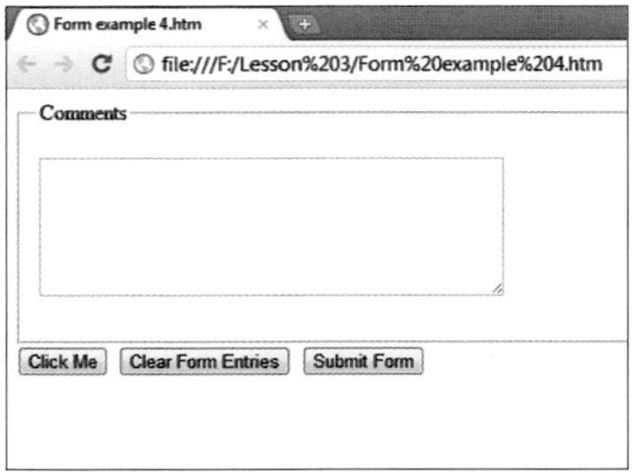

Figure 3-10

Summing Up

In this lesson, you learned how to set up a form in an HTML document, including all the following basics:

✔ The `<form>` element marks the beginning and end of the form. The attributes `action`, `name`, and `method` enable the form to work with scripting.

✔ You can organize a form into sections using the `<fieldset>` element. The `<legend>` tag, which is a child of `<fieldset>`, adds labels to each section in a form.

✔ You create many of the features visitors use to fill out a form with the `<input>` element. Its `type` attribute determines what type of `<input>` element appears onscreen. A `name` attribute enables the browser to send name/value pairs to a web server.

✔ The `type` attribute for a basic text box is `text`. Among the new `type` attribute values that HTML5 offers are `email`, `url`, `number`, `range`, and `search`. If you want text that visitors type into a text box to be hidden, set the `type` attribute's value to `password`.

✔ A new form element in HTML5, `<textarea>`, enables visitors to enter longer amounts of text into a form.

✔ To create check boxes, which enable visitors to select more than one option, use a `type` attribute value of `checkbox` and a `name` attribute value that describes the box. Remember, too, to label each check box with text that tells the visitor what option he's selecting.

✔ When you want users to select only one option, use the radio button form element. To create a group of radio button options, give each radio button in the group the same `name` attribute and then add a `value` attribute that reflects whatever option visitors select. The `text` attribute value that creates a radio button is, predictably, `radio`.

✔ A drop-down list enables visitors to choose an option from a menu. The `<select>` element tells the browser to display the drop-down list, and `<option>` elements, which are child elements of `<select>`, contain each choice visitors see in the list.

✔ HTML5 adds new input options for selecting the time and date: `time`, `date`, `datetime`, `datetime-local`, `week`, and `month`. You can use any of these options as a `type` attribute value in the `<input>` element.

✔ You can use the `<input>` element to create three types of buttons: generic, reset, and submit.

Try-it-yourself lab

If you worked with the Practice activities throughout this lesson, you've had a chance to play with creating some of the different form elements. To further build your experience creating form elements in HTML, look at the following figure and decide what form elements are the best choices for each part of the form. In your text editor, create an HTML document that includes all the elements shown in the figure. If you need help, view the source code in the companion file, `L3_01.htm`, which you can download from this book's companion website (see the Introduction for details).

Know this tech talk

> **label:** Text associated with an input field; it generally indicates to the user what she should type or select.
>
> **name/value pair:** A way of storing or transmitting data in which a text name is assigned to represent another piece of data. Examples include `name=Ed`, `quantity=4`, and `phone=555-555-5555`.
>
> **validation:** The process of checking user input for expected or required data or data formatting.

Table 3-2 outlines important tags, what the tags do, and important unique attributes when relevant.

Tag	What It Does	Important Unique Attributes
`<fieldset>`	Organizes form elements into groups.	`name`, `form`
`<form>`	Creates a `<form>` in an HTML document.	`action`, `name`, `method`

`<input>`	Creates many types of form elements that enable visitors to input data into a form. The type of input created depends upon the value of the `type` attribute.	`name` attribute
		
		`value` attribute
		
		`type` attribute values:
		
		  `text`, `password`
		
		  `email`, `url`, `number`, `range`, `search`
		
		  `checkbox`, `radio`
		
		  `time`, `date`, `date-time`, `datetime-local`, `week`, `month`
		
		  `button`, `reset`, `submit`

`<label>`	Holds text that labels, or provides instructions for how to select items from, an `<input>` element.	`for`, `form`
`<legend>`	Labels groups of form elements created with `<fieldset>`. Child of the `<fieldset>` element.	This item has no unique attributes.
`<option>`	Contains values for a drop-down list. A child of the `<select>` element.	`disabled`, `label`, `selected`, `value`
`<select>`	Makes a drop-down list.	`autofocus`, `disabled`, `form`, `multiple`, `name`, `size`
`<textarea>`	Creates a text box for entering paragraphs of text.	`autofocus`, `cols`, `disabled`, `form`, `maxlength`, `name`, `placeholder`, `readonly`, `rows`, `wrap`

Lesson 4

Creating Basic CSS Rules

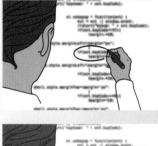

- ✔ *Put together selectors, properties, and values* in the CSS rule syntax.

- ✔ *Decorate your background* with a simple color or an image.

- ✔ You can *center your elements and create columns* on a web page.

- ✔ CSS rules *can be saved externally, internally, or inline* on a web page.

- ✔ Child elements *inherit styles* and browsers *resolve style conflicts.*

Cascading Style Sheets (CSS) gives you control over every aspect of how an HTML page is presented to the user. For example, you may use CSS to set the fonts, sizes, weights (or boldness), and colors of text. You might also use CSS to arrange pictures and blocks of text on a page. Or, if you want a page to look different when it's viewed on a mobile device versus when it's viewed on a desktop browser, CSS is the key to that, too.

In this lesson, I give you a taste of just how powerful CSS is and how you can make the best possible use of it in your web pages.

Introducing the Fundamentals of CSS Rules

The basic unit of CSS is the CSS rule. In this section, you take a close look at a CSS rule's syntax. Each part of a rule — selector, properties, and values — tells a browser something about how to display a web page. CSS has several types of selectors, and you discover how to choose among them. CSS also offers a bevy of properties and values you can assign to those properties, so you find an introduction to how those work in this section. Later sections in this lesson and Lesson 5 explain properties and values in more detail, in the context of formatting text, images, layout, and so on.

Knowing the parts of a CSS rule

CSS is short for Cascading Style Sheets. A *style sheet* consists of CSS rules and was introduced specifically to style HTML documents. The following is a simple example of a CSS rule:

```
p {
    color: red;
}
```

The following bullets walk you through the details of how the CSS rule works:

- The whole construct is known as a CSS *rule*, statement, or an instruction.

- The first item, p, is known as a *selector* and tells the browser what the style applies to. In this case, the selector tells the browser to apply the style to *all* the <p> elements in the HTML.

- Next comes a list of *declarations*. This example shows only one declaration. Curly brackets enclose all the declarations. Within a declaration, you need a property and a value separated by a colon.

- In this example, the only CSS property is `color`, which defines the color of the text. In this case, the value is a string, or keyword, with a value of `red`. You can describe the color in several ways, and you look at these later in this lesson, in the section "Introducing different value types," which looks at value definitions.

- The semicolon terminates the declaration.

- The browser ignores whitespace. The example could just have easily been written as

```
p{color:red;}
```

The results would have been just the same.

The syntax is easy, but unforgiving. Make the slightest mistake, and at best, your results will be not what you wanted. At worst, the mistake will invalidate the whole style sheet. For example, you don't need the semicolon on the final declaration, but you do need it after every declaration that isn't final. If you leave out a semicolon, the declaration will not be read and will cause unpredictable behavior with any other declarations. I typically include the semicolon after the final declaration because I think doing so is a good practice.

- A selector can have several declarations, and all the declarations that apply to that selector are contained in curly brackets. The syntax looks like this:

```
selector {
    property: value;
    property: value;
    property: value;
}
```

Styling elements with simple selectors

CSS3 provides several kinds of selectors, many of them introduced in CSS2. In a CSS rule, the selector's job is just what it sounds like: The selector selects elements in an HTML document. What it selects depends on the type of selector you use.

The following list introduces you to four important simple selectors:

✔ **Type selector:** Selects content in the HTML based on the tags that mark up the content. If you marked up all the navigation elements on a page with the `<nav>` element, new in HTML5, you could use a type selector to select all those `<nav>` elements and, for example, color them red, like this:

```
nav {color: red ;}
```

TIP

In CSS, you don't use the angle brackets, as you would in the HTML tags.

EXTRA INFO

You can write CSS rules in ways that simplify your ability to check the syntax. One way is to put the opening bracket on the same line as the selector, and then write each property and value pair on its own line, indented five spaces, with the semicolon at the end. The closing bracket also has its own line. The idea behind this structure is to make spotting the curly brackets and semicolons easy. The structure also makes skimming through a longer list of CSS rules easier because the selectors stick out on the left. Different developers have slightly different conventions. Some, for example, put the semicolon at the beginning of a line so the semicolon (or lack thereof) is even easier to spot. Because whitespace doesn't matter, you can tinker with conventions so you can easily review your code.

✔ **Class selector:** Selects content in the HTML document if the HTML element's `class` attribute corresponds to the name of the class selector. So, with a class selector, you can select many types of HTML elements with one CSS rule, as long as they all have the same `class` attribute.

For example, say your HTML document uses a `class` attribute to designate administrative content, like this HTML snippet:

```
<h3 class="adminstuff">Legal notices and disclaimers
        </h3>
<p class="adminstuff"> All rights reserved. Copyright
        2008. Opinions expressed here are those of the
        author and do not necessarily reflect those of
        ExampleSite.com</p>
```

In the CSS, you could use a class selector to apply special formatting to only those elements. It doesn't matter which HTML tag marks up the content. If the tag contains a `class` attribute whose value is `adminstuff`, that content is styled with the CSS rule's declaration on the web page. Here's what the CSS selector for this example looks like:

```
.adminstuff {property: declarations;}
```

See the period in front of the class selector, `.adminstuff`? That period is what indicates a class selector.

✔ **ID selector:** Remember that in Lesson 1, I urge you to give all block elements in your HTML an `id` attribute? This selector is a key reason why.

If one specific element requires special styling — like, oh, the color red to make it stand out on the page — use the ID selector. For example, say an element at the top of a web page, urging site visitors to buy your product or attend your next presentation, needs to stand out. If that element has a unique `id` attribute in the HTML, the CSS enables you to style just that element with the ID selector. If you give that element an `id` attribute value of `"urgent"` in the HTML, like this:

```
<p id="urgent">Our next event is Tuesday, April 18!
        Sign up now!</p>
```

The CSS rule that makes this text red would look like this:

```
#urgent {color: red ;}
```

The number symbol (#) begins every ID selector.

✔ **Attribute selector:** If the class and ID selectors aren't enough, you can also make use of the attribute selector, which selects — I bet you can guess — attributes! If you need to highlight every table cell that spans multiple rows, you could easily select them with the attribute selector, which can select every HTML element on the page that contains a `rowspan` attribute, like this:

```
[rowspan] {color: red; }
```

You can narrow the selection further by specifying a value so that, say, only `rowspan` attributes with a value of 2 are selected, like this:

```
[rowspan="2"] {color: red; }
```

Table 4-1 summarizes what each type of selector does.

Table 4-1	Types of CSS Selectors			
Selector	*What It Selects*	*Syntax*	*Example*	*Use It to Style*
Type	Every instance of the specified HTML element, such as `<body>`, `<p>`, `<table>`, or `<nav>`	`element {declarations}`	`nav {color:red;}`	Page elements based on an HTML element
Class	Every HTML element with the specified `class` attribute value	`.classvalue {declarations}` **Remember:** A period must be before the `class` value.	`.adminstuff {color:red;}`	Different HTML elements on a page similarly
ID	The element with the specified `id`	`#idvalue {declarations}`	`#same {color:red;}`	A single page element **Remember:** Each `id` attribute on an HTML page should be unique to the page.
Attribute	Any element with the attribute of the given name	`[att] {declarations}` Or `[att=value] {declarations}`	`[rowspan] {color:red;}` `[rowspan="2"] {color:red;}`	Page elements with a common attribute or `attribute` value

To practice creating different types of selectors, follow these steps:

1. **Open a text editor and enter the following HTML5 document:**

```
<!DOCTYPE html>
<html>
  <head>
  <style type="text/css">
    p {
    font-color:red;
    }
  </style>
  </head>
  <body>
  <p class="bodytext" id="myparagraph">Style this
        text</p>
  </body>
</html>
```

2. **Save the document as `styledtext.htm` and then open it in a web browser. Change the selector type to select the `<p>` element in as many different ways as you can.**

   For example, to select it with an `id` selector, use the following declaration:

```
#myparagraph {
  font-color:red;
  }
```

Combining selectors

Combining selectors enables you to refine how styles are applied to content in your HTML file, providing more flexibility than the basic selectors on their own. The following sections explain methods you can use to combine selectors in CSS rules.

Apply the same style to several elements

When you want to apply the same style to several elements, you can use a type selector for each HTML element you want to select and separate them with commas. For example, if you want all the headings on your page to be blue so they stand out from the body text, you could create the following CSS rule . . . .

```
h1, h2, h3 {color: blue ;}
```

. . . .instead of creating three CSS rules that repeat the same declaration:

```
h1 {color: blue ;}
h2 {color: blue ;}
h3 {color: blue ;}
```

Walk the document tree to select an element

You can also combine selectors so that they walk through the HTML document tree. (I introduce the document tree in Lesson 1, in case you need a refresher.) The *document tree,* or the *DOM,* is the way HTML elements relate to each other in an HTML document. For example, say your HTML document contains a list within a paragraph, like this:

> **LINGO**
>
> The **document tree**, or the **DOM**, is the way HTML elements relate to each other in an HTML document.

```
<p><b>To sign up for the Robert Burns newsletter,</b>
        follow these steps:
    <ol>
        <li>Go the <b>Robert Burns newsletter</b>
        page.</li>
        <li>Enter your <b>name</b> and <b>email
        address</b>.</li>
        <li>Click the <b>Sign Me Up!</b> button.</li>
    </ol>
Signing up is that easy! Do it today!
</p>
```

The <ol> tag is considered a *child* of the <p> tag because the <ol> opening and closing tags are within the <p> tag. Conversely, the <p> tag is a parent of the <ol> tag. The <li> tag is considered a *grandchild* of the <p> tag.

In other words, the document tree refers to the way the tags are nested within each other in an HTML document. Every element has only one parent, except for the root element, which has no parent.

If you want to narrow down what a selector selects using the document tree, you can combine selectors following the order in which items appear in the tree, from parent to child to grandchild and so on. For example, say that you want the bold words in the list to appear blue so that the bold keywords further stand out on the page. However, in the sentence that introduces the list, you don't want bold to be blue. The solution is the following CSS rule (assuming that the <p> tag in the example is a child of the root element):

```
p ol li b {color: blue ;}
```

The order of the elements in the selectors reflects how the elements are nested within each other in the HTML, starting from the oldest, p, on down to the youngest, b.

If you wanted the bold to apply to bold in the list items of both <ol> and <ul> lists, you could use the universal selector, which is an asterisk, and modify the selector as follows:

```
p * li b {color:blue}
```

The universal selector is usually used in conjunction with other selectors and will select any element in that position.

TIP

Commas tell the browser to apply the same CSS style to multiple elements. Selectors that walk the document tree use only spaces, not commas, between multiple elements in a selector.

Drilling down with pseudo-class selectors

Pseudo-classes are used to select elements that are not represented in the document tree. For example, most browsers show links in different colors depending on whether they've been visited, but these unvisited and visited links are the *same object* in the document tree.

A pseudo-class enables you to distinguish between the two. In the case of the <a> element

- ✔ :link refers to unvisited links.
- ✔ :visited refers to visited links.

The general syntax for pseudo-classes is

```
element:pseudo-class {declarations}
```

The following CSS rules use pseudo-class selectors to specify colors for different link states:

- ✔ **a:link {color: blue ;}:** Unvisited links appear in blue.
- ✔ **a:hover{color: red ;}:** Links turn red when the mouse pointer is over them.
- ✔ **a:visited {color: violet ;}:** Visited links appear in violet.

Pseudo elements

A *pseudo-element*, like a pseudo-class, enables you to style an entity that does not appear in the document tree; for example, the first letter of a line or the first line of a paragraph are such entities.

LINGO

A **pseudo-element** enables you to style an entity that doesn't appear in the document tree.

The general syntax is

```
element::pseudo-element {declarations}
```

TIP

Note the double colon, which is new syntax in CSS3 and differentiates pseudo-elements (two colons) from pseudo-classes (one colon). The difference between the two is beyond the scope of this lesson. Just know that when using pseudo-elements, the double colon is considered the correct way to go. If you happen to use a single colon, the CSS rule will still work; it just won't be compliant with CSS3.

The following CSS rule uses a pseudo-element to color the first *letter* of every paragraph red:

```
p::first-letter {color: red ;}
```

And this rule colors the first *line* of every paragraph red:

```
p::first-line {color: red;}
```

Choosing properties and values

Earlier examples introduced you to the `color` property, but CSS does much much more than apply color. This section offers a whirlwind overview of different types of properties and values to give you an idea of how they work and how different types of properties and values are different from one another.

GO ONLINE

To find out what the specification says about selectors in CSS3, including more ways to combine selectors, point your browser to the CSS3 recommendation: www.w3.org/tr/2011/rec-css3-selectors-20110929.

REMEMBER

The syntax for a CSS rule looks like this:

```
selector {property: value; property: value; property:
          value; }
```

The following style properties are often used to style HTML code:

- **Font properties:** In Figure 4-1, notice how the fonts in the page title, navigation, and copyright information change from the default font to Arial.

  A CSS rule changes the font to Arial — specifically a combined CSS rule for the heading 1, <nav>, and <p> elements with a `class` attribute value of `adminstuff`. Here's what the CSS rule looks like:

  ```
  h1, nav, p.adminstuff {font-family: arial; }
  ```

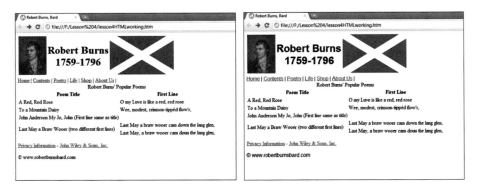

Figure 4-1

Find out all the ins and outs of formatting text in Lesson 5.

- **The color and width of borders and outlines around elements, such as tables or images:** The following CSS rule applies top and bottom border styles to the `table` element in the example page, so it looks like Figure 4-2.

  ```
  table {border-top: 10px solid blue; border-bottom:
         thick solid blue }
  ```

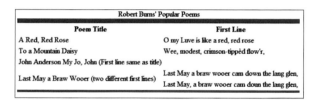

Figure 4-2

In this example, `border-top` and `border-bottom` are the properties. The values include `thick`, `10px`, and `blue`. You also see two property-value pairs separated by the all-important semicolon. Remember that without the semicolon, a CSS rule with more than one property-value pair won't work.

The next section, "Introducing different value types," explains different ways to set color and length values. Lesson 5 covers your many options for setting borders, shadows, rounded corners, and so on.

✓ **Background colors and images:** The `background-color` property turns the background color of the `<nav>` element silver, as shown in Figure 4-3, so it stands out from the body content and looks more like a navigation bar.

```
nav {background-color: silver; }
```

Background colors and images have their own set of properties in CSS, and the section "Decorating Backgrounds with Colors and Images" later in this lesson explains how they work.

✓ **Dimensions, such as height and width:** You can use CSS to set images to the same height, for example.

✓ **Whitespace:** You can set the amount of space between HTML elements with margins or padding. To add whitespace around the table in Figure 4-3, I added a `margin`, as shown in the following CSS rule:

```
table {border-top: 10px solid blue; border-bottom:
      thick solid blue; margin:25px;}
```

Margins and padding work with CSS rules that position elements on the page; you find details about positioning, margins, and padding in "Positioning Elements on the Page" later in this lesson.

GO ONLINE

To find a complete reference of CSS properties, check out `www.w3schools.com/cssref/default.asp` or the CSS specification at `www.w3.org/tr/#tr_CSS`.

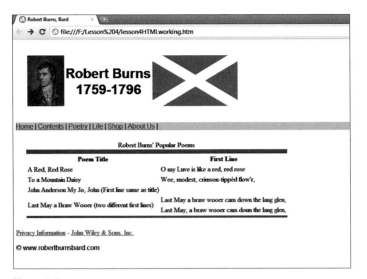

Figure 4-3

Introducing different value types

All properties take one or several values. I discuss these values in greater depth as you look at the individual properties, but an overview of these values and how they work is helpful as you start writing your own CSS. Generally speaking, the CSS property value falls into one of the following categories:

- ✔ Length
- ✔ Percentage
- ✔ URL
- ✔ Keyword
- ✔ String
- ✔ Number
- ✔ Color

Table 4-2 introduces property value types, except for color values. You see the value types in the specification when you look up what values a property can take.

Table 4-2	Types of Property Values in CSS	
Item	*Description*	*Example*

Relative lengths	The HTML5 specification recommends relative units wherever possible. These units (em and ex) are relative to something else. The element's current font size is 1 em. The height of the x character in the element's font is 1 ex. In the example, the heading font size is 2.5 bigger than the paragraph font size.	`h1 {font-size: 2.5em}`
		
		 `p {font-size: 1em}`

Absolute lengths	These units aren't relative to other elements but are absolute. CSS recognizes the following absolute lengths: in (inches), cm (centimeters), mm (millimeters), pt (points), pc (picas), and px (pixels).	`table {border-top: 10px solid blue }`
Percentages	The format for a percentage is a number followed by the % sign.	`body {font-size: 100%}`
URLs	Some properties take URLs as values. Unlike a keyword, the address should be quoted.	**Syntax:** `url("address")` `body { background: url("http://www. example.com/ pinkish.png") }`
Keywords	These values don't take quotes. The example code has three keywords.	`table { border-bottom: thick solid blue }`
Strings	A string value is a group of characters within single or double quotations.	`p {font-family: "Times New Roman"}`
Numbers	Very few properties accept a plain number. When the CSS notation calls for `<integer>`, use a whole number, such as 1, 5, and 27. A real number, or `<number>` in the notation, is a decimal: 1.0, 5.4, and 29.6.	`{z-index:1}`

In CSS, layouts can be flexible, also known as *fluid,* or they can be fixed. (Or they can be a hybrid, but for simplicity's sake, this section just compares flexible and fixed.) In a nutshell, *flexible* layouts use percentages and other relative values to determine how elements are positioned on a page whereas *fixed* layouts use absolute values. Flexible layouts are generally preferable to absolute layouts because a flexible layout can more easily adapt to whatever device or browser displays the page. This adaptability becomes increasingly important as more people access web pages from different types of devices, including desktop computers, laptops, mobile phones, and tablets.

The colors on a web page help communicate important information about the website's identity and message. Designers, understandably, want fine-grained control over colors and how they appear to the user. With this demand comes increasingly better ways to communicate colors to a browser. Both RBG and HSL color notation work with color values familiar to anyone who works with digital graphics. Table 4-3 shows the various ways to specify colors in CSS.

Table 4-3	Color Values in CSS	
Item	*Description*	*Example*
Keyword colors	Sixteen keywords indentify specific colors: maroon, red, orange, yellow, olive, purple, fuchsia, white, lime, green, navy, blue, aqua, teal, black, and gray.	`h1 {color:red;}`
Hexadecimal RGB colors	Hexadecimal colors use a six-character code (which includes a value for red, green, and blue, or an RGB value) to define colors. Hexadecimal values offer more color options than keywords. The example is a coral color.	`h1 {color: #FF7256;}`
Decimal RGB colors	Decimal RGB colors include a value for red, green, and blue. The example color is yellow.	Syntax: `rgb(<red value>,<green value><blue value>)` `h1 {color: rgb(255,255,0) ;}`

Item	Description	Example
RGBa	New to CSS3, RGBa controls the *alpha* value of a color, also known as transparency. The alpha value in RGBa, the fourth one in the list, takes a decimal value from 0 (no transparency) to 1 (fully transparent). For the alpha value, use only integers, not percentages. Because of browser implementation problems, provide an RGB value as a backup to any RGBa value.	A semitransparent blue: `aside {back-ground-color: rgba(0,0,255,0.5);}` A very transparent orange: `aside {background-color: rgba(100%, 50%, 0%, 0.1); }`

HSL colors	New in CSS3 and adopted by all browsers, this intuitive system is becoming increasingly popular. *HSL* stands for hue, saturation, and luminosity. You enter a value for each to create the desired color. Both example colors display the color red.	Syntax: `hsl(<hue>, <saturation>%, <luminosity>%)`
		
		`h1 {color: hsl(360,100%,50%) ;}`
		
		`h1 {color: hsl(0,100%,50%) ;}`

The advantage of the HSL notation is that it produces a color wheel. Artists have used color circles from time immemorial to select the correct colors. These circles help decide which colors clash and which supplement, complement, or contrast. All these combinations have their use and, when used appropriately, lead to good design.

More elaborate wheels show the saturation, with full saturation on the outside circumference and no saturation (black) in the center. Conversely, you find more luminosity toward the center and less outside. Most design texts are based on the traditional color wheel, but it's easy to convert these to the HSL wheel, hence the usefulness of HSL.

You can learn how the hue, saturation, and luminosity settings interact by playing around with a wheel-based color picker like the one shown in Figure 4-4, which converts values to HSL notation.

Select a color here...

...See its HSL values here

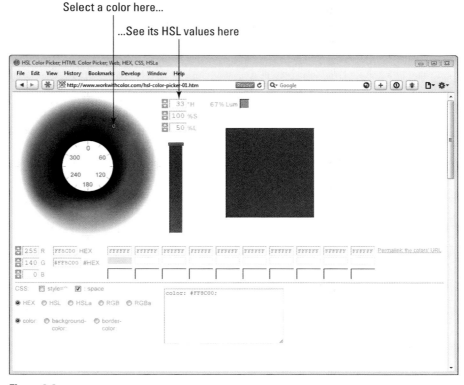

Figure 4-4

Decorating Backgrounds with Colors and Images

The background of a web page is kind of like the canvas on which it's painted (although most websites are meant to be more functional and less works of art). On your web page background, you can show a simple color or an image, which can tile across the background or show itself only once. The

GO ONLINE

Visit the following web page to experiment with different color values and convert them into different types of color notation, including HSL. Point your browser to www.workwithcolor.com/hsl-color-picker-01.htm.

following sections walk you through the details of setting backgrounds and all the options for repeating, positioning, and sizing a background image, if you choose to use one.

Coloring the background of a page or element

An easy way to add color to your web pages is by using a background color. You can add a background color to the whole page or to an element with the `background-color` property. Just add a value for the desired color using any of the accepted color value notations (hexadecimal, RGB, HSL, and so on).

Change the background color of a whole page by selecting the `<body>`. For example, the following CSS rule gives the page shown on the right in Figure 4-5 its light blue background:

```
body {background-color: hsl(210, 100%, 95%); }
```

A type selector of `body` selects the whole page. The `background-color` property tells the browser to color the background instead of all the text within the `<body>` element. The color is indicated using HSL color notation.

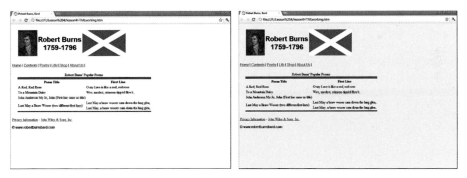

Figure 4-5

Open the HTML document you created earlier and apply a background color to the whole page by selecting the `<body>` element. Experiment with different ways to specify the color, such as by using color keyword and hexadecimal RGB values. Preview the page in a browser to see the results!

Change the background of an element by selecting the desired element instead of the whole page. For example, the following code changes the background of the <nav> element to yellow, as shown in Figure 4-6:

```
nav {background-color: hsl(49, 100%, 72%); }
```

This code still uses the `background-color` property and a color value in HSL color notation, but the type selector of `nav` tells the browser to color just the <nav> element, not the whole page.

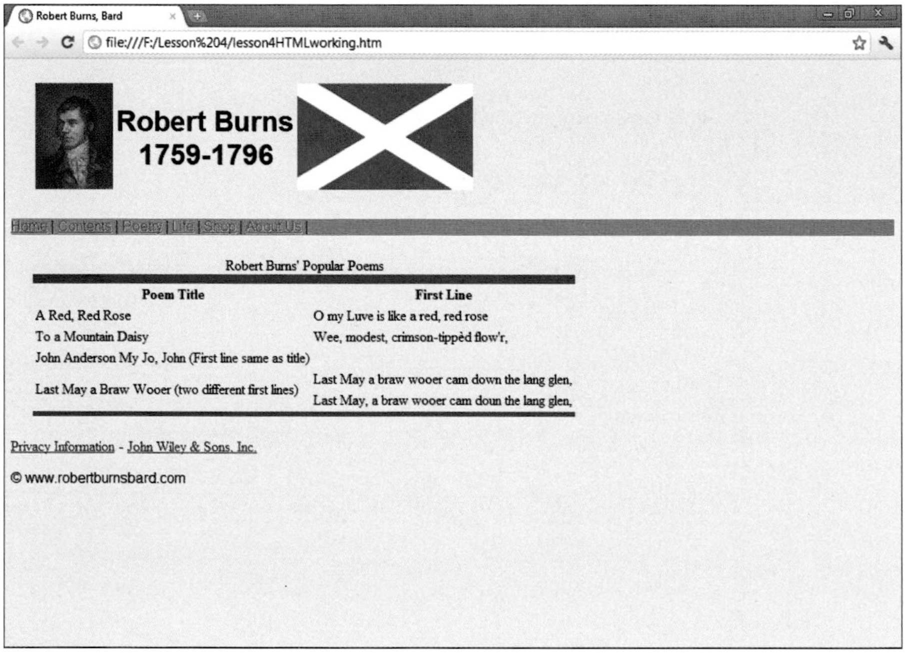

Figure 4-6

Inserting a background image

Early websites went hog-wild using background images, like the example shown in Figure 4-7, but it's rare to find a modern site that makes heavy use of them for design. Used judiciously, however, background images can be very useful, such as the Scottish thistle motif in the bottom-right corner of the page in a Robert Burns site or a parchment image repeated to make the web page background look like old paper.

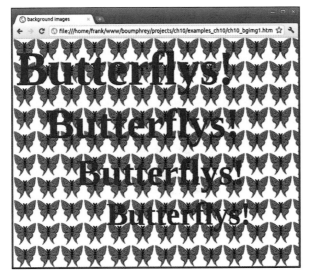

Figure 4-7

The syntax for loading a background image is as follows:

```
selector {background-image: url("absolute or relative
         URL"); }
```

In the Robert Burns site, the CSS that inserts the background image shown in Figure 4-8 looks like this:

```
body {background-image: url("images/thistle.png"); }
```

The body selector tells the browser to insert the image in the page body, or the background of the entire page. The background-image property tells the browser to insert the image as a background layer. The URL value points to the image file that you want to insert, which is either an absolute or relative URL. In this case, the thistle.png file is saved in the website's images subfolder.

Background image

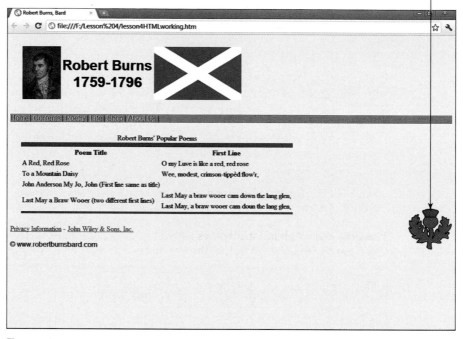

Figure 4-8

Control how a background image repeats

The `background-repeat` property tells the browser how to repeat the image. The following list explains how the possible values impact the look of the resulting web page:

- ✔ **repeat-x:** Repeats the image across only the x-axis.

- ✔ **repeat-y:** Repeats the image across only the y-axis.

- ✔ **repeat:** Repeats the image so that it fills the whole space available to it. This is the default value (refer to Figure 4-7).

- ✔ **no-repeat:** The image is shown once.

- ✔ **space:** The image repeats to fill the background but is spaced evenly so that no instance of an image is clipped.

- ✔ **round:** If the whole image doesn't fit into its allotted space, the image is resized so that it does fit.

Browser support for `space` and `round` is erratic, so test carefully
before you use these values in your CSS code.

In Figure 4-9 you see four `<div>` elements displayed in the browser, each
with a different `id` attribute. Each `<div>` has a background image with a different value for `background-repeat`. The first shows the default behavior
of `repeat`, the second `no-repeat`, the third `repeat-x`, and the fourth
`repeat-y`. Here's what the CSS looks like:

```
div {background-image:url("image.gif");}
#div2 {background-repeat:no-repeat; }
#div3 {background-repeat:repeat-x; }
#div4 {background-repeat:repeat-y; }
```

The first `<div>` element displays the default value because, whenever the
CSS doesn't set a repeat value, the default is automatically in effect.

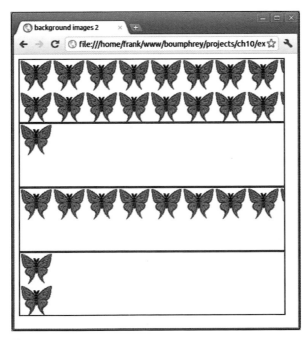

Figure 4-9

Inserting multiple images in a background

The background property enables you to layer more than one image in the background. Figure 4-10 shows two examples of layered background images. In the first example, the image of the purple butterfly is listed first in the CSS, so it appears in the top layer. The green butterfly, which is a GIF image with a transparent background, is listed second. You can also specify the position and repeat value for each image. In the first example, the purple butterfly is set to no-repeat, whereas the green butterfly does repeat.

Figure 4-10

The CSS rule for the first example looks like this:

```
#div1{
    background: url(image2.jpg) 0 0 no-repeat,
        url(image.gif) 0 0 repeat;
}
```

In the bottom example, the order of the images is switched: The green butterfly is listed first and appears on top. Because the green butterfly image is a transparent GIF, you can see more of the purple butterfly on the lower layer. Also, the position of the green butterfly, 75px 75px, located the image 75 pixels across and down from the upper-left corner of the page, which is considered position 0 0. Here's the CSS rule for the bottom image in Figure 4-10:

```
#div2{
      background:url(image.gif)75px 75px,url(image2.jpg);
      background-repeat:no-repeat;
}
```

To set the position for multiple background images, you could use the following position keywords, as well: top, bottom, center, left, and right.

Positioning a background image on the page

To position a background image, use the background-position property, which positions the image within the box that holds it.

What do I mean by *box,* you ask? Generally speaking, a parent element sets dimensions for the content within it. So, if the image's parent element is the <body>, the <body> is the box that holds the background image. If the image is inserted into a <div> element, the <div> and its dimensions form the box that holds the background image.

To position the background image where you want it, here's what you need to know:

✓ **The background-position property can take a percentage or a length as a value.** The following keyword values are also valid: left, center, right, top, and bottom.

✓ **For basic background image positioning, you can use one or two values:**

- *If you use one value,* the second is assumed to be center.

- *If you use two values,* the order of keyword values, such as bottom right, which positions the image in the bottom-right corner of the page (refer to Figure 4-8), doesn't matter.

  However, if you use a percentage or length value, the first value is for the horizontal position and the second is for the vertical position, where the value is an offset from the upper-left corner of the box/background that contains the image.

So {background-position: 40px 50px; }applied to the <body> element would place the image 40 pixels to the right and 50 pixels down from the upper-left corner of the web page.

✔ **Percentage values are relative to the width and height of the background area and the background image (as indicated in the background-size property).**

So, say the horizontal value for background-position is 50%. This would tell the browser to position the background image in the background at the 50-percent point (or halfway point) for each of the widths, as indicated by the red markers in Figure 4-11.

If the percentage value for the vertical positioning is 80%, the browser lines up the image on the vertical axis where each height value equals 80 percent. See the blue markers in Figure 4-11.

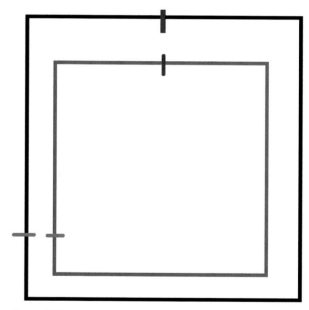

Figure 4-11

Positioning background images in a scrolling box

If the content is too large for the containing box and you use the overflow:scroll property on the box, a scroll bar appears. If you also have a background image in that box, you can use the background-attachment property to determine the behavior of the image when the box is scrolled. Values are

✔ **fixed:** The background image remains fixed with reference to *the ancestor* of the containing box. In the top box of Figure 4-12, notice how the butterfly image is a bit cut off by the border in the upper left. The text scrolls over the image, and the image stays in view.

✔ **scroll:** The background image is attached to the box's border, so the text scrolls over it and the image stays in view. In the second box of Figure 4-12, you can see how the image moves out of sight as the text scrolls down. This value is the default.

✔ **local:** The background image is attached to the contents in the scrolling box so that the image moves out of view with the text, as you can see in the bottom box of Figure 4-12.

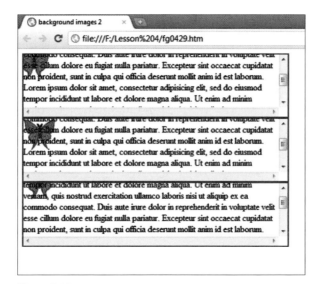

Figure 4-12

Sizing a background image

If you want to specify a size for your background image, you can do so with the `background-size` property. To set the values, you have the following options:

✔ **Use one or two length or percentage values.** If you use one value, the second value is assumed to be the keyword value, `auto`. If you use two values, the first sets the width and the second sets the height.

✔ **The keyword auto can be used with a length or percentage value or on its own.** auto sets the image size to its intrinsic value. So an image that's sized to 300 pixels wide in a graphics program will appear 300 pixels wide in the browser.

✔ **Instead of a length or percentage, you can use the keywords cover or contain.** The cover keyword sizes the image as small as possible while still completely covering the background area and maintaining the image's aspect ratio. The contain keyword makes the image as large as possible within the background area while maintaining the image's aspect ratio.

WARNING!

The layering of the cover and the contain size differs slightly from browser to browser. If you want to use either of these keyword values, make sure you test the web page in multiple browsers to ensure the page displays as you wish.

Table 4-4 shows how different background size values affect the way an image appears in a background area.

Table 4-4	Values for the background-size Property		
Value	*What It Does*	*Code Example*	*Image Example*
auto	Uses the intrinsic value of the image. This is the default value.	{background-size: auto;}	
per-centage	Sizes a background image relative to the background area.	{background-size: 100% 50%;}	
length	Sizes a background image with a fixed length value.	{background-size: 100px 50px; }	

Value	What It Does	Code Example	Image Example
cover	Sizes the image as small as possible while still completely covering the background area and maintaining the image's aspect ratio.	`{background-size: cover; }`	
contain	Sizes the image as large as possible within the background area while maintaining the image's aspect ratio.	`{background-size: contain;}`	

Positioning Elements on the Page

In this section, you find basic techniques for positioning content using CSS. To start, you need to understand whether you're working with block or inline elements. You then discover how to center content on the page. You learn how to structure content so that the layout can adapt to different browsers and devices, even when creating layouts with columns. You also find out the difference between the `margin` and `padding` properties and how they enable you to add whitespace between elements on the page.

Working with block versus inline elements

In HTML, any element that displays on the page has a default property of block or inline. (You may remember the discussion of block versus inline elements in Lesson 1.) *Block* elements, by default, take the whole width of the page and break to a new line before and after the element. Examples of block elements include <h1>, <p>, <div>, and so on.

Inline elements don't create new lines; they just take up the space they need to display on the page. Examples of inline elements include <b> for bold and <input> for forms.

When you start positioning elements on a web page with CSS, knowing the difference between block and inline elements is important. When you're working with a block element, you get the extra line breaks that the browser adds by default, and the element takes up the whole width of the page. When you're working with an inline element, you can still apply formatting just to that element. However, an inline element takes up only the space it needs (not the whole page width), and the browser won't add the breaks above and below the element.

If needed, you can change a block element to an inline element, or vice versa, by setting the element's display property in CSS:

```
{display: block;}

{display: inline;}
```

CSS also enables you to change the width of elements and other default properties of block and inline elements.

To see the difference between block and inline elements:

1. **Open a text editor and enter the following HTML document:**

```
<!DOCTYPE html>
<html>
  <head>
  <style type="text/css">
    p.block{
      display:block;
    }
    p.inline{
      display:inline;
    }
  </style>
  </head>
  <body>
  <p class="block">This is a block.</p>
```

```
    <p class="block">This is also a block.</p>
    <p class="inline">This is inline.</p>
    <p class="inline">This is also inline.</p>
    </body>
</html>
```

2. **Save the document as block-inline.htm and preview it in a browser.**

   Notice that the block elements always display on a new line, whereas inline elements display without inserting a line break.

Introducing grids and columns

Because the development of CSS3, like HTML5, is still in progress, a few new positioning techniques are available but not practical to use in the broader field of web development — at least not yet. The following sections introduce two game-changing and eagerly anticipated features — grid positioning and columns — as well as the caveats you need to keep in mind before using them.

CSS3 grid positioning

The aim of the *grid positioning module,* which Microsoft introduced and which became part of the CSS3 working draft in 2007, is to bring the same layout capabilities available in the desktop publishing programs to the web. Placing everything in a grid makes fine positioning possible.

As this book goes to press, browsers other than Microsoft's Internet Explorer haven't implemented grid positioning, and the CSS3 working group hasn't rated grid positioning as a high priority. As CSS3 progresses, however, keep an eye on the grid model, because browsers will begin to support it eventually.

The grid module can be found at www.w3.org/tr/css3-grid-layout . At its simplest, the grid module produces a column-like layout. For example, the following code creates a grid with two columns and three rows. The first column will be resized to fit its content. The second column will always be 250 pixels wide. The three rows will all adjust to the height of the content.

```
#grid {
    display: grid;
    grid-columns:auto 250px;
    grid-rows: auto auto auto
}
```

A more complex layout might have objects within the grid that span multiple columns, or even grid items that overlap each other. Figure 4-13 shows a sample layout that's possible with grid positioning.

In many ways the grid module duplicates what's possible with columns, but then goes far beyond the capabilities of columns. After columns become a full recommendation and have been fully implemented, development will likely begin to move forward on grids. Grids are certainly something that all developers should keep on their radar screen.

Figure 4-13

"Hooray for columns!"

Web developers have been clamoring for columns almost from the beginning. CSS3 promises a feature dedicated to presenting text in columns that flow from one column to another. However, to date, browsers each have their own implementation of columns, which isn't necessarily standard. To indicate that support for a feature is a work in progress, browser makers came up with the vendor prefix.

Vendor prefixes are simply characters that you put before the CSS properties to trigger that feature in specific browsers. So, for example, if you want to use columns in Firefox, you can prefix the columns CSS properties with -moz-; to use columns in Chrome or Safari, you can use the prefix -webkit-. In practice, vendor prefixes require you to write at least twice as much CSS code for features that require them. It's a messy solution, but you're stuck with it for now. When columns become standardized, you can use them without vendor prefixes and know that columns mean the same thing in every browser (or, that's the idea, anyway).

The following code is an example of the columns feature implemented with browser prefixes:

```
-webkit-column-width: 7em;
-webkit-column-count: 3;
```

```
-webkit-column-rule: 4px solid green;
-moz-column-width: 7em;
-moz-column-count:3;
-moz-column-rule: 4px solid green;
```

Notice the width, count, and rule properties. The property width sets the column width, count sets the number of columns, and rule puts a border around each column.

The following code shows a complete HTML5 document that uses columns. Figure 4-14 shows how this document renders in a browser. Notice that the text at the bottom of the first column continues in the second column.

```
<!DOCTYPE html>
<html>
<head>
  <title>3 columns</title>
  <style>
  #content{
    -webkit-column-width: 7em;
    -webkit-column-count:3;
    -webkit-column-rule: 4px solid green;
    -moz-column-width: 7em;
    -moz-column-count:3;
    -moz-column-rule: 4px solid green;
    }
  </style>
</head>
<body>
<div id="content">
<p>Lorem ipsum dolor sit amet, consectetur adipiscing elit. Curabitur mauris
            mi, cursus ut mattis eget, faucibus vitae mi. Nulla dictum
            facilisis venenatis. Nam consequat congue lorem, ac tincidunt
            nibh dictum id. Integer consectetur ultricies orci, a faucibus
            ante suscipit eget. Pellentesque fermentum vestibulum magna id
            venenatis. Nam lacinia condimentum risus a mollis. Nam porta
            sodales tempor. Ut accumsan ipsum in arcu mattis ut congue enim
            malesuada. Mauris vulputate lectus vel sem convallis laoreet.
            In ut varius est. Fusce convallis, lorem vel facilisis euismod,
            lectus urna porttitor urna, vitae adipiscing odio purus id dolor.
            Nulla facilisi.</p>
    <p>Nam id tortor sed nisl interdum feugiat. In condimentum lorem nec tortor
            mollis mattis. Fusce ornare lobortis sem quis fringilla. Quisque
            molestie augue vel neque dapibus condimentum. Praesent hendrerit
            euismod leo, eget eleifend erat scelerisque id. Quisque at sem
```

nisi, a sodales urna. Maecenas vulputate dolor sed felis aliquet tincidunt. Maecenas faucibus, elit et adipiscing venenatis, ante augue egestas justo, nec fringilla nulla turpis in est. Fusce bibendum posuere lorem, quis viverra nisl congue quis. In felis nisl, gravida vitae porta sit amet, eleifend eu tortor. Lorem ipsum dolor sit amet, consectetur adipiscing elit. Integer egestas imperdiet convallis. Mauris laoreet sem nulla, a egestas erat. Nunc accumsan, arcu sed luctus iaculis, augue velit egestas leo, a porta magna est at nisi. Aliquam dignissim blandit est, sit amet mollis libero molestie congue. Aenean adipiscing elementum venenatis.</p>
<p>Vestibulum sit amet libero velit, at vehicula arcu. Mauris ornare sagittis lacus, euismod vulputate tortor suscipit ut. Duis feugiat, velit nec molestie aliquet, turpis massa venenatis ante, vel venenatis diam tortor nec nisl. Fusce adipiscing auctor blandit. Aliquam erat volutpat. Aliquam eu sapien lorem, a venenatis dui. Vestibulum placerat pellentesque nulla, et pretium ligula accumsan sed. Vestibulum ante ipsum primis in faucibus orci luctus et ultrices posuere cubilia Curae; Nullam molestie tellus at nisl malesuada a pellentesque nunc tempor. Curabitur ut augue augue, in scelerisque ligula. Aliquam iaculis augue sed nibh sodales dictum. Fusce dui nisi, facilisis sit amet tempor sit amet, lacinia pellentesque eros. Cras nec nisl libero, a placerat elit. Suspendisse potenti. Sed ante libero, placerat vitae iaculis sit amet, sodales pulvinar justo.</p>
<p>Suspendisse luctus malesuada magna at rhoncus. Phasellus malesuada iaculis laoreet. Suspendisse leo nunc, congue ac blandit eu, varius ac dui. Etiam tempor elementum laoreet. Sed iaculis tellus sed nibh tincidunt at malesuada urna semper. Nullam adipiscing dui condimentum arcu euismod eu consequat dui mattis. Fusce aliquam risus vel odio viverra ut blandit purus auctor. Ut sed nulla eget nulla gravida dapibus. Fusce interdum, neque at luctus sollicitudin, mauris purus pulvinar mauris, ut aliquet velit libero et risus. Donec magna nibh, dapibus a ultrices vitae, convallis sed enim. Phasellus in sodales ante. Suspendisse in nisi dolor, ac ullamcorper nulla.</p>
<p>Proin pretium iaculis placerat. Etiam massa ipsum, pretium quis mattis et, feugiat ac quam. Vestibulum suscipit bibendum enim, eu aliquam nisi euismod fringilla. Maecenas placerat, libero id aliquam interdum, quam nisi tincidunt erat, a pretium eros leo ut nibh. Quisque sodales aliquam fringilla. Pellentesque non mi sed nunc aliquet aliquam. Aenean sollicitudin lobortis consectetur.</p>
        </div>
    </body>
</html>

Lorem ipsum dolor sit amet, consectetur adipiscing elit. Curabitur mauris mi, cursus ut mattis eget, faucibus vitae mi. Nulla dictum facilisis venenatis. Nam consequat congue lorem, ac tincidunt nibh dictum id. Integer consectetur ultricies orci, a faucibus ante suscipit eget. Pellentesque fermentum vestibulum magna id venenatis. Nam lacinia condimentum risus a mollis. Nam porta sodales tempor. Ut accumsan ipsum in arcu mattis ut congue enim malesuada. Mauris vulputate lectus vel sem convallis laoreet. In ut varius est. Fusce convallis, lorem vel facilisis euismod, lectus urna porttitor urna, vitae adipiscing odio purus id dolor. Nulla facilisi.

Nam id tortor sed nisl interdum feugiat. In condimentum lorem nec tortor mollis mattis. Fusce ornare lobortis sem quis fringilla. Quisque molestie augue vel neque dapibus condimentum. Praesent hendrerit euismod leo, eget eleifend erat scelerisque id. Quisque at sem nisi, a

viverra nisl congue quis. In felis nisl, gravida vitae porta sit amet, eleifend eu tortor. Lorem ipsum dolor sit amet, consectetur adipiscing elit. Integer egestas imperdiet convallis. Mauris laoreet sem nulla, a egestas erat. Nunc accumsan, arcu sed luctus iaculis, augue velit egestas leo, a porta magna est at nisi. Aliquam dignissim blandit est, sit amet mollis libero molestie congue. Aenean adipiscing elementum venenatis.

Vestibulum sit amet libero velit, at vehicula arcu. Mauris ornare sagittis lacus, euismod vulputate tortor suscipit ut. Duis feugiat, velit nec molestie aliquet, turpis massa venenatis ante, vel venenatis diam tortor nec nisl. Fusce adipiscing auctor blandit. Aliquam erat volutpat. Aliquam eu sapien lorem, a venenatis dui. Vestibulum placerat pellentesque nulla, et pretium ligula accumsan sed. Vestibulum ante ipsum primis in faucibus orci luctus et ultrices posuere cubilia Curae; Nullam molestie tellus at nisl malesuada a pellentesque nunc tempor. Curabitur ut augue augue, in

libero, placerat vitae iaculis sit amet, sodales pulvinar justo.

Suspendisse luctus malesuada magna at rhoncus. Phasellus malesuada iaculis laoreet. Suspendisse leo nunc, congue ac blandit eu, varius ac dui. Etiam tempor elementum laoreet. Sed iaculis tellus sed nibh tincidunt at malesuada urna semper. Nullam adipiscing dui condimentum arcu euismod eu consequat dui mattis. Fusce aliquam risus vel odio viverra ut blandit purus auctor. Ut sed nulla eget nulla gravida dapibus. Fusce interdum, neque at luctus sollicitudin, mauris purus pulvinar mauris, ut aliquet velit libero et risus. Donec magna nibh, dapibus a ultrices vitae, convallis sed enim. Phasellus in sodales ante. Suspendisse in nisi dolor, ac ullamcorper nulla.

Proin pretium iaculis placerat. Etiam massa ipsum, pretium quis mattis et, feugiat ac quam. Vestibulum suscipit bibendum enim, eu aliquam nisi euismod fringilla. Maecenas placerat, libero id aliquam interdum,

Figure 4-14

GO ONLINE

For the latest information about columns, see the specification at www.w3.org/tr/css3-multicol.

Centering content on the page

By default, HTML elements are positioned on the left side of the page and display one block element after another. However, most websites center content in the middle of the page, so the layout looks balanced. The following steps explain how to center the web page content:

1. **Use a type selector to select the <body> and then set the margin property to auto:**

   ```
   body {margin: auto;}
   ```

   At this point, you don't see any changes in your web page, but they're coming.

2. **To add whitespace on either site of the web page content to create a more balanced look, decrease the width of the body child elements.**

   For example, the following CSS rule adds a declaration that sets the width of all elements in the body to 60% of the width of the page:

   ```
   body {margin:auto;
   width: 60%;}
   ```

The positioning looks a little different, as shown in Figure 4-15. The image on the right shows the web page after the width is decreased to 60 percent.

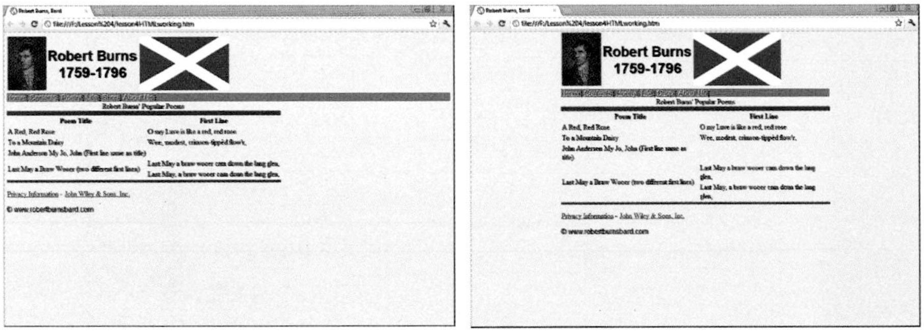

Figure 4-15

Remember that using percentages and other relative values makes the underlying code more flexible so that a web page adapts to the display in a variety of different devices more easily than one whose code uses fixed, or absolute, values.

Floating to the left and right

In addition to being centered, web page layouts often divide content in two columns (see Figure 4-16) or three columns (see Figure 4-17). To achieve this effect but still keep the layout flexible, use the float property to make the page elements float to either side of the page.

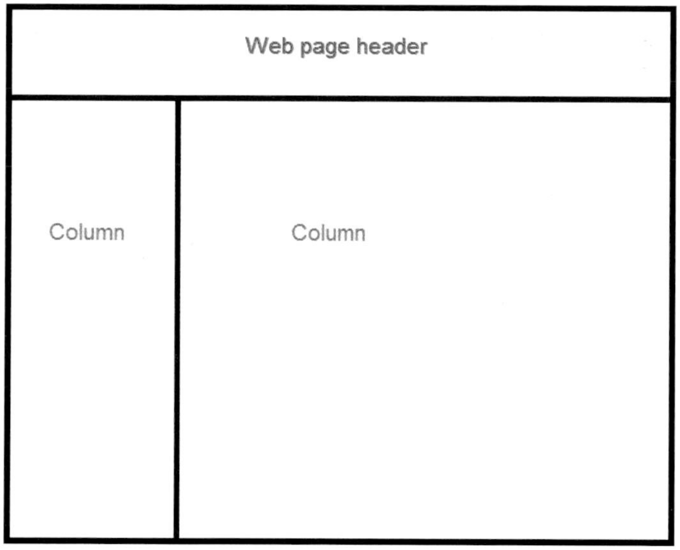

Web page header

Column	Column

Figure 4-16

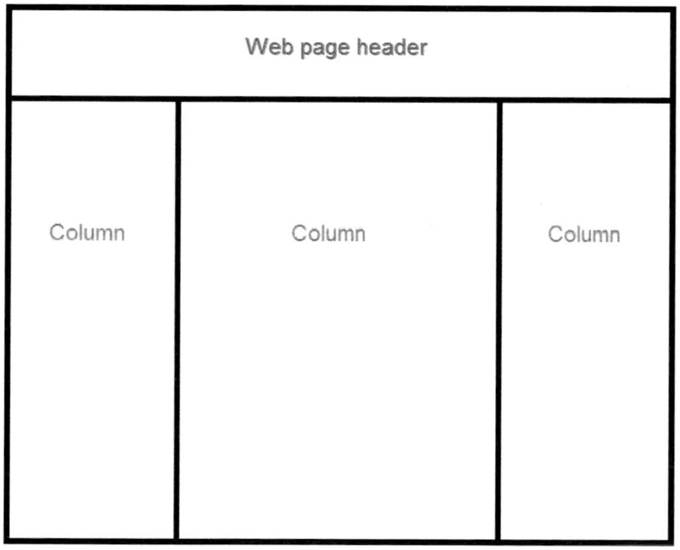

Web page header

Column	Column	Column

Figure 4-17

Say, for example, you want the page navigation to appear in a narrow column on the left, next to the page content, instead of across the top. The following steps walk you through creating a two-column layout that uses the `float` property, using the Robert Burns site as an example:

1. **Add the `float` property with a value of `left` to the CSS declarations for the `<nav>` element (or whatever element you want to put on the left; it might be a `<div>` or something else).**

   The CSS looks like this:

   ```
   nav {background-color: hsl(49, 100%, 72%);
   float:left;
   }
   ```

   This pushes the `<nav>` element to the left, as shown in Figure 4-18.

2. **Add a `float` property to the table that contains the poem information (or whatever element you want to position on the right).**

   You want to float the table to the right:

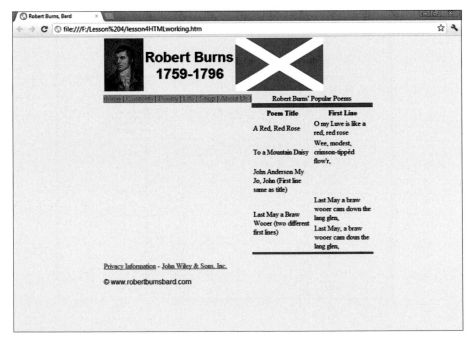

Figure 4-18

```
table {border-top: 10px solid hsl(207, 100%, 29%);
border-bottom: thick solid hsl(207, 100%, 29%);
float: right; }
```

At this point, the page looks quite messy, as shown in Figure 4-19. The two floated elements need their widths adjusted.

3. **Add a `width` value of 20% to the `<nav>` element and a `width` value of 75% to the table.**

For your own content, you can adjust these depending on the desired widths for the elements you want to position.

This tells the browser how much space you want the elements to take up relative to the entire width of the page (which is, remember, only 60 percent of the width of the browser window). Also notice that the total percentage adds up to 95 percent, leaving 5 percent of the space to create a little breathing room between the elements.

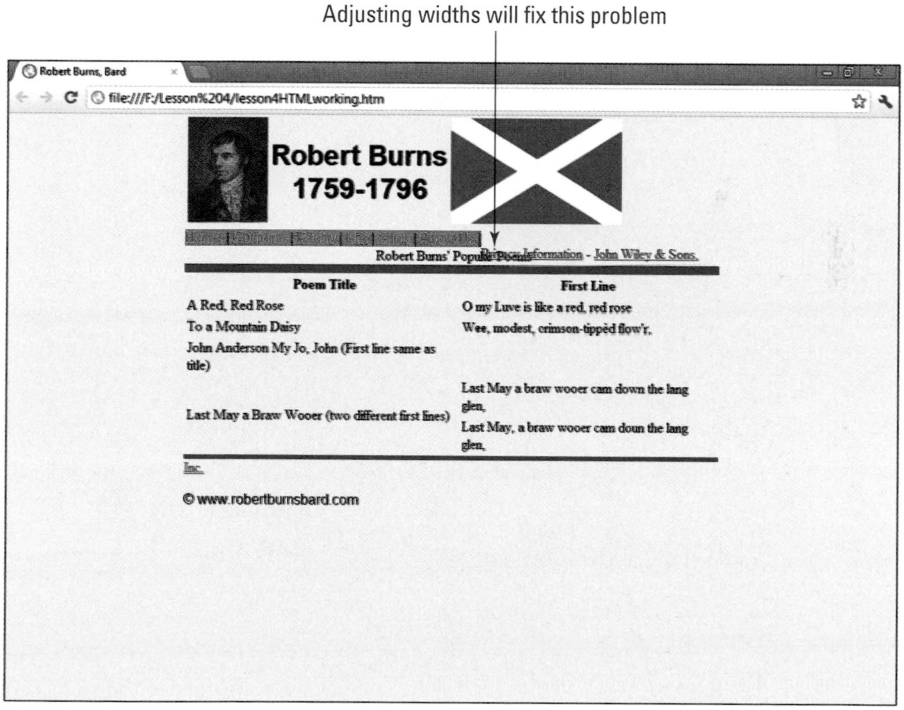

Figure 4-19

```
nav {background-color: hsl(49, 100%, 72%);
float:left;
width: 20%;
}
table {border-top: 10px solid hsl(207, 100%, 29%);
border-bottom: thick solid hsl(207, 100%, 29%);
float: right;
width: 75%; }
```

With this change, the footer jumps into the left column under the `<nav>` element. (See the image on the left in Figure 4-20.)

4. **To put the footer back at the bottom of the page where it belongs (or in your code, any elements that follow the floated elements), give the footer a `float` and `width` value as well:**

```
footer {float:left; width:100%; }
```

5. **To balance the height of the `<nav>` element with the height of the table, add a `height` value to the `<nav>` element, with a value in ems so that the positioning and sizing of elements on the page remains flexible.**

The image on the right in Figure 4-20 shows how the web page display changes in a browser.

```
nav {background-color: hsl(49, 100%, 72%);
float:left;
width: 20%;
height: 15em;
}
```

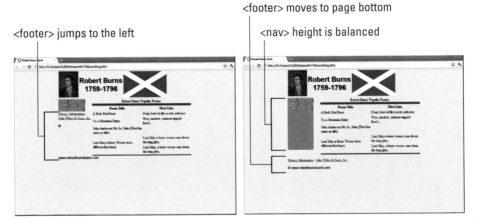

<footer> jumps to the left

<footer> moves to page bottom

<nav> height is balanced

Figure 4-20

Working with the position property

The position property enables you to move elements around the page as well. You can use the following values for the position property: static, fixed, relative, and absolute:

- ✔ The default value is **static**, which shows the box in the position of normal flow.
- ✔ The value **fixed** positions the box in relation to the browser window.
- ✔ **relative** positions the box in relation to its normal space, and the reserved space for the element is still preserved in the normal flow.
- ✔ **absolute** positions the box in relation to the parent box that has a value other than static.

In the following example, the box is positioned according to its top and left properties.

```
{ position:relative;
top:-75px;
left:125px;  }
```

Notice the minus sign, which enables you to position elements in the opposite direction of a positive value.

The position property is handy when you want to be more specific about where elements are placed in the browser window. For example, you might want your company logo to display 10 pixels from the left edge of the browser window and 50 pixels from the top of the window. In that case, you'd use the following declaration:

```
#logo {
  position: fixed;
  top: 50px;
  left: 10px;
}
```

And here's how you might use this style in a full HTML document:

```
<!DOCTYPE html>
<html>
<head>
    <title>position logo</title>
    <style>
    #logo {
      position: fixed;
      top: 50px;
      left: 10px;
    }
    </style>
</head>

<body>
<div id="logo">
    Logo Goes Here
</div>
</body>
</html>
```

Adding margins and padding

Block element boxes can have margins and padding:

- ✔ A **margin** is the distance between the *outside* of the border and the containing or adjacent styling box.
- ✔ **Padding** is the distance between the *inside* of the border and the box's content.

In Figure 4-21, two <div> elements have been given the margin *and* padding value of 50px:

```
{margin:50px;}
{padding:50px;}
```

Note how the margin between the top and the bottom box is 50px and not 100px. In other words, the margins collapse on one another.

Also note that the distance between the left of the boxes and the window is 60px. The default body margin of 10px is not collapsed.

10px

50px   Margin   Padding   Collapsed margin

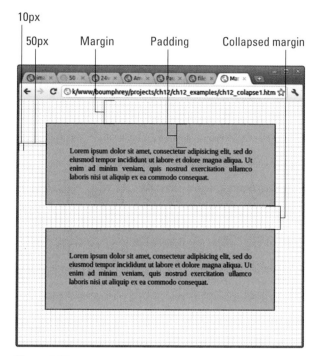

Figure 4-21

Saving CSS Instructions

You can apply CSS style rules to your page in three ways:

- Link to an outside CSS file with the `<link>` element.
- Embed a style sheet in a document using the `<style>` element.
- Use the `style` attribute on an element.

The difference among each of these methods is where you place the style instructions for the browser. The placement matters because it determines how the styles *cascade,* or which style is ultimately applied if any styles are in conflict with another style. In this section, you find out best practices for saving your styles and learn the basics of how styles cascade.

Choosing where to place CSS3 styles

Embedding a style sheet in a document using the `<style>` element has certain limitations: A separate sheet has to be written for each HTML page; site maintenance is difficult; and the style sheet is document-specific.

The preferred way to apply style to documents throughout a site is by using a separate file containing the CSS rules. This file is usually given the extension `.css`.

Table 4-5 introduces how each method of placing styles works and how each method impacts the way styles work with the HTML document. The following sections explain how each method works in more detail.

Table 4-5	Placing CSS Styles	
Location	*How It Works*	*Important to Know*
External CSS	Link to an outside CSS file by adding the `<link>` element to the HTML document.	This is the preferred way to apply styles to documents throughout a website.
Internal CSS	Embed styles in the `<head>` of an HTML document using the `<style>` element.	With this method, the style sheet is document-specific. You have to write a style sheet for each HTML page, making site maintenance difficult.
Inline CSS	Add style instructions as a value in the `style` attribute on an HTML element.	The rules in a `style` attribute apply only to that element. Placing style rules inline can be useful for prototyping. Instead of a `style` attribute, the preferred way to style a single element is to use an `id` attribute and selector.

Creating and linking an external style sheet

The CSS file is simply a text file listing CSS rules and saved with the file extension `.css`.

A style sheet can be as simple as this example, `mystyles.css`:

```
/*mystyles.css*/

p{
     font-size:1.2em;
     color:green;
}
```

In reality, your style sheets will likely contain at least a handful of styles. In addition to CSS statements, the file can contain blank lines and comments (denoted with the `/*` before the comment, and the `*/` at the end of the comment).

Comments enable you to leave notes in the code for yourself or anyone else who might read it or work with it. If you use comments, follow the style for CSS. Do not use HTML (`<!-- ... -->`) or JavaScript (`// ...`) comments. Unfortunately, you can get away with JavaScript comments in some browsers, but doing so will invalidate your style sheet in other browsers (Chrome and Firefox). No browser lets you get away with HTML/XML style comments in a style sheet.

A style sheet is just a text file! To link your CSS file to an HTML document, you can use the `<link>` element or the `@import` construct in a `<style>` element.

Using the <link> element

The `<link>` element is the preferred way of linking to a style sheet. You insert the `<link>` element into the `<head>` tag of your HTML document. For example:

```
<head>
     <title>Robert Burns Popular Poems </title>
   <link rel="stylesheet" type="text/css" href="mystyles.
          css" />
</head>
```

Here's what the attribute values mean:

- ✔ **rel:** The `stylesheet` value tells the browser it's dealing with a style sheet.

- ✔ **type:** The value indicates the type of the document you're linking to and is always `"text/css"` for a CSS file.

✔ **href:** This tells the browser what file you're linking to. The value can be a relative or absolute URL. The example here is relative. An absolute value is a full URL, like this one:

```
http://www.somesite.com/styles/corporatestyles.css
```

If using an absolute value, be sure to include the `http://`.

Using the @import construct

Although the `<link>` element is the preferred way of linking a CSS file, the `@import` statement can be useful in certain circumstances, such as when you want to load a CSS file only when certain conditions are met (such as the screen width being a certain size, or even whether the viewer is using a color monitor). I discuss more about the reasons why you might use `@import` when I discuss media types in Lesson 5. For now, just know that CSS *media types* allow you to change the way an HTML document is presented based on the device being used to view it.

To use the `@import` method, insert a `<style>` element into the `<head>` of the HTML document (instead of a `<link>` element) as follows:

```
<style type='text/css'>
    @import url("mystyles.css");
</style>
```

Where the example shows *mystyles.css*, use the filename of the style sheet you want to link.

Inserting internal styles

You can insert internal styles into the `<head>` of an HTML document with the `<style>` element, like this:

```
<head>

    <title>background images</title>

    <style type="text/css">

    .bgimage{background-image:url("image.gif");
    }
```

```
        p{margin-top:.1cm;
        margin-bottom:.1cm;
        font-weight:bold;
        color:red;
        }

        </style>
 </head>
```

When would you want to use a `<style>` element to style your page as opposed to an imported style sheet? Here are a few times:

- ✔ You want a particular style to apply to just a single page.

- ✔ You are prototyping a style.

- ✔ You want a style to apply to just a single element. (Use the ID selector.)

- ✔ You think your pages may be used offline. If you are offline, your link can't find the style sheet, unless the style sheet file has been cached.

Inserting CSS inline with the style attribute

The final way to incorporate CSS statements into your page is to use a `style` attribute in an HTML element. The rules in a `style` attribute apply just to that element.

The HTML5 specification strongly discourages adding inline CSS with the `style` attribute — the preferred way to style a single element is to use an `id` locator — but recognizes that inline CSS is useful for prototyping. It can also be useful if you're generating page content with JavaScript.

The syntax is very simple. Each rule must be separated by a semicolon, as shown here:

```
style="rule1;rule2;rule3;"
```

The following example changes the text color in a `<div>` element to silver:

```
<div style="color:silver;">
</div>
```

Note that styles placed on an element are inherited by child elements; all the child elements of this `<div>` have silver text.

Understanding inheritance and cascading

LINGO

In CSS, **inheritance** means that child elements inherit properties from the parent. **Cascading** refers to what happens when the declarations of one style sheet combine with other declarations.

In CSS, *inheritance* means that child elements inherit properties from the parent. Most properties are inherited; a few are not. Here's a brief example to illustrate how inheritance works. Say your style sheet has a single CSS rule to set the font color:

```
body{color: green;}
```

When you display the page in browser, all the text is green, as shown in Figure 4-22. The child elements of the `<body>` have inherited the style.

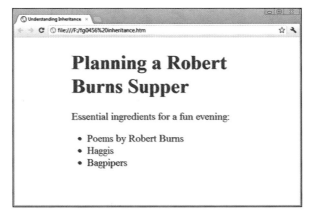

Figure 4-22

If you then add the following rule . . .

```
p{color: black;}
```

All the text *not* in a `<p>` element is still green, but the `<p>` text is black, as shown in Figure 4-23. The specific rule for `<p>` takes precedence over the more general rule for `<body>`, so the `<p>` element does not inherit the style applied to the `<body>` element.

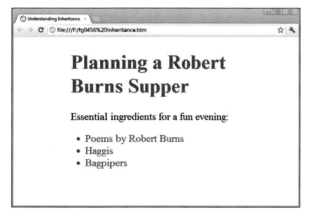

Figure 4-23

Cascading refers to what happens when the declarations of one style sheet combine with other declarations. The browser needs a way to figure out which styles to display when styles combine or conflict. Say you have

- ✔ A style for the color and font size of the <h1> element in an external style sheet.
- ✔ A style for the font color of the <h1> element in an internal style sheet.

The rules of cascading say that

- ✔ The <h1> element inherits the font size rule from the external style sheet.
- ✔ The font color rule in the internal style sheet overrides the external style sheet.

The CSS specification has a complicated algorithm for calculating what styles take precedence, but the basic rule is that the style closest to the HTML element is what appears in the browser. This means that

- ✔ External CSS is farthest from what appears in the browser.
- ✔ Internal CSS rules take precedence over rules in an external style sheet.
- ✔ Inline CSS rules take precedence over internal CSS and external CSS rules. Similarly, style rules that use an ID selector trump inherited style attribute rules.

A rule declared important trumps every other rule. The `important` declaration looks like this:

```
!important
```

Experiment with cascading by following these steps:

1. **Open one of the other practice HTML documents from earlier in this lesson and try the following:**

    a. *Apply a font color to the* <body> *element.*

    b. *Apply a different font color to a child of the* <body> *element (such as* <p>*), using an element selector.*

    c. *Apply a different font color to the same child of the* <body> *element, but this time use an* id *selector.*

2. **Save the file, and then guess which color the content of the <p> element will be.**

3. **Preview your document in a browser.**

    Were you right? Why did one color prevail over the others?

 Summing Up

In this lesson, you learned the basics of creating CSS rules that select HTML elements, add backgrounds to a web page, and position elements:

✔ The syntax of a CSS rule includes a selector, a property, and a value.

✔ A simple selector can select content in a web page according to the HTML tag that marks up the content, or the value of a `class` or `id` attribute.

✔ Combined selectors, such as a list of HTML elements, a document tree-based selector, or a pseudo-class, give you more control to select and style a web page.

✔ Properties take different types of values, depending on the property. Values may include integers, URLs, lengths, or color values.

- The `background-color` property enables you to change the background color of a web page and specific page elements.

- If you insert a background image, you can set properties that determine how the image repeats, where the image is positioned, and how the image is sized.

- A web page can have more than one background image.

- The `display` property enables you change block elements to inline elements, or vice versa.

- CSS grid positioning and columns are two up-and-coming new methods for more precisely controlling how content is arranged on a page and how text flows within different elements of a page.

- Several properties work together to center content on the page and create column-like layouts.

- `margin` and `padding` properties enable you to add whitespace around elements on a web page.

- You can save CSS instructions in an external style sheet, in the `<head>` of an HTML document, or inline with a `style` attribute. External style sheets are the preferred method for saving styles because this method streamlines the organization of styles applied to several web pages from one style sheet.

- In general, when style rules overlap, the rule closest to the HTML is the rule that the browser applies, and child elements inherit the properties of a parent element.

Try-it-yourself lab

The Practice activities throughout this lesson have given you a chance to experiment with applying CSS. To further build your CSS skills, download the HTML file `L4_01.htm` from the companion website for this book (see the Introduction for details). Then, take a look at the following figure and create an external CSS style sheet that mimics the design shown here, based on what you've learned in this lesson. (Some features, such as rounded corners and text alignment and formatting, you learn in Lesson 5.) Here's a quick list of what your CSS rules need to do:

- Choose a background color, margins, and width for the `<body>` element.

- Insert a background image in the `<div>` with an `id` of `burnsimage`. Decide how the image will repeat and what its position within the `<div>` will be.

✔ Add a `width`, `height`, and `float` for `<div id="burnsimage">`.

✔ For `<div id="burnspage">`, set a `width`, `height`, and `float` value. Select a color that enables the text to stand out on the page and padding that adds a little whitespace between the page elements.

✔ Give the `<nav>` element a different background color and change the colors of the unvisited, hover, and visited link colors so they complement the color scheme of the page.

✔ Float the labels in the Contact Information area to the left. Change the `<input>` elements from inline into block elements and add a left margin that adds a little whitespace between the label and the text box.

You can also find the CSS style sheet (`form.css`) I created among the downloads for this lesson. Try creating these styles on your own, and if you like, compare your approach to the one shown in the example style sheet.

Know this tech talk

You learned the following terms in this lesson:

absolute value: A value that points to an online resource with the full URL.

attribute selector: A CSS selector with a syntax that enables it to select any element based on whether it contains a specified attribute.

background image: An image inserted into the background of a web page via CSS instead of an `<img>` element in HTML.

block element: An HTML element that automatically inserts a line break and space after the element when it displays in a web page.

cascading: The way CSS styles that conflict determine which style will display in a browser.

class selector: A CSS selector that selects content in an HTML document based on the value of a `class` attribute.

columns: A way to create multi-column layouts, similar to how magazines and newspapers are arranged, with CSS.

declaration: The part of a CSS rule that appears between the curly brackets.

document tree: A way to model an HTML document with all the elements in the document arranged as branches and sub-branches of the root element, `<html>`.

external styles: CSS styles that are saved in an external style sheet with a `.css` file extension.

grid positioning: A proposed standard for allowing the precise layout of objects in web pages by arranging them on a grid.

hexadecimal RGB: A color value that begins with a # symbol and contains two characters to represent values for red, green, and blue respectively.

HSL: A color value that contains a value for the hue and a percentage for the saturation and luminosity.

ID selector: A CSS selector that selects content in an HTML document based on the value of an `id` attribute.

inheritance: The process of child elements inheriting the CSS values of their parent element.

inline element: An element that takes up only the space it needs to appear in the browser. This type of element doesn't add extra space or line breaks.

inline style: A CSS rule applied directly to an HTML element with a `style` attribute. Not recommended.

internal style: CSS rules applied to an HTML document via a `<style>` element in the `<head>` of an HTML document.

keyword: A property value in CSS that uses a word to apply a type of formatting and shouldn't be quoted.

margin: Area of whitespace outside of an HTML element.

padding: Area of whitespace within the border of an HTML element.

property: A part of CSS syntax that indicates what feature a CSS rule modifies.

pseudo-class selector: Allows you to select elements based on properties that are not represented in the document tree, such as whether a link has been previously visited or whether the user's mouse is currently hovering over the element.

pseudo-element selector: Selects sub-parts of an element, such as the first word in a paragraph.

relative value: A URL value that points to an online resource or file relative to the location of the current web page.

RGB: A color value that creates a color based on a specified value for red, green, and blue.

RGBa: Like the RGB value, but also includes a fourth value for opacity.

selector: In the syntax of a CSS rule, the selector determines what part of an HTML document is selected.

type selector: A CSS selector that selects content in an HTML document based on the HTML tag that marks up the content.

value: The part of a CSS rule that tells the browser how the selected content should be styled. Values can be lengths, percentages, URLs, keywords, and more.

The following table lists CSS elements covered in this lesson.

Element	*Description*	*Element*	*Description*
`a:link`	Pseudo-class selector; sets the color of unvisited links.	`@import`	Inserted into the `<style>` element, an `@import` statement can connect an external style sheet to an HTML document.
`a:hover`	Pseudo-class selector; sets the color of the link when a mouse cursor hovers over it.	`<link>`	Links an HTML document to an external style sheet. Includes the attributes `rel`, `type`, and `href`.

Element	Description	Element	Description
`a:visited`	Pseudo-class selector; sets the color of the link after it's clicked.	`margin`	Property that sets the amount of whitespace outside an element. Values are a length or a percentage.
`background-color`	Sets the background color of a web page. Use any accepted color value.	`padding`	Property that sets the amount of whitespace inside an element. Values are a length or a percentage.
`background-image`	Property that inserts an image into a web page background. Use a URL value.	`<style>`	Holds internal style rules and `@import` statements.
`background-position`	Property that positions a background image. Values include a percentage, a length, `left`, `right`, `top`, `bottom`, and `center`.	`style` (attribute)	Contains inline styles. Not recommended.
`background-repeat`	Property that determines how a background image repeats. Values include `repeat-x`, `repeat-y`, `repeat`, `no-repeat`, `space`, and `round`.	`width`	Property that sets an element's width. Value can be a length or percentage.
`background-size`	Property for sizing a background image. Values include a percentage, a length, `auto`, `cover`, and `contain`.	`display`	Property that can change a block element to a inline element or vice versa. Values are `block` or `inline`.
`float`	Moves an element left or right of other elements on a page, overriding the default behavior of block elements. Value can be either `left` or `right`.	`height`	Property that sets an element's height. Value can be a length or percentage.

Lesson 5

Styling Page Elements with CSS3

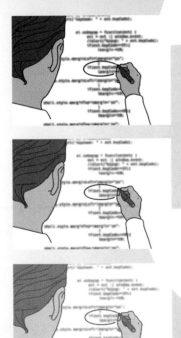

- ✔ You learn how to *choose fonts and apply font and text styles.*

- ✔ You can *customize bulleted and numbered lists.*

- ✔ *Apply common CSS rules for images,* such as margins and padding, floating elements left or right, and setting width and height.

- ✔ You can *draw borders, round corners, and add shadows.*

- ✔ *Customize CSS to different types of devices* by using media types and media queries.

Although today, graphics rule the web, text is still important, and how you style it can improve readability and the overall look and feel of a website.

In this lesson, you learn all about the basics of styling text elements with CSS, including some of the newest features in CSS3. You start with an introduction to properties that enable you to set the font family, size, width, and so on. You also discover how aligning and indenting work.

Among the new CSS3 features you learn about are applying a shadow to text and downloading whatever font you like with your web page (instead of hoping your website visitors have the font you want to use loaded on their computers).

Formatting Text

Before you get started, knowing the difference between text and font is helpful. In CSS, you find properties that modify text and properties that modify fonts. Here's what you need to know about the two:

- ✔ **Text** is the series of characters that make up a word, a line, or a paragraph. A *character* represents a letter, a number, a symbol, or a special character.

- ✔ A **font** on the other hand, is the way a character is rendered. That is, a single text character can be rendered in many different ways, depending on the font that renders the character.

Choosing fonts for font-family

A group of similar fonts is known as a *font family.* Typically, a font family has fonts of various sizes and fonts for italic, bold, and small caps text.

Use the `font-family` property to style text on your web pages. The general syntax is

```
selector {font-family: family-name1, family-name2, …
          generic name;}
```

For the property values, use the names of fonts that likely exist on the user's computer as well as a generic name. The order of the font names is the order in which the browser searches for the font. So, if the user's computer has the first font in the list, the web page displays in that font. If not, the browser moves to the second in the list, then the third, and so on.

Generic names tell the browser to select a font of the type indicated that's loaded on the user's computer. Basically, a generic name is a fallback in case none of the other fonts are available. Your options for a generic name are `serif`, `sans-serif`, `cursive`, `fantasy`, and `monospace`.

To illustrate how `font-family` works, take a look at a couple of examples. The first example CSS rule shows a `font-family` for selectors that should appear in a serif font:

```
body {font-family: Georgia, Times,
          "Times New Roman", serif;}
```

A second CSS rule indicates which selectors display text in a sans-serif font:

```
h1, h2, h3 {font-family: Verdana,
          Arial, Helvetica,
          sans-serif;}
```

So how to choose what fonts to use? The following fonts are among the most common fonts loaded on computers: Verdana, Georgia, Courier, Helvetica, Arial, and Times New Roman.

If you're expecting to have a lot of text that needs reading, select a serifed font. Research shows that this kind of font is much easier to read. (However, many people prefer the *look* of sans-serif type, so you may have to choose between a font that's attractive at a glance or a font that's practical for reading.)

Some fonts, such as Verdana and Georgia, are designed for the screen. Fonts better suited for the printed page include Times New Roman and Helvetica.

Fine-tuning font properties

After you set up the fonts you want to use, you can further refine how fonts look and feel. Common changes include the following:

- Sizing some fonts larger or smaller than the main body text

- Applying boldface for emphasis on headings or other elements that should stand out

- Adjusting the width so that letters are packed closer together or spread farther apart

To set the height of a font, use the `font-size` property. Setting a value as a percentage or ems is recommended. The following examples show percentage values that set the font size relative to other paragraph text in a document:

```
p.big { font-size: 125%; }
p.normal {font-size: 100%; }
p.small {font-size: 60%; }
```

In Figure 5-1, you can see these font-size styles applied to the title, a quotation, and the byline of a poem by Walt Whitman.

To set how bold or not bold a font appears, use the `font-weight` property, which takes the keyword values `normal` (the default), `bold`, `bolder`, or `lighter`. Figure 5-2 shows the following three CSS rules applied to the same snippet of a Walt Whitman poem:

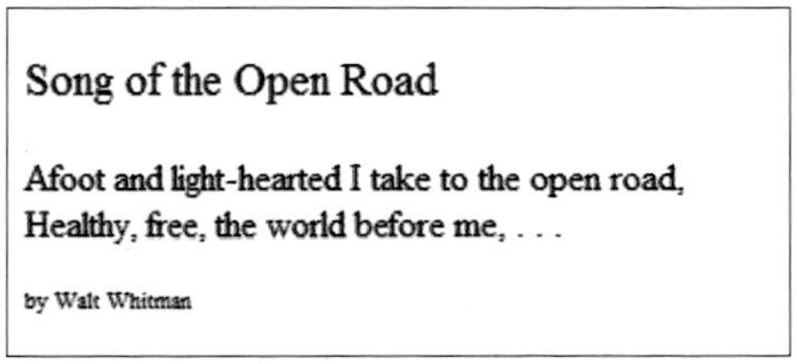

Song of the Open Road

Afoot and light-hearted I take to the open road,
Healthy, free, the world before me, . . .

by Walt Whitman

Figure 5-1

```
p.bolder { font-weight:
          bolder; }
p.normal { font-weight:
          normal; }
p.lighter { font-weight:
          lighter; }
```

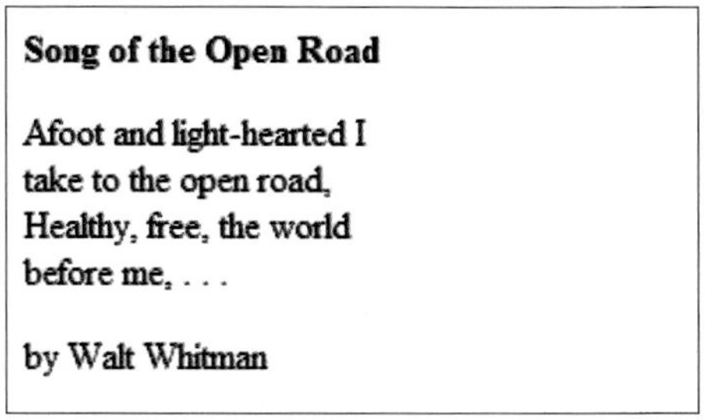

To stretch out lines of text, the `font-stretch` property is at your service. This property also takes keyword values, including `expanded`, `normal`, and `condensed`. In Figure 5-3, you can't see much difference, but your mileage may vary:

```
p.expanded { font-stretch:
            expanded; }
p.normal { font- stretch:
          normal; }
p.condensed { font-stretch:
             condensed; }
```

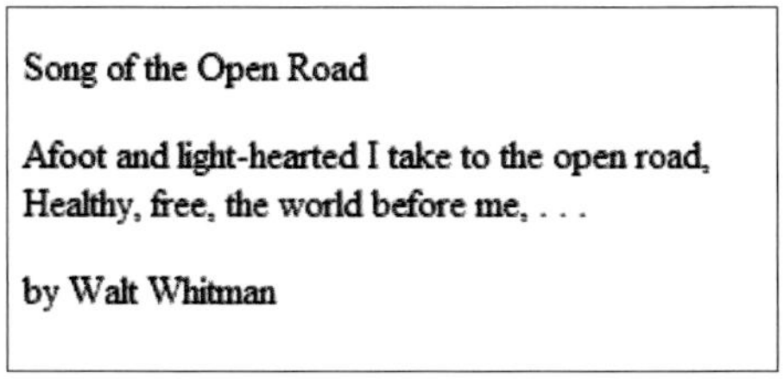

Figure 5-2

Figure 5-3

Tapping into text properties

When you want to align, indent, or apply some fancier visual effects, you need the text properties.

Aligning text

To start, look at `text-align`, which enables you to align text left, right, and so on, just as you can in a word-processing program. The `text-align` property takes the following keyword values: `left`, `right`, `center`, and `justify`. The following CSS rule aligns text to the right, as shown in Figure 5-4:

```
{ text-align: right; }
```

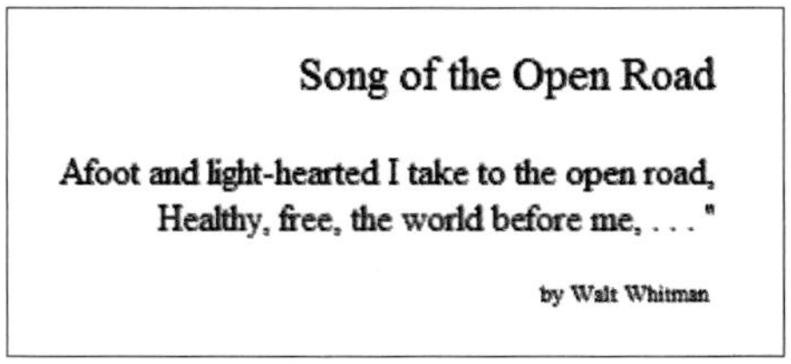

To change the alignment to centered, change the value of the `text-align`

GO ONLINE

You find out about the basic font properties in this topic. The CSS3 specification explains *all* the font properties and their possible values. You can find the the specification at `www.w3.org/tr/css3-fonts`.

Figure 5-4

property, as shown in the following CSS rule and in Figure 5-5:

```
{ text-align: center; }
```

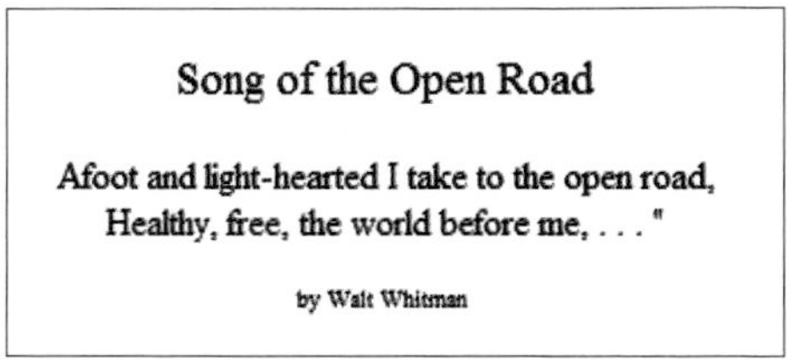

Indenting paragraphs

The `text-indent` property enables you to indent the first line of text after a hard break. Use a length or a percentage as a value, as shown in the following code:

```
{ text-indent: 3em; }
```

Figure 5-6 shows how the paragraph of the text is indented.

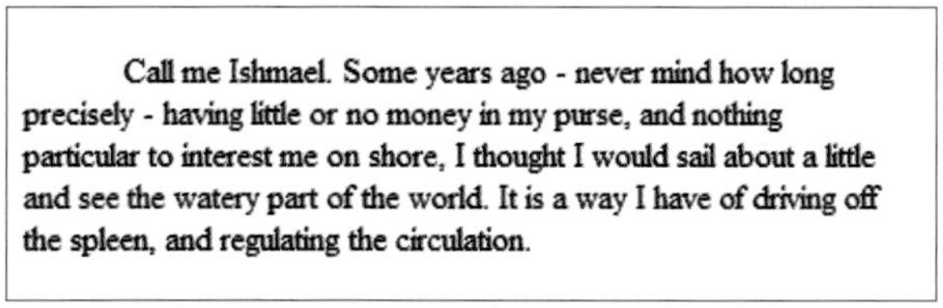

Song of the Open Road

Afoot and light-hearted I take to the open road,
Healthy, free, the world before me, . . . "

by Walt Whitman

Figure 5-5

Call me Ishmael. Some years ago - never mind how long precisely - having little or no money in my purse, and nothing particular to interest me on shore, I thought I would sail about a little and see the watery part of the world. It is a way I have of driving off the spleen, and regulating the circulation.

Figure 5-6

Transforming the case

Changing the case of text with CSS enables you to create and adjust stylistic effects quickly and easily. For example, in the HTML for the example shown in Figure 5-7, I applied a `<span>` tag with an `id` attribute value of `ishmael` to the first sentence of the paragraph. Then using an ID selector in CSS, I selected this snippet of text and changed it to uppercase using the `text-transform` property. The CSS rule looks like this:

```
#ishmael {text-transform: uppercase; }
```

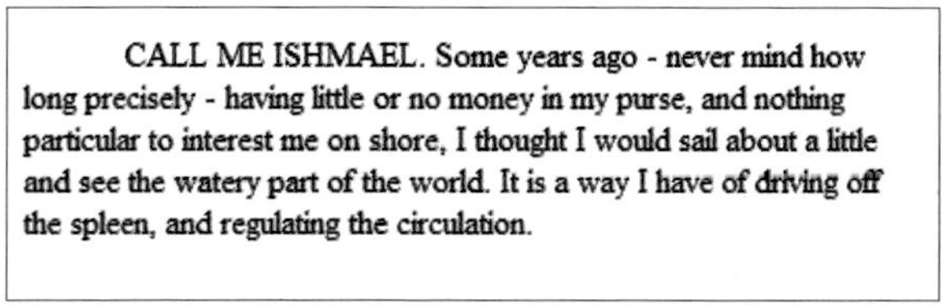

CALL ME ISHMAEL. Some years ago - never mind how long precisely - having little or no money in my purse, and nothing particular to interest me on shore, I thought I would sail about a little and see the watery part of the world. It is a way I have of driving off the spleen, and regulating the circulation.

Figure 5-7

Other values for `text-transform` include `capitalize` and `lowercase`.

Adding underline, strikethrough, and overline

To control how underline, strikethrough, and overline appear on text, turn to the `text-decoration` property. You can include up to three values for this property, one from the following three groups of keyword values:

- `underline`, `no-underline`, `replace-underline`
- `overline`, `no-overline`, `replace-overline`
- `line-through`, `no-line-through`, `replace-line-through`

You can also include `none` or `remove-all`. Most browsers support the `text-decoration` property, and you can use it to control whether underline appears, such as on links, or to add strikethrough.

Creating shadows

Text shadows are new in CSS3, a feature many designers are happy to see because the more HTML5 and CSS3 can do with text natively, the less web designers need to rely on images of text to get the look they want or settle for text effects they find ho-hum. You create shadows in CSS3 with the intuitively named `text-shadow` property. What's not so intui-

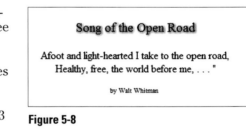

Song of the Open Road

Afoot and light-hearted I take to the open road,
Healthy, free, the world before me, . . . "

by Walt Whitman

Figure 5-8

tive are all the values this property can take. Here's an example CSS rule that adds an orange text shadow, and you can see how the effect displays in a browser in Figure 5-8:

```
{ text-shadow: 1px 1px 5px hsl(33, 100%, 50%); }
```

The first three values must be absolute and are, in order from left to right, as follows:

- **Horizontal shadow:** Specifies how far the shadow reaches horizontally.
- **Vertical shadow:** Specifies how tall the shadow stretches vertically.
- **Blur:** Determines how hard-edged or soft the shadow appears. If you want the shadow to look blocky, just like the text, don't add any blur. Conversely, the more blur you add, the softer the shadow looks.

The last value is a color value, in this case in HSL notation, but you can use any valid color notation that you like. Most new browsers support `text-shadow`. (The exception is IE9.)

Spacing the text

Space is often used to make text easier to read or to rest the eye. When you want to add different types of spacing, these properties are at your disposal:

- ✔ **Line height:** Specifies how much vertical space each line of text should take up. Negative values are not allowed, of course (because a line of text has to take up some space). But, you can set the line height to less than the height of the characters, in which case, the lines of text overlap each other.

- ✔ **Letter spacing:** Specifies how much space should be between characters.

- ✔ **Word spacing:** Used to increase or decrease the default amount of space between words.

Emerging CSS3 properties

Many text properties in CSS3 haven't yet been adopted in browsers. Here's a quick introduction to text properties that have limited or no browser support but that will likely be supported in the future:

- ✔ **Alignment:** You'll find no, or limited, support for the new CSS3 values for `text-align`, `start` and `end`. The same is true for new CSS3 properties, `text-align-last` and `text-align-justify` properties. `text-align-last` is not supported in any major browser, and `text-justify` is supported only in IE.

  The `text-align` property also has a string value, which must be a single character. Ideally, the text aligns on this character. However string values for `text-align` are not supported in most browsers, which is a pity because this feature would be very useful, especially in tables.

- ✔ **Decoration:** The following `text-decoration` properties are new to CSS3 and have not been fully implemented in all browsers: `text-decoration-color`, `text-decoration-style`, and `text-decoration-line`.

- ✔ **Wrapping:** The `text-wrap` property is new to CSS3. It allows you to control whether and how lines of text wrap inside an element. It has not yet been implemented in any of the major browsers.

EXTRA INFO

For the most current information about CSS3 text properties, see the specification at `www.w3.org/tr/css3-text`.

Downloading fonts with a web page

The @font-face rule in CSS3 enables you to use fonts on a web page without worrying about whether your site visitors have the font loaded on their computers. With the @font-face rule, your web page links to a font file that downloads with the page so the web page can display the font.

The basic CSS syntax for the @font-face rule is as follows:

```
@font-face { font-family: value;
src: url(address) format("filetypestring");
}
```

✔ The value for font-family is the name of the font.

✔ The value for the url address is an absolute or relative address to the font file you want the browser to download with the page. You might keep font files in a subfolder called fonts, just as you do for images.

✔ The value for format is whatever file type string corresponds to the file type that the url links to.

In practice, you currently need to link to several different font file types because not all browsers recognize a single file type. In the future, WOFF (Web Open Font Format) may emerge as the standard, but that hasn't happened yet. Table 5-1 lists the most common font file types and which browsers support each file type:

Table 5-1		File Types for @font-face		
File Type	*What It Means*	*File Type String*	*Browser Support*	*Good to Know*
TTF	TrueType	"truetype"	Safari 3.1, Firefox 3.5, Opera 10, and Mobile Safari (in iOS 4.2), IE9	An established format closely associated with Microsoft, but vendors beyond Microsoft have adopted it.
SVG	Scalable Vector Graphics	"svg"	iOS prior to 4.2, Chrome, and Opera	File sizes can be large and slow to download. This is the only format that iOS (for iPhone and iPad) supported prior to iOS version 4.2.

File Type	What It Means	File Type String	Browser Support	Good to Know
EOT	Embedded Open Type	`"embedded-opentype"`	IE4 to IE9	Microsoft is the only browser vendor to support this file type.
WOFF	Web Open Font Format	`"woff"`	IE9, Firefox 3.6, and Chrome 6	The proposed standard for web graphics files.

To link to more than one file type, you include all the `url` values you need in `src` and separate each one with a comma. The user agent uses the first file type that it recognizes, so prioritize the order of the files, if needed. Here's how the CSS code for the `@font-face` rule looks for a font called Muncie:

```
@font-face { font-family: Muncie;
src: url(fonts/muncie.ttf) format("truetype"),
     url(fonts/muncie.woff) format("woff"),
     url(fonts/muncie.eot) format("embedded-opentype");
}
```

When you set up this rule in the CSS, you can then refer to the `font-family` name when you later style HTML elements in your style sheet. So if you wanted all your `<h1>` and `<h2>` elements to appear in the Muncie font, the CSS for those elements would look like this:

```
h1, h2 {font-family: Muncie, Verdana, Arial, sans-serif; }
```

The CSS still specifies fallback fonts (Verdana, Arial, and finally the generic sans-serif font), just in case Muncie doesn't load. Specifying fallback fonts is still recommended when using the `@font-face` rule.

The `@font-face` rule is a great way to use fonts that complement a website's content and tone, as well as to display a larger array of fonts with confidence that your users can see the chosen font in their browsers. When choosing a font to use, keep the following tips in mind:

- ✔ **Check whether the font is easy to read and displays well onscreen.** Not all fonts do.

- ✔ **Check the copyright information and the end-user license agreement (EULA) for the font to make sure you have permission to use the font on your site.** Just because you can pay for a font doesn't mean you can use it online; or a free font that you can use with @font-face may ask that you give the font designer a credit.

✔ **Check out Font Squirrel, a popular resource for fonts that you can use with @font-face fonts.** Font Squirrel offers a converter that enables you to convert a font file into any other file type that you need; check it out in Figure 5-9. (www.fontsquirrel.com)

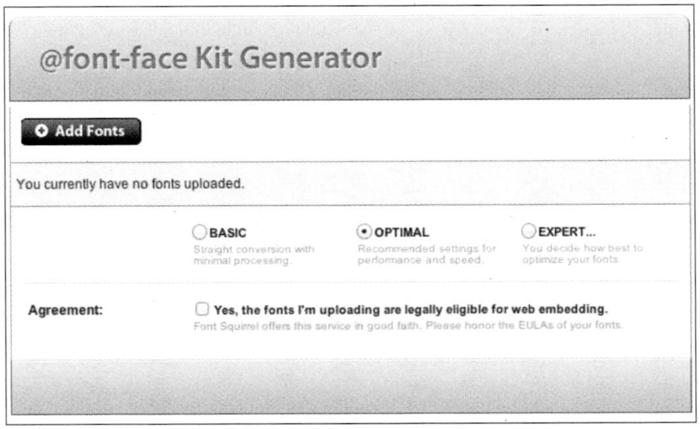

@font-face Kit Generator

⊕ **Add Fonts**

You currently have no fonts uploaded.

○ BASIC	⊙ OPTIMAL	○ EXPERT...
Straight conversion with minimal processing.	Recommended settings for performance and speed.	You decide how best to optimize your fonts.

Agreement: ☐ **Yes, the fonts I'm uploading are legally eligible for web embedding.**
Font Squirrel offers this service in good faith. Please honor the EULAs of your fonts.

Figure 5-9

Styling list bullets

CSS enables you to customize the bullet that appears next to unordered lists, customize the numbering system used in ordered lists, and adjust the position of the list bullet or number.

To change the appearance of a bullet, select the list you want to change, use the list-style-type property, and choose from the following keyword values:

✔ disc (the default)

✔ circle

✔ square

Here's an example of a CSS rule that changes the bullet style to circle:

```
ul.circle {list-style-type: circle; }
```

You can also use an image for a bullet, instead of the keywords. The syntax for the CSS is

```
selector {list-style-image: url("image.png"); }
```

You use the `list-style-image` property and a `url` value that points to the image file you want to use. The URL for the image file can be either relative or absolute. Here's an example of a CSS rule that uses an image:

```
ul.star {list-style-image: url("starbullet.png"); }
```

Figure 5-10 shows an example list with three different bullet types. The first is an image of a star, the second uses the `circle` keyword value, and the third uses the `square` keyword value.

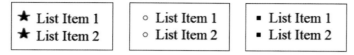

Figure 5-10

 Sometimes, part of an image bullet is cut off in the browser. To fix the problem, increase the size of the left margin in the `<ul>` or `<li>` element, using the `margin-left` property.

Customizing numbering in ordered lists

To change the numbering in an ordered list, use the `list-style-type` property, just as you do for unordered lists.

 The `list-style-type` property doesn't differentiate between `<ol>` and `<ul>` elements, so you can use any of the options discussed whether you tag the text as `<ol>` or `<ul>`. However, most of the keyword values were clearly meant to work with bullets or numbering. The `none` value works well for either.

Table 5-2 contains the possible values and what the resulting automatic numbering looks like when displayed in a browser.

Table 5-2	Keyword Values for Ordered Lists
Value	**What It Looks Like**
decimal	1. List Item 1 2. List Item 2
decimal-leading-zero	01. List Item 1 02. List Item 2
lower-roman	i. List Item 1 ii. List Item 2
upper-roman	I. List Item 1 II. List Item 2
lower-greek	α. List Item 1 β. List Item 2
lower-latin	a. List Item 1 b. List Item 2
upper-latin	A. List Item 1 B. List Item 2
armenian	Ա. List Item 1 Բ. List Item 2
georgian	ა. List Item 1 ბ. List Item 2

Value	What It Looks Like
lower-alpha	a. List Item 1 b. List Item 2
upper-alpha	A. List Item 1 B. List Item 2
none	List Item 1 List Item 2

Positioning bullets and numbering

By default, a bullet or number hangs out in the whitespace to the left of the text. This default option is great because it's the style most people want and expect.

When you want something different, however, CSS enables you to change the positioning with the list-style-position property. Values include the keywords inside, outside, and (new in CSS3) hanging.

EXTRA INFO

You can generate content on web pages by combining pseudo-elements with CSS. The process is beyond the scope of this lesson but useful to know about as you expand your knowledge of HTML and CSS.

Generated content is content that's automatically inserted before or after an item, such as a list or a heading. The content can be a text string, an image, a counter, or anything else the CSS specification allows. To make generated content work, you combine pseudo-elements with the content property. The pseudo-elements indicate where the generated content goes, and the content property tells the browser what content to generate.

Here's an example of a CSS rule that generates the text string *Wow!* before a list element:

```
li::before{content:"Wow!";}
```

You can find out more about generated content at www.w3.org/tr/css2/generate.html.

A working draft to update lists and counters lives at www.w3.org/tr/2011/wd-css3-lists-20110524.

Styling Images and Borders

This section introduces you to the basics of styling images and borders. You find out how to make text wrap around images and create borders using different line styles. You also discover how to to round corners and add shadows behind boxes, two popular new features in CSS3.

Setting image styles

You've already learned about several properties that are typically applied to images, including those for margins and padding, floating elements left or right, and setting width and height. Images are so important to most websites that the impact these properties have on images deserves its own section. You can combine these with borders, as well, which are the main focus of the next section.

The `margin` and `padding` properties can determine how much whitespace appears between the image and surrounding text *(margin)* and between the border and the image *(padding)*. The following CSS rule is applied to the image in Figure 5-11.

```
img {padding: 50px;
margin: 50px;
}
```

Often, you want the text to wrap around an image that goes with that text. For that, use the `float` property. The following CSS rule creates the effect shown in Figure 5-12.

```
img {float: right; }
```

EXTRA INFO

Tables are, by default, block images, and as such, follow the general rules and take the same styling properties as all block images. The `<td>` cells, however, are inline elements, and they behave like inline images. If you change an entire table from a block to an inline element, however, you can float the table so that the surrounding text wraps around it. The effect is like that of floating images and can be handy if you want to display a small, related table of data amid paragraphs of text.

The other concepts for styling tables are similar to other styling covered in this lesson.

For more about styling tables, check out the CSS specification at `www.w3.org/tr/css2/tables.html`. You can also find details about styling tables via the W3Schools website at `www.w3schools.com/css/css_table.asp`.

Figure 5-11

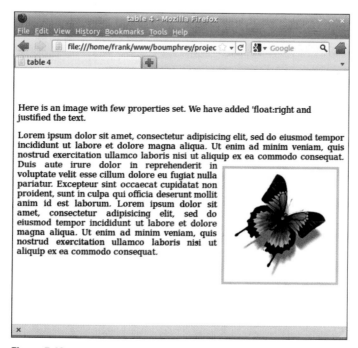

Figure 5-12

When using the width and height properties on an image, remember that although the image appears small in a browser window, site visitors are downloading the full-size image. Also if you enlarge the image, you aren't increasing the pixel size. Sizing images with CSS can be helpful when you don't have a large size difference, but if you can, sizing images and optimizing them in a graphics program is your best option. Then the browser displays the image at what size you chose in the graphics program, and you don't need to write extra CSS code. Figure 5-13 illustrates how width and height have the potential to distort an image.

Here's how the width and height properties were applied in Figure 5-13:

- **Top left:** No width or height specified
- **Top center:** img {width: 100px; }
- **Top right:** img {width: 100px; height: 204px; }
- **Bottom:** img {width: 300px; height: 100px; }

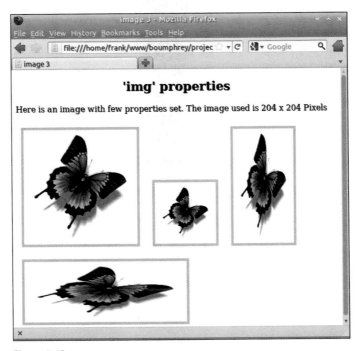

Figure 5-13

Creating borders

Borders are pretty simple, but you can do a lot of different things with them. You can add a basic border to an image or any other block element with the following syntax:

```
{ border: style color width
        ; }
```

Figure 5-13 showed an image with a plain gray border. Here's an example of a CSS rule that adds a dashed border, which is used to suggest the old cut lines on a coupon, even though it's displayed in a browser in Figure 5-14 (and today, a real online coupon takes the form of a bar code or a QR code).

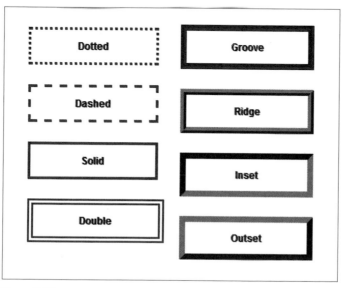

Figure 5-14

```
img.coupon {border: dashed green 0.2em}
```

The default value for a border's style is none, and you can change the style using any of the following keyword values. A border created using each value is shown in Figure 5-15.

Figure 5-15

✔ dotted

✔ dashed

✔ solid

✔ double

✔ groove

✔ ridge

✔ inset

✔ outset

For more control over the appearance of each side of a border, you can use the `border-style`, `border-color`, and `border-width` properties:

- ✔ **border-style** takes any of the keyword values noted in the preceding list, as well as `none`.

- ✔ **border-color** takes a color value in any of the recognized color notations: keywords, hexadecimal, RGB, or RGBa.

- ✔ **border-width** can take a relative or absolute value. Remember that relative values, such as ems, keep your design flexible so that it's more likely to display well in a broad range of browsers and devices.

The main reason these properties offer you more control is that each can have one, two, or four values:

- ✔ **If you use one value,** the border is the same on all four sides.

- ✔ **If you use two values,** the first value applies to the top and bottom, the second to the left and right.

- ✔ **If you use four values,** the values are applied clockwise: top, right, bottom, and left.

Figure 5-16 illustrates how the values are applied to different parts of a border. I used contrasting colors that aren't necessarily the best looking but stand out so you can see how the values display.

One value
{border-color: red;}

Two values
{border-color: red blue;}

Courtesy of the U.S. Fish and Wildlife Service

Courtesy of the U.S. Fish and Wildlife Service

Four values
{border-color: red green blue black;}

Courtesy of the U.S. Fish and Wildlife Service

Figure 5-16

Using border images

The border-image property is new to CSS3. Its purpose is to let you create any type of border that you want around an element by using images. At present, it needs a vendor prefix to make it work, and the only browser in which this property behaves correctly is Chrome. To give you a sense of what it can do, check out the code in L5_01.htm, which uses border.png. You can download these files from this book's companion website (see the Introduction for details). Figure 5-17 shows the output displayed in Chrome.

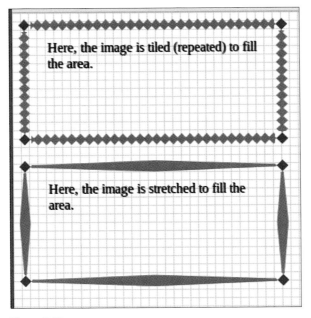

Here, the image is tiled (repeated) to fill the area.

Here, the image is stretched to fill the area.

Figure 5-17

Compare Figure 5-17 with Figure 5-18, which shows the original image used to create the effects.

Rounding corners

Rounded corners are new to CSS3. To create them, apply the border-radius property to the element whose corners you want to round, like the photo of a chameleon shown in Figure 5-19, which has a border-radius property set to 3em.

Figure 5-18

The value, in this case 3em, is the radius of a circle. The radius tells the browser the size of the circle and thus how much rounding to add. The bigger the radius, the more rounded the element. You give the value as a length: ems, percentages, and so on.

As shown in Figure 5-20, you can give one, or more than one, value:

- ✔ If just one value is given, all borders are rounded the same.

- ✔ If two values are given, the first value is the y-axis of the ellipse and the second value is the x-axis.

- ✔ Each separate corner can take its own values: `border-top-right-radius`, `border-bottom-right-radius`, `border-bottom-left-radius`, and `border-top-left-radius`.

GO ONLINE

Details about the `border-image` property can be found at `www.w3.org/tr/css3-background/#border-images`.

Figure 5-19

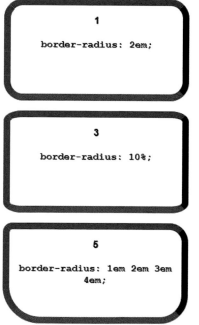

1

border-radius: 2em;

2

border-radius: 3em 1em;

3

border-radius: 10%;

4

border-radius: 10% 25%;

5

border-radius: 1em 2em 3em 4em;

6

border-radius: 2em 3em/5em 2em;

Figure 5-20

✔ To load different values on to the composite `border-radius` property, separate them with a forward slash.

To take a closer look at how the different boxes in Figure 5-20 were created, check out the CSS style sheet that created this web page in Listing 5-1. The ID selectors, #d1, #d2, #d3, and so on correspond to the box numbers shown in the figure.

Listing 5-1:   Rounding Corners with CSS3

```
body {margin:auto;
width: 80%;
}

#left {float:left;
width: 45%;
}

#right {float: right;
width: 45%;
}

div.example {border-style: solid;
border-color: red black green blue;
border-width: 0.7em;
margin: 5%;
width: 80%;
height: 150px;
}

p {font-family: Arial;
font-weight: bolder;
text-align: center;
}

span {font-family: courier; }

#d1 {border-radius: 2em;}

#d2 {border-radius: 3em 1em;}

#d3 {border-radius: 10%;}

#d4 {border-radius: 10% 25%;}

#d5 {border-radius: 1em 2em 3em 4em;}

#d6 {border-radius: 2em 3em/5em 2em;}
```

Adding shadows behind box elements

Box shadows are new to CSS3 and add a shadow behind any block element, such as the chamelon image you saw in the preceding section. See how, in Figure 5-21, the image now has a shadow?

To create a shadow, use the box-shadow property, which must have at least two values: the horizontal position and the vertical position of the shadow. The following example code shows the two values in action:

Figure 5-21

```
{box-shadow: 1em 1em;}
```

You can also add optional values, which you must put in the following order for the values to work:

1. *Horizontal position*

2. *Vertical position*

3. *Blur:* The amount of blur added to the shadow

4. *Spread:* The amount of the shadow that appears on the left and top edges of the box

5. *Color:* Use any accepted color value

6. *Inset:* A keyword value that flips the shadow with a background color

In Figure 5-22, you can see how adding each of the optional values to the yellow square's shadow impacts its appearance in the browser.

Here's what the final CSS code for the yellow and green box shadow example looks like:

```
div {background-color: yellow;
height: 20em;
width: 20em;
box-shadow: 1em 1em 1em 1em green inset;
}
```

{box-shadow: 1em 1em;}   {box-shadow: 1em 1em 1em;}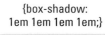

{box-shadow:
1em 1em 1em 1em green;}   {box-shadow:
1em 1em 1em 1em green inset;}

Figure 5-22

Introducing Media Types and Media Queries

HTML documents can be used on and by a variety of different devices — not just desktop computers. Media types and media queries are two ways to make sure that you give users the best experience on every device that you intend your web pages to be viewed with.

Introducing media types

Media types, from CSS2, enable you to present your site in different ways based on the type of media your visitor uses. For example, you may want to present a web page that visitors will print differently from the one that visitors see onscreen. Or you may want to show visitors using a mobile device with a small screen a different layout from those viewing your web page on a larger desktop monitor or laptop screen.

Here's a list of the recognized media types:

- ✔ **all**: Suitable for all devices.
- ✔ **braille**: Intended for Braille tactile feedback devices.
- ✔ **embossed**: Intended for paged Braille printers.
- ✔ **handheld**: Intended for handheld devices (typically with a small screen and limited bandwidth).
- ✔ **print**: Intended for paged material and for documents viewed on screen in print preview mode.
- ✔ **projection**: Intended for projected presentations, for example projectors.
- ✔ **screen**: What most people write web pages for. Intended primarily for color computer screens.
- ✔ **speech**: Intended for speech synthesizers. *Note:* CSS2 had a similar media type called `aural` for this purpose. `aural` is deprecated in HTML5. Although you're now encouraged to use the `speech` media type, no browsers as of yet recognize `speech`.
- ✔ **tty**: Intended for media using a fixed-pitch character grid (such as teletypes, terminals, or portable devices with limited display capabilities).
- ✔ **tv**: Intended for television-type devices (low resolution, color, limited-scrollability screens, and sound available).

Here's the basic syntax for applying CSS based on the `@media` rule:

```
@media mediatype {
selector {property:value; }
}
```

Basically, you start with the `@media` rule and indicate the media type — such as `print`, `handheld`, `screen`, and so on — that you want certain CSS rules to apply to. You then insert CSS properties and values that you want to use inside the curly brackets of the `@media` rule, as you would in a typical CSS rule.

Listing 5-2 shows a style sheet snippet that uses the @media construct and gives you an idea of how you might set up @media rules for different media types in a style sheet.

Listing 5-2:   A Sample @media Rule

```
@media print{

    h1{font-size:40pt;
        text-decoration:underline;
        font-style:italic;
    }

    #lcol,#rcol{display:none;
    }

    table{border:none;
    }

    #printbadge{display:block;
    }
}


@media screen{

    #webbadge{display:block;
    }
}
```

Figure 5-23 shows the output in print mode, and Figure 5-24 shows the output in screen mode.

GO ONLINE

See www.w3.org/tr/css2/ media.html and www. w3.org/tr/css3-media queries for the relevant specifications.

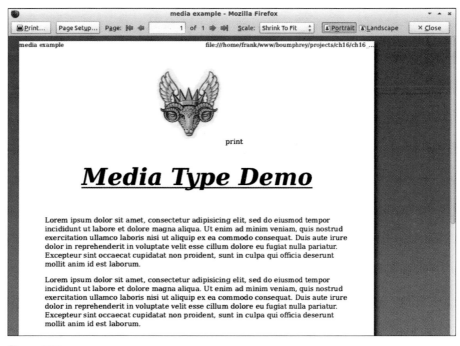

Figure 5-23

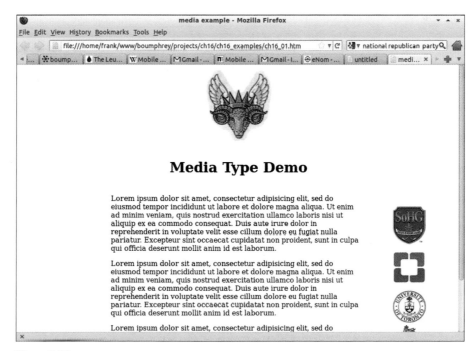

Figure 5-24

Creating media queries

Media queries, new in CSS3, extend what media types can do and give you a little more control over when a set of styles is applied. Whereas media types allow you to use different style sheets depending on the type of device, media queries allow you to use different style sheets depending on the capabilities of the device. Media queries are becoming a popular way to handle the display of websites on a variety of devices for two reasons:

- Not every web browser on a handheld device responds to the `handheld` media type.
- Screen sizes of mobile phones and tablets are becoming increasingly diverse.

With a media query, you can ask the browser what its screen resolution is and tell the browser what CSS to use based on the information the browser provides. For example, if you want to display your page in a single column when the browser width (technically called the *viewport*) is less than 800 pixels, you can create a media query like this:

```
@media screen and (max-width: 799px) {property:value;
          property:value; }
```

The following list offers a little more detail about how the browser interprets each element when it encounters this media query:

- **@media screen** tells the browser this query applies to any device, such as desktop computers, smartphones, and tablets, that's valid for the `screen` media type.
- **and (max-width: 799px)** tells the browser to check whether the screen width has 799 or fewer pixels. Whatever properties and values you needed to add in order to create the single-column layout would go where they usually do — between the curly brackets.

In a media query, you still use the `@media` rule and a media type. You also add an expression that's either `true` or `false`. If the expression is `true`, the browser applies the CSS in the media query. In this case, if the width of the viewport is 799 pixels or fewer, the CSS rules within the curly brackets apply.

Creating a Style Sheet for the Mobile Web

A common use of media queries is to detect small-screen devices and to serve them a style sheet that's optimized for use on smartphones.

To detect a small-screen device, you can use the following `<link>` tag in the header of your HTML document:

```
<link rel="stylesheet" type="text/css" media="only screen
       and (max-width:480px), only screen and (max-
       device-width: 480px)" href="/css/smallscreen.
       css" />
```

This tag loads the `smallscreen.css` style sheet if the size of the browser is 480px or less or the size of the device's screen is 480px or less. On mobile devices, the width of the browser is typically the same as the width of the screen (the browser takes up the whole screen width, in other words).

To create a mobile style sheet, follow these three tips:

✔ **Specify widths as percentages, which is a fluid layout.** Notice the difference in these two styles:

```
#content {
  width: 960px;
}
```

```
#content {
  width: 100%;
}
```

The first example doesn't adjust for small devices. The second example always takes up 100 percent of the horizontal space available to it — whether this is 960px or 320px.

✔ **Turn off auto-scaling by setting the `viewport` meta tag.** Although this isn't something you can set in the style sheet, it's vital to optimizing your site for mobile devices. The following meta tag, when placed in the header of an HTML document, indicates to browsers that the width of the website should be set to the width of the display:

```
<meta name="viewport" content="width=device-width,
       initial-scale=1.0, maximum-scale=1.0" />
```

✔ **Make clickable areas large enough to be touched.** Apple's guidelines for mobile apps say that buttons should be at least 44px by 44px for users to easily press them with their fingers. This is a good guideline for designing mobile websites as well.

 Summing Up

This lesson gave you a tour around the many CSS properties you can use for different types of elements you'll likely want to style. Here's a brief recap:

✔ CSS groups properties that style text into two categories: font properties and text properties. When you want to format the appearance of the characters, check out the font properties. The text properties enable you to format the words and paragraphs.

✔ Typically, you choose one of a few fonts users are likely to have loaded on their computers, as well as a series of fallback fonts. When using an uncommon font is important to you, the @font-face rule tells the browser to download the font you want with the rest of the page.

✔ In addition to properties that align, indent, adjust spacing, and change the case of a page's text, new text properties in CSS3 can add shadows and wrap text within a box. CSS3 also adds the ability to align text on a specific character, which will be useful for tables when more browsers begin supporting the feature.

✔ You can customize the look of bullets in unordered lists with keyword values or an image. Similarly, customize the numbering of ordered lists by choosing from a variety of numbering schemes.

✔ Borders can be as simple or as complex as you need. Use the border property or customize each side of a border with the more specific border properties for style, color, and width.

✔ The border-radius property, new in CSS3, enables you to round the corners of any block element by specifying a radius size. The bigger the radius, the bigger the circle, the more rounding is applied to an element.

✔ The @media rule allows you to use media types and media queries. The media type enables you to present your site in different ways based on the type of media your visitor uses. Media queries build upon the media type and allow you to use different style sheets depending on the parameter the media query specifies.

✔ To create a mobile style sheet, specify widths as percentages, turn off auto-scaling by setting the viewport meta tag, and make clickable areas large enough to be touched.

Try-it-yourself lab

In this lesson, you learned about a formatting text with CSS. Time to experiment with some of the things you've learned:

1. **In your text editor, start with the following basic HTML document:**

```
<!DOCTYPE html >
<html>

<head>
<title>CSS Experiments</title>
<style type='text/css'>
  h1 {
    /*replace this*/
  }
  h2 {
    /*replace this*/
  }
  h3 {
    /*replace this*/
  }
</style>
</head>

<body>
  <h1>Make this text huge.</h1>
  <h2>Align this to the right and make it blue.</h2>
  <h3>Compress This (reduce the space between
        letters).</h3>
</body>
</html>
```

2. **Follow the instructions in the document to style the three headers.**

   If you need some help, you can download the completed document from the website (L5_02.htm).

3. **After you complete the initial instructions, try some of the other styles you've learned.**

   Go nuts! See how good or bad (your choice!) you can make this simple document look by just changing the CSS. Feel free to add your own text as well.

Know this tech talk

blur: Determines how hard-edged or soft the shadow appears.

character: Represents a letter, a number, a symbol, or a special character.

font: How a character is rendered.

font family: A group of similar fonts.

letter spacing: Specifies how much space should be between characters.

line height: Specifies how much vertical space each line of text should take up.

margin: How much whitespace appears between the image and surrounding text.

media query: Allows you to use different style sheets depending on the capabilities of the device. Tells the browser what CSS to use based on the information the browser provides about its screen resolution.

media type: Enables you to present your site in different ways based on the type of media your visitor uses.

padding: How much whitespace appears between the border and the image.

text: The series of characters that make up a word, a line, or a paragraph.

word spacing: Used to increase or decrease the default amount of space between words.

The following table outlines some important text and font-related properties and what they do.

Property	What It Does
font-family	Sets the font family.
font-weight	Specifies the weight of a font.
font-size	Sets the size of the fonts.
color	Sets the color of the text.
text-align	Specifies the horizontal alignment of the text.
letter-spacing	Increases or decreases the spacing between letters.
line-height	Sets the line height of the text.
word-spacing	Increases or decreases the spacing between words.

Adding Interactivity with Scripting

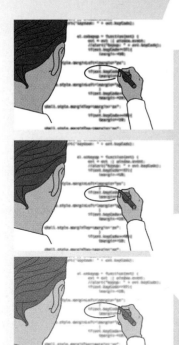

- ✔ The `get` or `post` protocol can be used to *return data from the server.*

- ✔ The `if` keyword *tests for the truth of a statement.*

- ✔ You can *link externally or inline with JavaScript.*

- ✔ You can *validate forms with the forms array.*

- ✔ You need to *follow rules for security when dealing with geolocation.*

This lesson and Lesson 7 deal with several topics that need scripting. So far, how you make a form interactive has been the elephant in the room, but unless you're content with writing decorative pages, you need to know something about scripting. This lesson won't make you a JavaScript guru, but it covers enough to allow you to understand what's going on. JavaScript (and its server-side cousin, PHP) is a very powerful programming language, but this lesson is not going to teach JavaScript as such. I show you how to use them in the context of specific examples.

GO ONLINE

Dummies.com has some very good pages on JavaScript. Point your browser to www.dummies.com/how-to/computers-software/programming/javascript.html.

Sending Forms

In Lesson 3, you looked at how to construct a form in order to send information to the server. But what happens when a user clicks the Submit button?

The answer depends on whether the `<input>` element that creates the button has a `type` attribute of `submit` or `button`.

In most cases, the button is a `submit` button so that's what I focus on in this section. (Find out what happens if the button is of the type `button` in the section, "Validating Forms" later in this lesson.) The following code snippet is an example of a simple form:

```
<form method='get' action='forms1.htm'>
<br/>First Name:-<input type='text' name='fname'/>
<br/>Last Name:-<input type='text' name='lname'/>
<br/><input type='submit' value='submit form'/>
</form>
```

Type this text (or download L6_01.htm from this book's companion site and save it as forms1.htm), open it in your favorite browser, fill in a name (like

John Doe), and click the Submit Form button. The form will reload, but when you look at the address bar, you see something like this:

```
...forms1.htm?fname=John&lname=Doe
```

The address bar reveals what's happened behind the scenes when you clicked the Submit Form button. The browser made up a string of name/value pairs and sent them to the address given in the form's `action` attribute. In Figure 6-1, you see how the address bar looks in Chrome after I fill in the example form with my name.

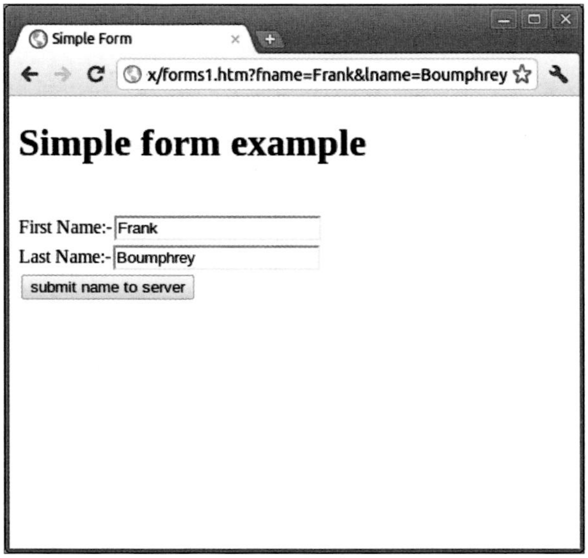

Figure 6-1

Understanding how browsers handle form data

Now that you've had a look at the address bar, you're ready to take a close look at what's happening in the `<input>` elements:

- ✔ Each `<input>` element has been given a `type` and `name` attribute. The value is what the user enters in the text box.
- ✔ When the user clicks the Submit Form button, the browser first builds a string of name/value pairs, of the form `name=value`.
- ✔ An ampersand (&) separates each name/value pair.
- ✔ The browser next goes to the `<form>` element to find out where to send the information and the protocol to send it by.

✔ The `action` attribute tells the browser where to send the information. The value of this attribute must be either an absolute or relative URL. In the preceding example, the `action` attribute contains the filename of the page with the form on it. In other words, the form is sending the information in the form to itself.

✔ The `method` attribute tells the browser which protocol to use: `get` or `post`. The preceding example form specifies the `get` protocol, which is also the default value.

✔ The `get` protocol sends the name/value pair string to the address as a query string attached to the name of the destination address. A *query string* is the part of a URL that comes after the `?`. Whereas everything to the left of a `?` in a URL is information about the address of a particular web page, the purpose of the query string is to communicate data that should be used by the web page.

> **LINGO**
>
> A **query string** is the part of the URL that follows the `?`. A query string communicates data that should be used by the web page.

The next section looks at the `method` values and then you take a look at what happens on the server-side.

PRACTICE

Experiment with the example form (`ch6_01.htm` in the companion files for this book) to see how the browser handles data that you enter into a form. Add a few values to the example form and check the address bar each time you click the Submit Form button. Do the following:

✔ **Enter more than one word into one of the fields.** Notice how the browser replaces spaces with + signs. Because spaces aren't allowed to be in URLs, the browser uses a substitute character.

✔ **Enter very long strings of characters into one of the fields.** URL query strings have a limit to how much data they can contain (which varies depending on the browser). See if you can reach this limit!

✔ **Enter line breaks into one of the fields.**

✔ **Insert special characters (such as ?, / and :), which have other meanings in URLs, into one of the fields.** Notice how the browser automatically replaces these characters with a combination of characters (such as `%26`). Because spaces are one of the characters that aren't allowed in URLs, the browser uses codes starting with percentage signs to represent these characters.

Lesson 6

Choosing between get and post protocols

A browser sends a request to a server whenever a user submits a form containing data to a web server. The request travels as a formatted text file, dubbed an *HTTP request header*, and this text file contains

- ✔ The name of the protocol to be used in returning the data from the server: get or post.
- ✔ The URL of the requested file from the server.
- ✔ A list of file types the browser is willing to accept from the server.
- ✔ The name/value string.

If you specify the get method, the name/value string is attached to the URL. If the post method is used, the string is embedded in the request file itself, and thus doesn't appear in a browser address bar.

Which method to use? The post method is more secure in that the form information isn't so easily accessible. Also, the post method isn't limited in how many characters it can contain. The get method has the advantage that if a page is bookmarked, the requested information is also bookmarked.

EXTRA INFO

The limit to the number of characters that can be sent in a query string differs by browser. Web developers generally use 2,048 characters as the effective limit because this is the maximum number of characters that Internet Explorer will accept in the query string.

Introducing the Building Blocks of Scripting

In this lesson and Lesson 7, you use JavaScript quite extensively. This section introduces the key elements in the JavaScript language and what these elements do. This section gives you the grounding in JavaScript basics that you need to start working with the examples in this lesson and Lesson 7.

Values

JavaScript, indeed any programming language, is about manipulating values. JavaScript recognizes three types of values:

✔ **Strings:** Strings are simple pieces of text quoted with either single or double quotation marks. You can glue together two strings by using the plus sign, a process called *concatenation*. Thus `"This is a string"` `+ " which is just text"` is the same as `"This is a string` `which is just text"`.

✔ **Numbers:** Numbers are just unquoted numbers and can be positive or negative. `67` is a number and so is `3.14`. However, `"3.14"` is not a number but is a string because it's quoted.

✔ **Boolean:** A Boolean value is either `true` or `false`.

Variables

Variables are like buckets or containers that hold a value or an object. You can also place an array in a variable, as I explain a little later in this lesson.

You declare a variable name in JavaScript by using the keyword `var`. For example, `var myname` creates a variable `myname`. When you create a variable name, you need to know the following rules:

> **LINGO**
>
> JavaScript uses a number of reserved words called **keywords.** Examples are `var`, `true`, `for`, `if`, `while`, and numerous others. I point them out as you learn about them. Note that keywords are case-sensitive.

✔ You can use alphanumeric characters or underscores.

✔ You can't use spaces or a JavaScript keyword in the name.

✔ Variable names are case-sensitive; `myvar` is not the same as `myVar`.

To fill a variable, you assign it a value using the equals sign, technically known as an *assignment operator*. Here are a couple of examples:

```
var myName='Jane Roe';
var Num=1.414;
var myBool=true;
```

In each of these examples, I declared a variable name and assigned a value in one fell swoop. The semicolon indicates the end of a statement, explained in the next section.

After you declare a variable name, you can change its value. For example, the following code changes the value contained in `myNum`:

```
myNum=49;
```

After a variable has been created, you can modify its value as many times as you want, and the new value will be remembered until you change it again. This is part of what endows scripting with its ability to make web pages perform useful tasks.

Statements

JavaScript code is made up of a series of statements. A semicolon (;) or a line break terminates a statement. Never rely upon a line break, however. Always make a habit of terminating statements with a semicolon.

Comments

You've already come across two kinds of comments:

```
<!--HTML Comment-->

/*CSS Comment*/
```

JavaScript, however, uses these two kinds of comments:

- ✔ A pair of forward slashes //, which comment anything up to the next line break.
- ✔ A comment identical to CSS, which can comment multiple lines:

```
/*This is also a JavaScript Comment*/
```

Objects

Everything is an *object,* and objects consist of other objects. For example, my body is an object, which has a torso object, and a head object. My head has an eyes object, an ears object, and a hair object.

Objects also have things that they are, and things that they do. In programming, these are dubbed *properties* and *methods.* For example, my eyes have a color property and a seeing method. You have come across a special group of objects already when I talked about the HTML DOM (see Lesson 1 for a refresher).

JavaScript has numerous built-in objects. For example the `window` object contains information about the browser window; the `document` object contains information about the page that was loaded on the browser. In JavaScript, you use objects to modify and manipulate web pages.

For example, all the HTML elements within a web page have style objects, and these styles have properties. You can access the `color` style of an element object (you have to create these yourself, but more on this as you go along) called `myElement` by following the string `document.myElement.style.color`. `color` is the JavaScript equivalent of the CSS property of the same name.

Most JavaScript objects are read/write, so `document.myElement.style.color='red';` would set the `color` property value to `red`.

JavaScript does not like hyphens, so to get the equivalent of a hyphenated CSS property, just capitalize the second word; for example, the CSS `background-color` becomes JavaScript `backgroundColor`, `margin-left` becomes `marginLeft`, and so on.

JavaScript has numerous objects that have *methods* (things objects can do), too. In JavaScript, parentheses identify a method. For example, the `window` object has an `open` method that causes a new browser window to open. You use the `open` method of the `window` object like this:

```
window.open('http://www.example.com', 'examplewindow');
```

The result of this code is that the browser opens a new window named `examplewindow` and the web page at `http://www.example.com` opens in that window.

To help you see how objects with their properties and methods work together in JavaScript, here are a couple examples:

- An often used method of the `window` object is the `alert()` method, so `window.alert("Hello JavaScript");` makes a pop-up box appear and display the text `Hello JavaScript`.
- An often used method of the `document` object is the `write()` method. The following code displays the text `Hello JS Objects` on a web page:
  ```
  document.write("Hello JS Objects");
  ```

Arrays

It's often important to store *lists,* or groups of related variables, in a way that makes it easy to access them together. The way to do this is with arrays. An *array* is an indexed list of values or objects. For example, suppose I had a list of cat names: Ben, Pierre, and Daisy. I could make an array of these names and then, instead of referencing them by name, I could reference them by number. It's rather like what they used to do to you in the army! On induction, you ceased to be John Doe but became Pvt. 34578120!

In JavaScript, you can make an array as follows;

```
var myCats=new Array('Ben','Pierre','Daisy');
```

Indexing begins from 0, so to refer to `'Ben'` I could now use `myCats[0]` instead.

Another form of an array is the *associative array*. Here, instead of using a numbered index, the index is a string. So if I had a list of states and wanted to associate them with their postal codes, I could create an array `state` where the contents of the array are patterned as follows:

```
state["NY"]="New York";
state["OH"]="Ohio";
state["SC"]="South Carolina"
```

Associative arrays are important in reading forms and also on the server-side for reading name/value pairs.

Loops

Loops and arrays go hand in glove. A *loop* is a way of reading through an array. The two basic types of loops in JavaScript are the `for` loop and the `while` loop. To see how loops work, you take a quick look at `for` loops in this section.

The `for` loop is the workhorse of many programming languages, which all use the same syntax:

```
for(i=starting value;i < end value; value increment )
```

`for` tells the browser this is a `for` loop. Inside the parentheses, the `for` loop has three parts. The first is the starting value. Traditionally, you use `i` as the incrementing variable, but the variable name can just as easily be any other letter, or any valid variable name, such as cat or myLoopValue. The incrementing value will be changed in some way (as indicated in the third part) with each iteration of the loop, and the loop will continue to run until the condition in the second part of the for loop statement is met.

For example, the following reads off the myCats array:

```
<script type='text/javascript'>
var myCats=new Array('Ben','Pierre','Daisy');
    for(var i=0;i<myCats.length;i++){
        document.write(myCats[i] + "<br/>");
    }
</script>
```

Note the following:

- ✔ The code snippet is in a <script> tag with a type attribute of text/javascript. See the section "Linking JavaScript to Documents" later in this lesson for details.

- ✔ myCats.length uses the length keyword to figure out how many names are in the array. Remember that indexing begins at 0.

- ✔ i++ increments the value of i by one for each loop.

- ✔ document.write(myCats[i] + "<br>"); writes the cat name, followed by an HTML break tag.

Another loop, the for/in loop, is particularly good for reading through associative arrays. That's because a for/in loop offers a way of reading both the index and the value, as the following example illustrates:

```
<h1>Associative Array</h1>
<p>States and PC appear below</p>
<script type='text/javascript'>
    var states=new Array;
    states["NY"]="New York";
    states["OH"]="Ohio";
    states["SC"]="South Carolina";
    var state;
    for(state in states){
        document.write(states[state]+" - "+state +
        "<br/>");
    }
</script>
```

This uses a special form of a for loop to read the state name and its zip code. It does this by starting with the first element in the array and looping through every element until there are no more left. At each iteration of the loop, the `document.write` statement prints the index (`"NY"` or `"OH"`, for example) and the value.

Events

Events are very important in JavaScript. They are the ways by which a user communicates with the document. A user causes an event by moving the mouse (even just a pixel), clicking the mouse, pressing a key, loading an image or a page, submitting a form, and so on. The capture and trickle down of events are also important concepts to understand in order to work with events:

LINGO

An **event handler** hands off the event to more code that then processes that event.

- ✔ To be useful, an event must be captured, and JavaScript has numerous *event handlers* to do this.

- ✔ Events trickle down. When one HTML element is nested within another HTML element, the event will be fired on the top element, then the next, and so on.

The following code features a `<p>` element nested in a `<div>` element. An `onclick` event handler is used on each element to capture a click event. Type the following code:

```
<h1>Event Example</h1>
    <div onclick='alert("Div Capture")'>
    <p onclick='alert("P capture")'>Click Me</p>
    </div>
```

Note the order in which the pop-up boxes appear.

In the preceding code, the `click` event was simply handed to the `'window. alert()'` method. More usually though, a `click` event is handed off to a function for processing. Notice that in the preceding example, the `alert()` method is used without specifying the `window` object. When you do this, JavaScript assumes that you want the alert to happen in the current window, so specifying the `window` object isn't required.

Functions

A *function* is a piece of code that just sits there until it is *called*. Here's the syntax:

```
function functionName(parameters){
code to be executed
value to be returned
}
```

In the following example, clicking the text calls a simple function:

```
<p onclick='demofunct(this)'>Click Me to see what kind of
        element this is</p>
<script type='text/javascript'>
    function demofunct(a){
    alert("This is a '"+a.nodeName+"' element");
    return 0;
    }
</script>
```

After you type this code (or download L6_02.htm from this book's companion website) and click the text, you see an alert box saying: This is a 'P'
element. Here's how the code works to create this result:

✔ The click event is captured by an onclick handler, which calls the
function demofunct().

✔ The function is given a parameter, this, which is a JavaScript keyword
that refers to the element that captures the event.

✔ The JavaScript code is contained within <script> tags. (See the
upcoming "Linking JavaScript to Documents" section.)

✔ The first line of JavaScript in the <script> tag tells the browser that
I've created the function demofunct() that expects a single parameter,
which will be named a when received by the function.

✔ All the code within the curly brackets will run when the function is
called.

✔ The parameter is referred to as a in the function. In this case, the
parameter is an element object. Thus, a.nodeName uses the element's
nodeName property and will return P. (Note that even though I used a
lowercase p, JavaScript will always return uppercase.)

✔ An alert method and *concatenated* (or glued together) strings create
the window and the text that appears in the window.

✔ This function does not return anything. Because the purpose of a function is usually to accept one or more values and do something with that
value, many functions use the return statement to tell the function to
give its new value back to the code that called it. But, because this function doesn't return a value, I used the statement return 0; to indicate
that this is the case. I could have left out the return statement in this
case, and most programmers do.

The if statement

The `if` keyword tests for the truth of a statement; here's the general syntax:

```
if(statement is true){
execute code in curly brackets
}
else {execute this code}
```

In the following example, I want to see whether the style of the element is red. To do this, I use the equality operator, which is two equals signs `==`. If the `color` property is indeed `red`, the code converts the element to `black`. If it's *not* red, the `else` keyword changes the element to `red`. Note how the colors are quoted in JavaScript unlike CSS:

```
<p onclick='toggle(this)'>Click Me to toggle this text
        color</p>
    <script type='text/javascript'>
    function toggle(a){
        if(a.style.color=='red'){
            a.style.color='black';
        }
        else{a.style.color='red';}
    }
    </script>
```

The equality operator is one of several comparison operators. Here are a few more.

Operator	What It Means
!=	Not equal to
<	Less than
>	Greater than

Linking JavaScript to Documents

You can link JavaScript to HTML documents in one of three ways:

- ✔ Embed the JavaScript in `<script>` tags.
- ✔ Link to an external file that contains the JavaScript by using a special `<script>` tag.
- ✔ Place the JavaScript code inline with the HTML.

I use the first way in most of the examples (for simplicity's sake, to keep the code for each example in one file), although in real life, the second way is more commonly used.

> The advantage of putting JavaScript in separate files is that the same code can be re-used time and time again. As you will discover, JavaScript is very tedious to debug, and it's very useful to have reusable debugged code!

The `if` statement from earlier in this lesson can be used to demonstrate all three methods. First, I show you the `<script>` tag method:

```
<p onclick='toggle(this)'>Click Me to toggle this text
     color</p>
  <script type='text/javascript'>
  function toggle(a){
     if(a.style.color=='red'){
          a.style.color='black';
     }
     else{a.style.color='red';}
  }
  </script>
```

Linking to external JavaScript

To illustrate how external JavaScript works, you take the identical code from the preceding example and move it to an outside file. To start, you'd create two new files: `L6_03a.htm` and `L6_03b.js`.

Here's what `L6_03a.htm` looks like:

```
<p onclick='toggle(this)'>Click Me to toggle this text
     color</p>
  <script type='text/javascript' src='L6_03b.js'></script>
```

Basically, instead of inserting the JavaScript in the `<script>` tag, the `src` attribute refers to `L6_03b.js`. Remember that the closing `</script>` tag is essential when you link to an external JavaScript file.

In addition to `L6_03a.htm`, you have `L6_03b.js`, which simply contains the function and nothing else! No script tags are required. You could add a comment if you wish.

When you display `L6_03a.htm` in a browser, the result is identical to the internal file.

Inline JavaScript

The third way to embed script is to embed it inline. This method is rarely used, but here's what it would look like:

```
<p onclick="if(this.style.color=='red'){this.style.
        color='black';}
        else{this.style.color='red';}">Click Me to
        toggle this text color</p>
```

All the JavaScript and HTML would all have to be on one line.

Validating Forms

In Lesson 3, you discovered how to set up the HTML side of a form, and at the beginning of this lesson, you looked at what's submitted to the server. In this section, you look at how to prevent a user from sending junk information, such as a bad e-mail address or missing information in a form, either accidentally or knowingly.

The key is *form validation,* either on the browser-side or on the server-side. In the following sections, you look at ways to create JavaScript that validates a form, using the building blocks you just learned about.

Validating when the user clicks submit

The most common mistake users make is to leave out a required field, and you can use JavaScript to make sure all required fields are filled. The following example form requires the user to fill in a single field:

```
<form name="myForm" action="validate1.htm"
        onsubmit="return validateForm()" method="get">
First name: <input type="text" name="fname">
<input type="submit" value="Submit Name">
</form>
```

When the user clicks the Submit Name button, a submit event is fired. You can use this event to trigger JavaScript that checks the information before submitting it to a web server.

The following code shows the `validateForm()` function that's called by the `onsubmit` event handler. This function looks at the value that the `onsubmit` handler passes off to the event and tests whether it's completed. If it is, `true` is returned and the form is submitted. If it's not completed, a value of `false` is returned and the form will not be submitted. Note that you *must* put `return` before calling the function.

```
<script type='text/javascript'>
function validateForm()
{
var x=document.forms["myForm"]["fname"].value;
if (x==null || x=="")
  {
  alert("First name must be filled out");
  return false;
  }
}
</script>
```

The line `var x=document.forms["myForm"]["fname"].value;` creates a variable `x` whose value equals the value of the `fname` name/value pair. In other words, the `x` variable equals whatever the user types into the text box. The code accesses this via the `forms` object, which uses a special part of the DOM only applicable to forms (and makes use of the square brackets). The section "Working with the forms array" later in this lesson explains how the `forms` DOM works. For now, know that it enables you to specify what part of the form you want to access. The `value` at the end of the breadcrumb then accesses the value of whatever element the earlier part of the breadcrumb has specified.

In the next line, you see the double pipe-stem sign | | that stands for OR. So the statement is saying, "If the value is null or an empty string, display the alert." Don't worry about the exact meaning of `null`.

If the input field is empty, the `return` keyword returns `false` to the `onsubmit` event handler and the form isn't submitted.

Validating with a generic button

You can also use this form validating by using an `<input>` with a `type` attribute of `button` and adding the `onclick` event to the `<input>`. Remember a `button` input does nothing by itself and is just used for calling a function. The HTML for this form looks like this:

```
<form name="myForm" action="validate1b.htm" method="get">
First name: <input type="text" name="fname">
<input type="button" value="Submit"
          onclick='validateForm()'>
</form>
```

Note how the function is now called from the button itself, not the form.

The JavaScript function looks like this:

```
function validateForm()
{
var x=document.forms["myForm"]["fname"].value;
if (x==null || x=="")
  {
  alert("First name must be filled out");
  return false;
  }
  else{document.myForm.submit();}
}
```

Because the `<input>` doesn't use the `type="submit"` button, you must submit the form using the JavaScript `submit()` method, as shown in blue in the preceding code.

Working with the forms array

When I introduce arrays earlier in this lesson, I mention that HTML has a number of built-in arrays, and the `forms` array is one of them. The `forms` array can be both an indexed array and an associative array. By *associative,* I mean that you can retrieve a value by name rather than just by number. The `forms` array consists of two arrays, known as a *2-dimensional array:*

- ✔ An array of all the different forms on the page.
- ✔ An array for each form, which has all the form elements.

The validation examples in the previous sections use a single form named `myForm` and only one text input named `fname`. So you can access the value of `fname` with the breadcrumb trail:

```
document.forms["myForm"]["fname"].value;
```

This breadcrumb trail could just as easily have been written as

```
document.forms[0][0].value;
```

Because each array is also an object, the following would work:

```
document.forms.myForm.fname.value
```

Or more simply:

```
document.myForm.fname.value
```

The fact that `forms` is an array makes it quite easy for multiple fields to be evaluated for content.

Validating multiple fields

The previous examples validated a single field. In the upcoming example, you find out how JavaScript can check several fields. The following code sets up a sample form with several fields:

```
<p>Fill all fields</p>
<form name="myForm" action="validate1b.htm"  method="get">
First name: <input type="text" name="fname">
Last name: <input type="text" name="lname">
E-Mail: <input type="text" name="email">
<input type="button" value="Submit"
            onclick='validateForm()'>
</form>
```

And here's the script that validates these fields:

```
<script type='text/javascript'>
function validateForm(){
var formlen=document.forms[0].length;
    for(var i=0;i<formlen;i++){
            var x=document.forms[0][i].value;
            //alert(x);
            if(x==null || x==""){
                alert("All fields must be filled");
                return 0;
            }
    }
    document.forms[0].submit();
}
</script>
```

The script requires a little explanation because there are a couple new concepts:

- ✔ The first line of the function puts the length of the `forms[0]` array into a variable. `length` is a JavaScript keyword.

- ✔ A `for` loop reads through each value of the `forms[0]` element.

- ✔ The code in parentheses tells the `for` loop where to start and finish reading through the array. `i=0` tells the loop to start at the beginning (remember that indexing begins at 0). `i<formlen` tells the loop to check the value of `i` to see whether it's less than the length of the array (or, in other words, see whether there are still more values to go through). `i++` increments the value of `i` (one is added to it) if the test

in the previous part is passed, and the loop continues. Basically, it says the `for` loop is finished when it reaches the length of the loop.

✔ The code in curly brackets is executed with each loop. For each loop, the code checks whether the input value is empty. If it is, a message appears and the browser aborts the function by returning `false`.

✔ If the code can run until the end of the loop, the script submits the form using the `submit()` method.

If a form needs other types of validation, you can write separate code to check, for example, whether the e-mail address is a valid one or if a card number is required. However, writing that type of validation yourself is beyond the scope of this book. Indeed libraries, such as jQuery, can do the heavy lifting for you. Also, HTML5 introduces several new `<input>` types that do the validation for you, and I introduce you to these now.

Simplifying validation with HTML5 input types

In Lesson 3, I introduce input types that are new in HTML5, and now that you've learned more about validation and scripting, it's worthwhile to take a second look at them. Basically, these input types can help you with validation either behind the scenes or by limiting the options a user can enter with a picker. The catch is that the user's browser must support these input types.

At the time of writing, IE supports none of them (IE10 is not tested), and Opera supports only color but does not support URL.

The following list introduces you to some of these input types again, together with the browsers that support them. For a closer look at how the code works, check out the `L6_04.htm` file, which you can download from this book's companion website.

✔ The `placeholder` attribute

```
placeholder="descriptive text"
```

`placeholder`, a useful attribute to put on `<input>` elements that produce a text box, displays grayed out text in the box. This text will disappear as soon as a user begins to type, and if left alone, will not be sent as a value.

✔ `<input type="email" />`

If you try to enter something that doesn't look like an e-mail address to the browser, the Submit button does not let you submit the form. (This is supported in Firefox, Chrome, and Opera.)

✔ **The `required` attribute**

`required="required"`

This new `<input>` attribute is supported by the latest versions of Firefox, Opera, and Chrome but not by IE and Safari.

✔ `<input type="url" />`

Enter a bad URL, and you see a message (in Firefox and Chrome). Figure 6-2 shows how the message looks in Chrome after a bad URL has been typed in the box. (Try the validation yourself using the companion file, `L6_05.htm`.)

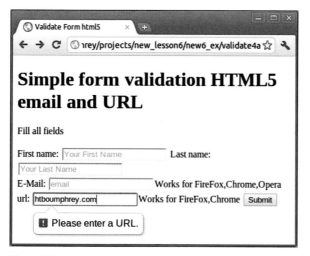

Figure 6-2

✔ `<input type="color" />`

In supporting browsers (only Opera at this time), a color picker appears, as shown in Figure 6-3. (You can check out how this type works using the companion file, `L6_06.htm`.)

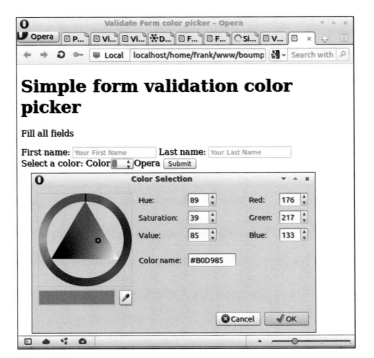

Figure 6-3

✔ Date and time inputs

All the following currently work in Chrome, Safari, and Opera. They usually include a date picker and expect input in the international date/time format: `yyyy-mm=ddThh:mm`. An example is 2012-02-07T15:57.

- *The following shows GMT:*

```
<input type="date" />
<input type="datetime" />
```

- *These show local time:*

```
<input type="datetime-local" />
<input type="time" />
```

- *The following enables a user to pick dates:*

```
<input type="month" />
<input type="week" />
```

All conforming browsers provide a date picker of some kind. Figure 6-4 shows the `date` option (`L6_07.htm`) in Opera. Figure 6-5 shows the same file in

Chrome after a non-valid date has been entered. (U.S. style is not a valid date format; international format yyyy-mm-dd is required.)

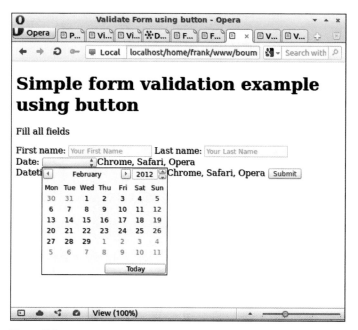

Figure 6-4

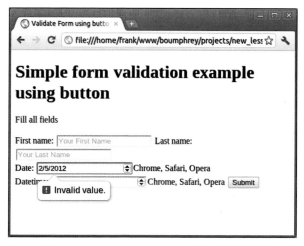

Figure 6-5

Note that if the browser does not support the type, the input will default to regular text input. Also, note that although these fields will enforce the correct data format if you enter data into them, they don't care and won't report an error if the person filling them out just leaves them blank.

These new HTML5 attributes are so useful that I'm sure that even IE will become fully compliant in the near future.

Swapping Images with JavaScript

When a user downloads a page, the page is downloaded first and then the images. You can change the image on a page with JavaScript, by simply changing the value of the image's `src` attribute. A request is sent to the server, and a new image is supplied. The main point is that a completely new page does not have to be downloaded, just a new image.

EXTRA INFO

Images, once downloaded, are cached by the browser, so if a new image is requested, the browser will look in its cache to see whether it's already there. This aspect of image swapping is the basis of animation that I explore in Lesson 7.

What makes image swapping work is the complete array of images that JavaScript keeps in the document. This array is known as an *images collection,* and you can access the array with the breadcrumb `document.images[]`.

The following example code shows image swapping in action:

```
<h1>Image swapping Demo</h1>
<img src='butterfly3.jpg' alt='butterfly'/>
<button onclick='swapimg()'>Click Me</button>
<script type='text/javascript'>
    function swapimg(){
        document.images[0].src='butterfly4.jpg';
    }
</script>
```

When you click the button, you call the function `swapimg()`. This simply sets the image's `src` attribute to a new value, and this replaces the old image. See how it works using companion file `L6_08.htm`.

To see how the function `swapimg ()` can become the basis of animation, replace the script in the preceding example with the following one:

```
<script type='text/javascript'>
        var imgnum=4;
    function swapimg(){
        document.images[0].src='butterfly'+imgnum+'.
         jpg';
        imgnum++;
        if(imgnum==7){imgnum=3;}
    }
</script>
```

Now when you click the button, it cycles through four images, as you can see if you download companion file `L6_09.htm`. Here's how it works:

- ✔ I set an `imgnum` variable *outside* the function. This is important because with the `imgnum` variable, you can now specify a starting value. It doesn't matter what the starting value is. In this case, I decided to make it 4. This number simply determines which image will be shown the first time the function is called.

- ✔ The function constructs a new image `src` with each click. This allows you to show `butterfly3.jpg` through `butterfly6.jpg`.

- ✔ The function increments `imgnum` with each click by using the increment operator (++).

- ✔ When `imgnum` reaches 7 (there is no `butterfly7.jpg`), it resets `imgnum` to 3 by using the following code: `if(imgnum==7) {imgnum=3;}`. What this is saying, in plain English is: "If the value of `imgnum` is 7, reset the value of `imgnum` to 3.

In Lesson 7, you find out how to automate the image swapping and thus create an animation.

Setting CSS Properties via JavaScript

Using the HTML DOM, all CSS properties can be applied, deleted, or changed. The process works like this:

1. Isolate an element or a collection of elements.

2. Modify the `style` property.

You can also use JavaScript to write HTML automatically. In Listing 6-1, the code toggles the color of a simple heading. See how it works with the companion file, `L6_10.htm`.

Listing 6-1:   Toggling Element Colors

```
<h1 id='h1' >Toggle Heading Colors</h1>
<button onclick='toggle()'>Toggle Heading Colors</button>
<script type='text/javascript'>
     var myhead=document.getElementById("h1");
     myhead.style.backgroundColor='red';
     myhead.style.color='black';
function  toggle(){
     if(myhead.style.color=='black'){
          myhead.style.color='red';
          myhead.style.backgroundColor='black';
     }
     else {
          myhead.style.color='black';
          myhead.style.backgroundColor='red';
     }
}
</script>
```

In Listing 6-2, I create a 6-x-6 table of HSL color values and add a matching `background-color` (written `backgroundColor` in JavaScript) to each using the HSL color value that the table displays.

Listing 6-2:   A Simple Color Table

```
<h1>HSL Colors</h1>
<table border='1'>
<caption><h2>Hues</h2></caption>
<tr>
     <script type='text/javascript'>
     for(var i=1;i< 37;i++){
          document.write("<td style='background-color:hsl(
          "+i*10+",100%,50%)'>"+i*10+"</td>");
          if (i%6==0){document.write("</tr><tr>")}
     }
     </script>
</tr>
</table>
```

Figure 6-6 shows the table of HSL hues that the code in Listing 6-2 generates. Imagine how much typing would be required if you did this all by hand!

Figure 6-6

Here's how the code in Listing 6-2 creates the table. There's not much new here except the use of the modulus operator (%), which you haven't seen previously.

- ✔ `for(var i=1;i< 37;i++)` { makes a loop that will run 36 times.

- ✔ For each loop, `document.write` creates a `<td>` cell with a `background-color` property calculated from the index of the loop.

- ✔ `"+i*10+"` multiplies the index (`i`) by ten, and this is used as the hue value for an HSL color value. The calculation is repeated on this line in order to also print this number in the cell.

- ✔ `if (i%6==0){document.write("</tr><tr>")}` uses the modulus operator to determine whether it's time to start a new table row. (The modulus operator is also known as the division remainder operator.) The modulus operator tells you what the remainder is after dividing a number by another number. For example, the remainder of dividing 6 by 5 is around 1. Every sixth time the loop runs, you write a new row.

Going Local with Geolocation

Geolocation is becoming increasingly important, especially with the increase of mobile devices — although you don't have to have a mobile device to use geolocation, just a compliant browser. In this section, I give you a brief insight into the workings of geolocation and make a small app that tells how many degrees of latitude or longitude the user is from Robert Burns' birthplace.

GO ONLINE

HTML5 provides a standard for geolocation, which you can find at `http://dev.w3.org/geo/api/spec-source.html`.

Following security best practices

Security is a primary concern for geolocation. A user doesn't want to identify his location to just any old web page that comes along. Compliant browsers deal with this issue in a number of ways, but all insist that a user takes positive action to reveal a site with geolocation. Firefox has probably the most user-friendly method: Before releasing a location to a website, Firefox makes the user click a consent box. (I use Firefox in the figures for the following geolocation sections.)

Establishing a location

The specification says nothing about how the browser should establish an exact location. From the browser's point of view, establishing a position is resource-intensive. Generally speaking, a browser typically establishes a location depending on what type of device is used to access a web page:

- **If the user downloads a webpage via a phone,** the browser will probably use GPS coordinates, and the position returned will probably be accurate to within a few meters.

- **With a browser connected by a WiFi or a landline,** the browser has to use much less precise information, such as the location of a WiFi point, of a shortwave tower, and so on, and the positioning will be much less precise. By and large, this location method is fairly precise in large cities, but could be several miles off in the country.

In the next section, you look at some code.

Making a geolocation application

The example in this section makes a simple page that returns the approximate latitude and longitude of a browser and the distance the browser is from Robert Burns' birthplace. You can experiment with this application using the companion file, `L6_11.htm`.

Conforming browsers have in their JavaScript DOM a `geolocation` object, which is a child object of the `navigator` object. The application uses this object to establish the coordinates.

Here's the HTML code:

```
<h1>Geolcation example</h1>

<div id="main">
    <button onclick='startSearch()'>Where am I?</button>
</div>

<div id="results">
</div>
```

A `button` element calls the `startSearch()` function. The second `<div>` element displays the result.

In JavaScript, I start by creating a `navigation.geolocation` object as follows:

```
<script type="text/javascript">
function possearch(){
        var gps = navigator.geolocation;
```

At this stage, the browser asks for the user's permission to continue, as shown in Figure 6-7. (Firefox uses a pop-up box. Other browsers have slightly different methods.)

The file /home/frank/www/boumphrey/projects /new_lesson6/new6_ex/geolocate3.htm wants to know your location.

Learn More...   Share Location ▼

Figure 6-7

Next, the code checks that an object has indeed been created by the browser, as follows:

```
if (gps){
     gps.getCurrentPosition(getmypos, myerror);
     }
else{
     alert("There were ERRORS:- No Geolocation object
          created");
     }
}     //end of possearch
```

✔ **if (gps) {:** This line simply checks for the existence of an object named gps.

✔ **gps.getCurrentPosition(getmypos,myerror);:** If there is a gps object, this code uses the getCurrentPosition method to determine the user's location. The parameters (in parentheses) tell getCurrent Position what to do with the position information (give it to the getmypos function) and what to do in case of an error (give it to the myerror function).

✔ **else {:** If no geolocation object was created, the following alert notifies the user that errors occurred.

✔ **alert("There were ERRORS:- No Geolocation object created");:** This code pops up an error message, and execution of the script is done. This is what a user with a non-compliant browser would see.

I return now to what happens when a user visits this page with a browser that supports geolocation. After the if/else statement, you create the functions that do the real work of the program. The first is the getmypos() function:

```
function getmypos(position){
    var myposinfo=document.getElementById("results");

//build a string showing position
    var strmypos="<br/>My current latitude is:- "+
        position.coords.latitude;
    strmypos+="<br/>My current longitude is:- "+
        position.coords.longitude;
    strmypos+="<br/>You are "+(position.coords.
        latitude-55.453941)+" degrees of Latitude from
        Robert Burns' birthplace.";
    strmypos+="<br/>You are "+(position.coords.
        latitude-(-4.62616))+" degrees of Latitude from
        Robert Burns' birthplace.";
//display this string
    myposinfo.innerHTML=strmypos;
}    //end of getmypos
</script>
```

✔ **function getmypos(position){:** When this function is invoked (by the getCurrentPosition method), it receives the position object, which was created by getCurrentPosition().

✔ **var myposinfo=document.getElementById("results");:** The current contents of the results element are copied into a new variable called myposinfo. (You update this variable with a new value after you determine what that value is.)

✔ **var strmypos="
My current latitude is:- "+ position.coords.latitude;:** The `position` object has a `coords` object with `latitude` and `longitude` properties. Here you use that object to populate the `strmypos` variable.

✔ **strmypos+="
My current longitude is:- "+ position.coords.longitude;:** You do the same thing with the longitude, and you use the `+=` operator to add this new string to the end of the preceding one. So, `strmypos` now contains two sentences.

✔ The next two lines of code calculate the difference between your current location and the location of Robert Burns' birthplace. These lines are also added to the `strmypos` variable.

✔ **myposinfo.innerHTML=strmypos;:** The string is read into `<div id='results'>`, which causes the contents of the string to display, as shown in Figure 6-8. You could give the distance in miles, but this would require some spherical trigonometry to do the longitude conversion — and I have forgotten all that I ever knew!

Figure 6-8

You can do much more with the `geolocation` object, and I hope this geolocation example has whetted your appetite to explore it.

When the `getCurrentPosition` method can't determine a location for the user, this function is called, which displays an error alert to the user.

Using jQuery and JavaScript Libraries

Before leaving this lesson, I need to say a little about libraries. The JavaScript for many functions can get quite complicated and difficult to maintain. For this reason, several libraries that contain reusable snippets of JavaScript are available.

You can import a snippet of JavaScript code into a document, saving a tremendous amount of time and debugging stress. Among the many commercial and free libraries is jQuery, which is one of the best free ones.

For more information, check out *jQuery For Dummies* by Lynn Beighly.

 # Summing Up

In this lesson, you looked at scripting and many of its uses:

- ✔ To submit a form to a server, the `action` attribute sets the destination for the user entry.
- ✔ The fundamentals of scripting include variables and values, statements, comments, objects, arrays, loops, events, functions, and `if` statements.
- ✔ To add JavaScript to an HTML document, use an external file or a `<script>` tag. You can also insert JavaScript inline, but this is rarely done.
- ✔ To validate forms, you start with `onsubmit` or `onclick`, depending on the button type. You then use the `forms` array to check whether the user entered content into the form inputs. You can also validate form input using the new HTML5 input types and JavaScript.
- ✔ Server-side includes enable you to streamline page maintenance.
- ✔ JavaScript enables you to swap one image for another using the `swapimg()` function.
- ✔ You can use JavaScript to set CSS properties when you want an event to trigger a change in the look of a web page.
- ✔ The `navigation.geolocation` object enables a web page to detect where a user is, if the user gives the web page permission to do so. This object is handy when you want to provide information to a user that's relevant to wherever she is.

Try-it-yourself lab

JavaScript has been around for a while and is an extremely popular scripting language. As a result, thousands of JavaScript programs are available for download on the web — and many of them are free!

To get a taste of what can be done with JavaScript, search for *free JavaScript code* online and then try some scripts that other people have written. You'll find many sites that specialize in categorizing or rating and make available free JavaScript code for use on your site.

Know this tech talk

client-side: Refers to a process on the browser that serves web pages.

concatenation: Glued together.

event handler: Hands off the event to more code that then processes that event.

forms DOM: An HTML collection of all the forms on a page.

geolocation: An HTML API (application program interface) for determining the geographic position of a browser.

image swapping: Using JavaScript to change the source of an image object.

jQuery: One of the more popular libraries.

keywords: Words that are reserved for a special purpose in a computer language.

libraries: Collections of pre-composed and debugged JavaScript.

name/value pairs: The format in which form information is sent to the server.

query string: Communicates data that should be used by the web page.

server-side: Refers to a process on the server that serves web pages.

Lesson 7
Exploring the Canvas and Animation

✔ You need to *follow six steps* to draw on the `<canvas>`.

✔ You can *alter images* in the `<canvas>` element.

✔ *Create a slider, interval timer, and marching animation* with CSS3 and JavaScript.

✔ You can *use transitions, transformation, and animations* with CSS3.

In this lesson, I take you to the cutting edge of HTML and CSS. You'll look at two of the coolest features of HTML5 and CSS3: animation and the `<canvas>` element. Both rely heavily on JavaScript, so I help you with this as much as possible as you go along. First, I cover the `<canvas>` element; now that it's generally supported, I'm sure you'll see more widespread use of it.

Drawing on the `<canvas>`

Look upon the `<canvas>` element as a bare canvas on which you can paint, but instead of using a paintbrush, you use JavaScript. This element can take all the usual attributes plus, like an image, a `height` and a `width` attribute, which act just like an image's `height` and `width` attribute, giving a height and width in pixels.

Walking through the overall process

Here's an overview of the steps for drawing on the `<canvas>`:

1. Create a `<canvas>` element.
2. Create a JavaScript element object from the `<canvas>` element.
3. Create a JavaScript function to draw on the `<canvas>`.
4. Create a JavaScript `context` object.
5. Draw on the `<canvas>`.
6. Load the function.

The following sections walk you through each step.

Create the <canvas> element

To start, create a file called L7_01.htm. The following creates a 300-x-500 pixel <canvas> element:

```
<canvas id='canvas1' height='300' width='500'
    style='border:solid 2px red;'>Your browser
    does not support canvas</canvas>
```

As I mention in Lesson 6, giving the element an ID enables you to take advantage of certain JavaScript features. Also, the text Your browser does not support canvas appears only if the user's browser really doesn't support canvas.

Create an element object

You do this in the usual manner by using the getElementById() method, as follows:

```
<script type='text/javascript'>
var mycanvas=document.getElementById('canvas1');
</script>
```

Create a JavaScript function

The function you add follows the format you learned in Lesson 6. For this <canvas> example, add the following to the JavaScript file:

```
function paintCanvas(){
}
```

The function needs to test that your browser supports <canvas>. The standard way to do this is by checking for the existence of the getContext method of the canvas object. Place the following if/else statement in the function between the curly brackets:

```
if(mycanvas.getContext){
}
else {alert("Couldn't create context.";}
```

Create a context object

A context object is what you'll be using to do your actual drawing on the canvas. You create a context object by using the getContext() method and giving the resulting object a name.

The following code (which should be placed inside the true condition of the if/else statement) creates a 2D object named ctx:

```
var ctx = mycanvas.getContext('2d');
```

Note that, in theory, you could create a 3-dimensional `context` object by changing the parameter you pass to `getContext` to 3d, but this isn't supported by any browsers yet.

Now that you have a canvas with a `context` object, you can use this context with the numerous canvas methods and objects.

Create code for the drawing

Think of yourself holding a pen and moving it to a specified spot; then draw a line on the canvas and without taking it off the canvas, draw another line.

The following code moves your "pen" to the x- and y-coordinates 50,50; then draws a line to coordinates 50,100; and finally draws a line to 100,100. The code then tells the canvas to draw the line as a stroke. If you're drawing several objects on a canvas, begin each one with a `beginPath();` method:

```
ctx.beginPath();
ctx.moveTo(50,50);
ctx.lineTo(50,100);
ctx.lineTo(100,100);
ctx.stroke();
```

This creates two strokes in the form of the letter L.

 In JavaScript, the coordinates are measured from the top-left corner.

To create another stroke, move the pen to a separate location. Add the following before `ctx.stroke`:

```
ctx.moveTo(100,150);
ctx.lineTo(400,150);
```

The default thickness for the line is 1 pixel. Thicken the lines with the `lineWidth` attribute. The default color is black, and you can change the color using the `strokeStyle` attribute. Add the following to your code *before* the `ctx.stroke`:

```
ctx.strokeStyle="red";
ctx.lineWidth=8;
```

Load the function

To execute the drawing, you must call the function you created earlier. This example uses the `onload` JavaScript event to call the function:

```
<body onload='paintCanvas()'>
```

This event fires when the page finishes loading. Check out all the code for this example in Listing 7-1.

Listing 7-1: Drawing Lines on the Canvas

```
<body onload='paintCanvas()'>
    <canvas id='canvas1' height='300' width='500'
style='border:solid 2px red;background-image:url(10px.
        png);'> Your browser does not support canvas
        </canvas>


<script type='text/javascript'>
    var mycanvas=document.getElementById('canvas1');
    function paintCanvas(){

        //create a JS context object
        if(mycanvas.getContext){
            var ctx = mycanvas.getContext('2d');


            ctx.moveTo(50,50);
            ctx.lineTo(50,100);
            ctx.lineTo(100,100);
            ctx.moveTo(100,150);
            ctx.lineTo(400,150);
            ctx.strokeStyle="red";
            ctx.lineWidth=8;
            ctx.stroke();

        }     //end if
        else{
            alert("could notcreate a context");
        }
    }     //end paintCanvas
</script>
</body>
```

Creating basic shapes

This section shows you a few more techniques that enable you to draw a triangle, a rectangle, and a circle on the canvas.

For each of the following shapes, create a file called L7_02.htm and use the preceding example, Listing 7-1, as your template. That is, use the <canvas> you created in the preceding section as a framework and simply add or replace the code that draws the lines with the code you see in this section:

✔ **To create a triangle,** add the `closePath()` method after the code that creates the first example. The `closePath()` method does just what it says: It closes any open path.

```
ctx.beginPath();
ctx.moveTo(50,50);
ctx.lineTo(50,100);
ctx.lineTo(100,100);
ctx.closePath();ctx.stroke();
```

Voilà! A right triangle!

✔ **To create a rectangle,** use the `rect(x,y,width,height)` method. Here's the code to draw a rectangle in the example:

```
ctx.rect(150,50,100,50);
```

You don't need to use the `moveTo()` method because `rect()` takes care of those details for you.

✔ **To create a circle,** the code is a bit trickier than the triangle or rectangle. Use `moveTo()` to move your `context` pen to where you want to start the circle. Then, create an arc of 360 degrees, using the following syntax:

```
arc(centerX, centerY, radius,
    startAngle, endAngle, clockwise||anticlockwise)
```

Here's how to draw the circle:

```
ctx.moveTo(375,75);
ctx.arc(350,75,25,0,Math.PI*2,false);
```

`Math` is another JavaScript object. `PI` is an accurate representation of the constant pi, which is slightly more than 3.14. There are pi radians in a semicircle circumference, and 2 pi radians in a circle circumference. So the preceding code draws a complete circle.

PRACTICE

Experiment with the code for drawing a circle to see the different effects you can create and develop a better sense for how the different parameters affect the final drawing. Try the following:

✔ Alter the value of the `moveTo()` x-coordinate to the same as the x-value (the first parameter) in `arc`. Can you predict what will happen?

✔ Draw various arcs.

✔ Use the `closePath()` method to make those arcs into a closed arc.

✔ See what happens when you draw a semicircle using `true` versus `false`.

Filling shapes and adding shadows

In this section, you look at methods that enable you to fill shapes you create on the <canvas> and add shadows.

✔ To fill the circle and triangle with color:

a. *Add the following code after* beginPath():

```
ctx.fillStyle="violet";
```

b. *Before* moveTo(), *add the following code:*

```
ctx.fill();
```

For a little more context, check out how these lines fit into the drawing of a triangle:

```
ctx.beginPath();
ctx.fillStyle="violet";
ctx.fill();
ctx.moveTo(50,50);
ctx.lineTo(50,100);
ctx.lineTo(100,100);
ctx.closePath();
ctx.stroke();
```

✔ To fill a rectangle, use the same method for a circle or triangle, or you can use the fillRect() method, like this:

```
ctx.fillRect(150,150,100,50);
```

For a color other than black, add a fillStyle attribute, too. The code that draws a blue rectangle on the <canvas> looks like this:

```
ctx.rect(150,50,100,50);
ctx.fillStyle="violet";
ctx.fillRect(150,150,100,50);
```

✔ To add a drop shadow to filled shapes, add the following lines of code before fill():

```
ctx.shadowOffsetX = 4;
ctx.shadowOffsetY = 4;
ctx.shadowBlur = 5;
ctx.shadowColor="silver";
```

The preceding example adds a silver color to your drop shadow. Also, note that the drop shadow will appear on all the succeeding shapes on the canvas. Switch off the drop shadow by setting the offsets to 0.

To have a look at the complete code, check out the file `L7_02.htm`, which you can download from this book's companion website. (See the Introduction for details.) Figure 7-1 shows how a few different triangles, rectangles, and circles look with different line colors, fill colors, and shadows, as displayed in Chrome.

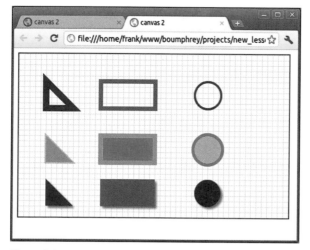

Figure 7-1

Drawing Bézier curves

If you've used a drawing program, you may be familiar with a *Bézier curve,* which is a curve with a handle at each end that contorts the line.

Here's the general syntax to draw a Bézier curve:

```
context.BezierCurveTo(controlX1, controlY1, controlX2,
          controlY2, endX, endY);
```

The following HTML creates the <canvas> in which you see a sample Bézier curve:

```
<canvas id='myCanvas'
    style='border:1px solid red;
    background-image:url(10px.png);
```

```
height' height='300'
      width='500'>
      Your browser does not
      support the canvas
      element
</canvas>
```

Listing 7-2 shows the code that draws the Bézier curve, as shown in Figure 7-2.

GO ONLINE

The following website is a handy online resource for learning more about Bézier curves: www. html5canvastutorials. com/tutorials/html5-canvas-Bezier-curves.

Listing 7-2:   A Bézier Curve on the canvas

```
<script type='text/javascript'>
window.onload = function(){

    var canvas = document.getElementById("myCanvas");
    var context = canvas.getContext("2d");

    context.moveTo(190, 120);
    context.BezierCurveTo(160, 260, 400,
        10, 400, 150);
    context.lineWidth = 10;
    context.strokeStyle = "black"; // line color
    context.stroke();
};
</script>
```

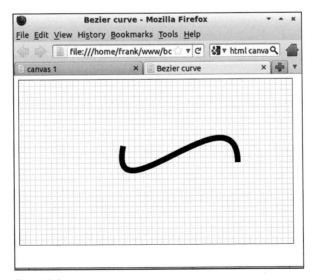

Figure 7-2

Try experimenting with the curve values to see how it changes. If you want to know what's really going on, check out the tutorial at www.html5canvas tutorials.com.

Typing text on the canvas

You can display two kinds of text on the canvas:

- ✔ **Stroke text** creates hollow text, similar to what you see if you apply outline formatting to text in a word processor. The syntax for stroke text looks like this:

  ```
  ctx2.strokeText("text",posX,posY,width);
  ```

- ✔ **Fill text** creates text that's all one color, much like the default text in a word processor. To create fill text, use the following syntax:

  ```
  ctx2.fillText("text",posX,posY,width);
  ```

You add the text you want to display where you see the text placeholder, between the quotation marks. The posX and posY values represent the position on the canvas where you want the text to appear. The width value is the maximum width in pixels that you want the text to be, so you can squeeze the text together or spread it out using this property.

To format the text, you have the following options:

- ✔ To alter the font size and font family, use the font attribute.
- ✔ Alter the color and stroke width of stroke text with the strokeStyle and lineWidth attributes.
- ✔ Alter the color of regular text with the fillStyle attribute.

Listing 7-3 creates text on the canvas with these formatting options applied. To see this code in a browser, look at the file L7_03.htm, which you can download from this book's companion website.

Listing 7-3:   Displaying Text on the canvas

```
var canvas = document.getElementById("myCanvas");
var context = canvas.getContext("2d");
    context.font ="36pt  arial";
    context.strokeStyle="navy";
    context.lineWidth=2;
    context.strokeText("To be or not to be?",10,50,270);

    context.font ="24pt times";
    context.fillStyle="red";
    context.fillText("Hamlet",10,105,250);
```

Blending color gradients

The <canvas> element enables you to create two patterns of color gradient: linear and circular (or *radial*), as illustrated in Figure 7-3.

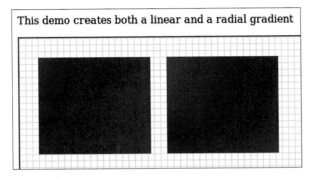

Figure 7-3

To create a color gradient, set up the gradient and then use that gradient to fill a shape. The following code creates the red-to-blue color gradient and then uses it to fill a rectangle (refer to Figure 7-3).

The general syntax to create a linear gradient is

```
context.createLinearGradient(startX, startY, endX, endY);
```

The startX and startY parameters are numbers that determine the starting point of the gradient on the canvas, and the endX and endY parameters are numbers that determine the ending point of the gradient.

Now, check out the following code, which creates the red-to-blue linear gradient on the left in Figure 7-3.

```
var grd=ctx.createLinearGradient(0,0,170,90);
grd.addColorStop(0,"#f00");
grd.addColorStop(1,"#00f");
ctx.fillStyle=grd;
ctx.fillRect(30,30,175,150);
```

Here's what each line of the preceding code does:

- ✔ var grd=ctx.createLinearGradient(0,0,170,90);: This creates a gradient object that spans from the upper-left of the screen to a position 170 pixels to the right and 90 pixels down on the screen.

✔ `grd.addColorStop(0,"#f00");`: This sets the starting color of the gradient. The first parameter of the `addColorStop` method is a number representing a position on the gradient. A value of 0 indicates the start of the gradient. A value of 1 indicates the end. Any number between 0 and 1 can be used to represent a point along the gradient.

✔ `grd.addColorStop(1,"#00f");`: This sets the ending color of the gradient.

✔ `ctx.fillStyle=grd;`: This sets the `fillStyle` to use the gradient. Think of it as similar to selecting a color from a program's toolbar prior to using a tool.

✔ `ctx.fillRect(30,30,175,150);`: This creates a rectangle and fills it with the gradient.

The best way to find out what effect altering the values has is to try it yourself:

✔ Change the values for `startx`, `endx`, `starty`, and `endy`.

✔ Change the values (any number between 0 and 1) for `addColorStop`.

✔ Try different colors.

The general syntax for a radial gradient is

```
context.createRadialGradient(startX, startY, startRadius,
                    endX, endY, endRadius);
```

The `startX`, `startY`, `endX`, and `endY` parameters all work similarly to how they work for a linear gradient. The `startRadius` and `endRadius` parameters specify the radius of the start circle and the end circle.

You can see the code for the linear and radial gradients in Figure 7-3 by downloading `L7_04.htm` from this book's companion website.

GO ONLINE

For more on gradients, see the specifications at the following websites:

`www.whatwg.org/specs/web-apps/current-work/multipage/the-canvas-element.html#colors-and-styles`

`http://sixrevisions.com/html/canvas-element`

Altering Images in the <canvas> Element

The canvas enables you to display image files and can alter the image after the file displays. This section introduces you to a few neat effects the canvas can create.

In order to work with an image, you need to *draw* it on the canvas using the `drawImage()` method. The syntax for `drawImage()` is as follows:

```
context.drawImage(image, x, y)

context.drawImage(image, x, y, w, h)

context.drawImage(image, sx, sy, sw, sh, dx, dy, dw, dh)
```

The following breaks down what the parameters of some of the preceding code means:

- ✔ s stands for *source,* or the part of an image you want to work with.
- ✔ d for *destination,* or where you want to put the source image.
- ✔ x and y stand for the respective axes.
- ✔ w stands for width.
- ✔ h stands for height.

The effect, depending on the number of parameters you use, is as follows:

- ✔ **Two parameters:** Simply places an image at the specified x- and y-coordinates (see the first line in the preceding code).
- ✔ **Four parameters:** Allows you to place and then scale the image by adjusting the width and height (see the second line in the preceding code).
- ✔ **Eight parameters:** Allows you to slice an image by selecting an area within the image and moving it to a new location on the canvas (see the last line in the preceding code).

The following no-frills example loads an image of a solider onto the canvas using the `drawImage()` method and uses only two parameters. (You can check out the actual file in `L7_05.htm` on this book's companion website.)

```
var img = new Image();
img.src = 'images/walk1.png';
//when the image finishes loading, draw it

    img.onload = function(){
        context.drawImage(img,0,0);
    }
```

Clipping the source image

Image clipping, or *slicing,* is the process of selecting part of an image and moving it elsewhere on the canvas. You can add a clipping effect to an image drawn on the <canvas>.

For example, the following parameters would clip an area from the source image and display it in a box that's 180 x 160 pixels:

```
context.drawImage(img,10,10, 90,70, 100,10, 180,160);
```

Figure 7-4 shows an unclipped image and a clipped image, which I created using the preceding code.

Normal | Clipped

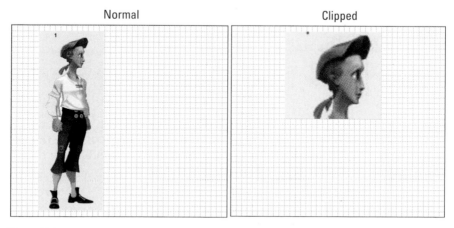

Figure 7-4

To see the example in action, check out L7_06.htm, available on this book's companion website.

Changing image data

After the `drawImage()` method captures an image, the `createImage Data()` method can capture the image's individual pixel data. The syntax looks like this:

```
imagedata = context.createImageData(imageData)
```

The `imageData` parameter represents an `imageData` object that you want to work with. After you capture the image with `createImageData`, the data can then be manipulated. `L7_07.htm` shows how to invert colors, and `L7_08.htm` shows how to convert them to grayscale. Figure 7-5 shows the result of manipulating the image data with these two files, with a normal for comparison.

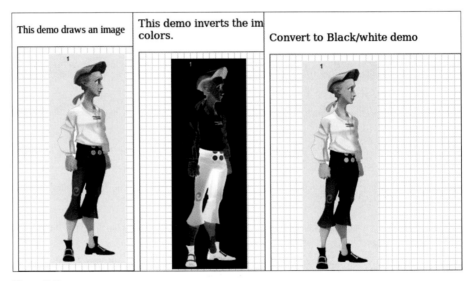

Figure 7-5

Note this will only work for documents served by a server, *not* served from your file system. Also note that the image *must* be in the same domain as the HTML document. If not, an error is generated.

GO ONLINE

For more information about working with images on the canvas, check out the following sites: `www.whatwg.org/specs/web-apps/current-work/multipage/the-canvas-element.html#images` and `www.html5canvastutorials.com/advanced/html5-canvas-get-image-data-tutorial`.

Now that you know about the `<canvas>` element and it uses, you're ready to look at animations.

Animating with CSS3 and JavaScript

One of the most exciting things about CSS3 is the possibilities it creates to improve animation. An animated picture is simply a series of pictures shown one after another at a set interval of time. You must still use JavaScript for animation, but HTML5 and CSS3 add new possibilities.

Two key skills you should be familiar with are finding the x- and y-coordinates of a point on a page and setting a time interval. The following sections introduce you to these skills. To learn how to find x- and y-coordinates, you create a simple slider. You then find out how to work with intervals of time in JavaScript.

You're introduced to a marching animation that demonstrates animation with images. You find out how to capture a keystroke, which is an important element in creating many different types of animations. And then you pull together the techniques in these examples to create a game.

Finding the x- and y-coordinates

As you move a mouse pointer across a page, you create a series of JavaScript events, specifically `onmousemove` events. This section shows you how to capture the x- and y-coordinates with these events.

To start, create an ordinary 200-x-200 pixel `<div>` element and give it an absolute position of 20 on the x-axis and 20 on the y-axis. If you want to follow along with this example, type the following code, careful to repeat it exactly (or check out `L7_09.htm`, which is on this book's companion site):

```
<body>
    <div id='d1' onmousemove='getposxy(event,this)'>
    </div>
    <script type='text/javascript'>
    function getposxy(e,a){
        var myx=e.pageX;
        var myy=e.pageY;
        a.innerHTML=(myx-20) + ", "+ (myy-20);
    }           }
</script>
</body>
```

When you move your mouse over the box shown in Figure 7-6, the coordinates of your mouse pointer are written out. The dot on the screen shot shows the approximate position of the mouse when the snap was taken, Here's how the code works:

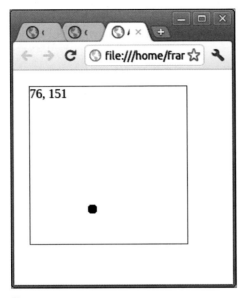

Figure 7-6

- ✔ `<div>`, `onmousemove='getposxy(event,this)'` captures the event and sends it to JavaScript for processing with two arguments: the `event` argument and the `this` argument.

- ✔ `event` and `this` are two JavaScript keywords:
  - `event` refers to the event that the code is capturing.
  - `this` refers to the element object that the event is being captured on.

- ✔ `var myx=e.pageX` creates an `object` variable that refers to the `pageX` property of the event. `pageX` is the position of the mouse from the top-left hand corner *of the page.*

- ✔ `var myy=e.pageY` similarly captures the `pageY` position.

- ✔ `a.innerHTML=(myx-20) + ", "+ (myy-20)` writes these positions to the `<div>` element using the `innerHTML` property:
  - The `a` represents the `<div>` where you're capturing mouse movements.
  - The `innerHTML` property simply says to change the value that's inside this `div`. In other words, write the numbers inside the `<div>`.

Making a slider

Sliders are often part of an animation. In this section, you apply the preceding example, finding coordinates, in order to make a simple horizontal slider. The example in Listing 7-4 includes some global variables and two new functions. You can see how the slider looks and works by opening L7_10.htm (found on this book's companion website) in a browser.

Listing 7-4:   Creating a Slider

```
<div id='d1'   onmousemove='getposxy(event,this)'>
    <div id='d2' onmouseover='spriteon(this)' onmouseout=
        'spriteoff(this)'> </div>
</div>
<p id='p1'></p>

<script type='text/javascript'>
var reader=document.getElementById("p1");
var sprite=document.getElementById("d2");
var animationon=false;
function getposxy(e,a){
   var myx=e.pageX;
   //var myy=e.pageY;
   if(animationon && myx > 19 && myx<221){
      sprite.style.marginLeft=myx-30+"px";
   //reader.innerHTML=sprite.style.marginLeft;
      reader.innerHTML=(myx-20) //+ ", "+ (myy-20);
   }
}
function spriteon(a){
   a.style.backgroundColor="rgba(0,200,0,0.5)";
   animationon=true;
}
function spriteoff(a){
a.style.backgroundColor="rgba(200,0,0,0.5)";
   animationon=false;
}
</script>
```

The following explains this code in greater detail:

- ✔ `var reader=document.getElementById("p1");` creates an object, `reader`, which will set the value of the div with id "p1", for the purpose of showing the numerical position of the slider.

- ✔ `var sprite=document.getElementById("d2");` creates an object to access the properties of the "d2" `<div>`, which is the sprite that you can adjust the position of.

✔ `function getposxy(e,a)` is a fuction that's called when the user's mouse moves via the `onmousemove` event handler attribute of the `d1 <div>`.

✔ `var myx=e.pageX;` creates a local variable containing the horizontal position of the sprite.

✔ `if(animationon && myx > 19 && myx<221){` checks the position of the mouse to make sure that it's within the width of the slider. You do this to make sure that you don't position the sprite off its slider!

✔ `sprite.style.marginLeft=myx-30+"px";` adjusts the position of the sprite by increasing or decreasing its left margin.

✔ `reader.innerHTML=(myx-20)` changes the value of the `reader` `<div>` so that it displays the current position of the sprite along the slider.

✔ `spriteon()` and `spriteoff()` simply change the color of the sprite depending on whether your mouse is currently hovering over it.

LINGO

A **sprite** is an image that you can integrate into a scene in order to create an animation. You see another example of a sprite in the marching animation later in this lesson.

Create your own code based on what you learned from the example slider (and using the hints that are commented out in the code). The following tasks enable you to practice modifying different aspects of the code:

✔ Use Listing 7-4 as a model to make a vertical slider.

✔ Make three sliders to set RGB or HSL colors. Display the resulting color as the background color of an element.

✔ Make the dimensions of the slider larger. See whether this increases its usability and performance.

✔ Use an image of your choice as a sprite.

You can see an improved slider in this book's companion file, `L7_11.htm`. The code, although simple, is too long to include here.

Creating an interval timer with JavaScript

Central to any animation is a timer. JavaScript uses the setInterval() function to call other functions at various intervals. The setInterval() function takes two parameters:

- ✔ The name of the function it must call
- ✔ The interval in milliseconds in which setInterval() should call the named function

The setInterval() function will continue calling the named function until the clearInterval() function is called.

The code in Listing 7-5 creates a simple counter. You can see the counter in action by viewing this book's companion file, L7_12.htm, in your browser.

Listing 7-5: A Simple Counter

```
<body>
<div id='d1'>0</div>
<form>
    <input type='button' value='start'
           onclick='startcounter()'/>
    <input type='button' value='stop'
           onclick='stopcounter()'/>
    <input type='button' value='reset'
           onclick='resetcounter()'/>
</form>
<script type='text/javascript'>
    var mydiv=document.getElementById("d1");
    //mydiv.style.color="lime";
    var intervalID;

    function startcounter(){
        intervalID =setInterval("startcount()",250);
    }
    function startcount(){
        mydiv.innerHTML=(mydiv.innerHTML-0) + .25;
    }
    function stopcounter()
    {
        var dummy=clearInterval(intervalID);
    }
    function resetcounter()
    {
    mydiv.innerHTML=0;
    }
</script>

</body>
```

Here's how the code in Listing 7-5 works:

- ✔ The HTML code creates a box to display the count and creates three form buttons.

- ✔ In JavaScript, `getElementById()` creates a global element object variable.

- ✔ `var intervalID;` creates a global variable to hold the ID of the `setInterval()` function that the code creates a little later in the listing.

- ✔ The `startcounter()` function sets up the `setInterval()` function and reads its ID into the `intervalID` variable created earlier. The ID is needed so the code can stop the function. Note that the function name is quoted. `250` means the code will call the `setInterval()` function every quarter second.

> **LINGO**
>
> A **global variable** is created outside of a function and can be used anywhere in a script. **Local variables,** on the other hand, are created inside of functions. They can be accessed only from within the function where they're created.

Time is set in milliseconds.

- ✔ The `startcount()` function simply adds a quarter second to the readout. Keep the function that's being called as simple as possible. This is the function that eats up your CPU!

- ✔ The `stopcounter()` function calls `clearInterval()` on the `setInterval()` function that was created earlier.

- ✔ The `resetCounter()` function sets the counter to 0.

To practice working with an interval timer, open this book's companion file `L7_013.htm` in your code editor of choice and try the following:

- ✔ Alter the speed of the bomber.

- ✔ Make the motion less jerky.

> **EXTRA INFO**
>
> You can alter this to create animations. A simple addition to Listing 7-5 (the companion file `L7_013.htm` found on the website) shows a bomber flying across the sky. Check it out.

Creating a marching animation

I'm not sure whether the animation in this section shows a revolutionary soldier marching off to join his unit, or Robert Burns off to visit the *Mauchline ladies!*

Generally speaking, though, the soldier in Figure 7-7 is an animation sprite, an image you can integrate into a scene. You can find numerous sprites on the web by Googling *animation sprites.* The images in this section are from `http://caja-de-luz.blogspot.com`. Figure 7-7 shows the image before it was sectioned. To make this example work, I used an image editor to crop this image into separate files, named `walk1.png` to `walk7.png`.

Figure 7-7

The program uses JavaScript to change the `img src` property of the image. All that needs to be done is make some minor modifications to the interval timer code from earlier in this lesson. To see the following code in full, check out this book's companion file, `L7_14.htm`. In this section, I break the code into chunks and explain the key points about how each section works.

First, I made the following additions to the style sheet and HTML, which create the landscape the soldier will march over and the container for the image. In the HTML, I load the image with the standing-at-attention image, `walk1.png`.

Here's the style sheet:

```
<style type='text/css'>
    #d1{border:solid 1px red;
    height:100px;
    width:200px;
    font-size:3em;
    color:lime;
}
</style>
```

And here's the HTML:

```
<div id='d0' style='height:350px;background-
        color:#e9e9e9;'>
    <img id='image' src='images/walk1.png'/>
</div>
```

Now make a few changes to the script. First, make an array of the image source names, which makes referencing the src attribute easy. Here's what the array looks like:

```
var imagelist=new Array(
     "images/walk1.png",
     "images/walk2.png",
     "images/walk3.png",
     "images/walk4.png",
     "images/walk5.png",
     "images/walk6.png",
     "images/walk7.png"
     );
```

Add the following global variables:

```
var imagenumber=0;
document.images[0].src=imagelist[imagenumber];
var paddingnumber=0;
```

The following explains these variables:

- ✔ var imagenumber=0; keeps track of the images.

- ✔ document.images[0] is the HTML Document Object Model (DOM) element that keeps track of the number of images on your page.

- ✔ 0 refers to the first image.

- ✔ var paddingnumber=0 keeps track of the padding.

Now, make a few changes to two of the functions. The changes are colored in blue, and the explanation for each change appears in a comment before each change. Here are the changes you need to make to the startcount() function:

```
function startcount(){
/*there are only 7 images. When the number reaches 7 go
        back to number1*/
     if(imagenumber>6){imagenumber=1};
/*at the end of the page, return to the beginning
     if(paddingnumber>24){paddingnumber=1};
/* the next two lines calculate the padding amount and
        applies it to mydiv2*/
```

```
        var padding=paddingnumber*50;
        mydiv2.style.paddingLeft=padding+"px";
//switch the images
        document.images[0].src=imagelist
            [imagenumber];
        mydiv.innerHTML=imagenumber;
/*increment imagenumber and paddingnumber by1*/
        imagenumber=imagenumber+1;
        paddingnumber=paddingnumber+1;
}
```

And here are the changes to make to the `resetcounter()` function:

```
function resetcounter()
{
mydiv.innerHTML=0;
document.images[0].src=imagelist[0];
mydiv2.style.paddingLeft="0px";
paddingnumber=0;
}
```

When you run the modified example in a browser, the soldier marches across the field and returns to the beginning.

Try the following tasks to practice your skills with JavaScript animation:

- ✔ Change the interval from 250 milliseconds to some other interval.
- ✔ Make an animation of your own.

JavaScript animation is useful, but it has its drawbacks, chief among them is that the animation tends to be jerky. CSS3 shows promise of changing this and of providing a great substitute for Flash. See the section "Animating with CSS3" later in this lesson.

Preloading images

If you look at the marching animation from a server for the first time, you'll notice that the soldier (or Robert Burns) makes a hesitant start — not at all like a brave swaggering revolutionary soldier going off to fight the Hessian Mercenaries of King George, and certainly not like Robert Burns off to visit his lady friends!

The reason for the delay isn't reluctance on the character's part, but rather that the animation starts before all the images are downloaded. Downloading images over the Internet takes time. To get around the downloading delay, you need to load the images *before* the animation plays, which you can do in one of two ways:

✔ **Actually download the images for display.** If you use this method, you don't need to actually display the images. Set the CSS `display` property to `none`, and the images are still downloaded.

✔ **Download the images to a JavaScript** `image` **object.**

This book's companion files, `L7_15.htm` and `L7_16.htm`, available on the website, show preloading images in action.

Capturing a keystroke

As you read through various articles on animation, you'll find that a number require you to capture a keystroke (that is, pressing a key on the keyboard). All you have to remember is that the only elements that can capture a keystroke are elements that can receive focus.

The simplest way to capture a keystroke is to give an element a `tabindex`. Here's a simple example that pops up an alert telling you what key you pressed:

```
<div id="div2" tabindex="1" style='height:200px;border:
        solid 2px red;'>Click or tab to give this
        element the focus</div>

<script type="text/javascript">
   var el = document.getElementById("div2");
   el.onkeyup = function(evt) {
      evt = evt || window.event;
      alert("keyup: " + evt.keyCode);
      if(evt.keyCode==65){alert("You clicked the 'A'
         key!");}
   };
</script>
```

In this code, I gave the `<div>` element a `tabindex`. The variable `el` selects the `<div>` in the HTML. I used the `onkeyup` method of the `el` object to detect when a user releases a key (which, of course, implies that she previously pressed the key). After that, I translated the keystroke into the numeric code that JavaScript uses to identify letters and display that code in an alert. The `if(evt.keyCode==65)` line demonstrates how the `keyCode` can be used to look for the pressing of a certain key — A in this case. Check out how the example works with the companion file, L7_17.htm.

Playing with games: The Bomber Game

Using a combination of several of the techniques and methods you've seen in this lesson, you can make some quite sophisticated effects. L7_18.html and L7_19.html show two simple games where the aim is to shoot down the bomber as it transverses the screen. Keystrokes control the "gun." Although the code is too long to print in the book, you can view the source code for the sample files on this book's companion site.

Download the games from the companion site and figure out how the code works line by line. (The code is just a combination of the preceding examples in this section.) Then, try altering the numbers: Speed up the bomber and change the size of the target area. (A gentle warning: When you start improving a game like this, you can waste several evenings. It's rather like Facebook!)

Animating with CSS3

CSS3 transitions, transformations, and animation enable you to do animations without any JavaScript. The drawback is that these techniques are still experimental and require vendor prefixes, as I discuss in Lesson 5. IE has only just started supporting these techniques in IE10.

CSS3 animations nevertheless show a lot of promise, and I'm sure they'll gradually become more popular.

Making smooth CSS transitions

Transitions allow the smooth change of CSS properties over a period of time. The best way to introduce transitions is with a simple example, which you can check out in your browser by displaying this book's companion file, `L7_20.htm`.

The HTML for the transition example looks like this:

```
<div id='div1' style='width:800px;
          text-align:center;
          border:solid 1px lime;'>
     <p>Hello Transitions!</p>
</div>
```

And here's the style sheet:

```
<style type='text/css'>
    #div1:hover{
        color:#f00;
        font-size:4em;
        padding-top:50px;
        padding-bottom:50px;
/*vendor prefixes*/
        -moz-transition:all 4s;
        -webkit-transition:all 4s;
        -o-transition:all 4s;
        -ms-transition:all 4s;
    }
</style>
```

When you hover over the <div>, the new style rules in the style sheet take effect over four seconds. The `#div1:hover` uses a pseudo-class selector that tells the browser to apply the color, font size, and padding only when the cursor hovers over the <div>. The CSS `transition` property is what makes the change happen over a specified period of time. The `all` value indicates that you want all the properties of the element (rather than just width or just height, for example) to transition, and the `4s` value sets the interval for the transition to four seconds.

GO ONLINE

Several other transitions demos can be found at `http://nettuts.s3.amazonaws.com/581_ csstransitions/demos.html` and `http://css3.bradshawenterprises.com/ transitions`.

To see the earlier bomber example as a transition, check out this book's companion file, L7_21.htm, on the website. (I added a new twist: The bomber climbs into the night sky.)

TIP

Try these examples on different browsers to see the animations all function slightly differently, depending on the browser. As I wrote this lesson, Opera is the closest to being correct, according to the CSS3 specification.

Transforming elements with CSS3

A *transformation* allows you to stretch, skew, rotate, and move the element, as shown in Figure 7-8.

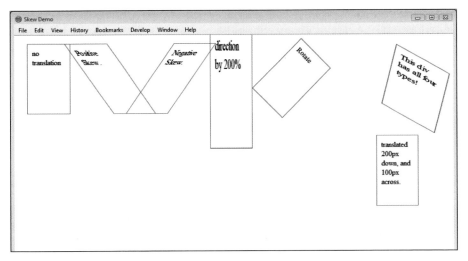

Figure 7-8

CSS3 has two categories of transform:

- ✓ **2D transforms:** Used for manipulating elements in two dimensions (x and y)
- ✓ **3D transforms:** Used for 3D transformations and animations

Transformations have been most fully developed by Chrome and other WebKit browsers, but the basic 2D values work in all the latest browsers. Listing 7-6 shows the style sheet that creates the transformations shown in Figure 7-7. Note that I show the vendor prefixes just once, and the code [vendor prefixes] is a placeholder that shows where the prefixes belong in subsequent CSS rules. Also, each unique ID selector and transform property (without the prefixes) is colored orange so you can easily scan the code.

Listing 7-6: A Style Sheet of Transformations

```
<style type='text/css'>
#container   div{
     width:70px;
     height:130px;
     margin:10px 20px;
     padding:10px;
     border:1px lime solid;
     float:left;
}
#container #skew {
     -webkit-transform:skew(35deg);
     -moz-transform:skew(35deg);
     -o-transform:skew(35deg);
     -ms-transform:skew(35deg);
     transform:skew(35deg);
}
#container #skew2 {
     [vendor prefixes]
     transform:skew(-35deg);
}
#container #scale {
     [vendor prefixes]
     transform:scale(1,2);
}

#container #rotate {
     [vendor prefixes]
     transform:rotate(45deg);
}

#container #translate {
     [vendor prefixes]
     transform:translate(100px, 200px);
}
#container #rotate-skew-scale-translate {
     [vendor prefixes]
     transform:skew(30deg) scale(1.1,1.1) rotate(40deg)
          translate(10px, 20px);
}
</style>
```

The HTML for the page in Figure 7-8 looks like this. The id attributes that correspond to the preceding selectors are colored green so you can more easily see how the HTML and CSS fit together:

```
<div id="container">
        <div >no translation</div>
        <div id="skew">Positive Skew.</div>
        <div id="skew2">Negative Skew.</div>
        <div id="scale">Scale in Y direction by 200%</div>
        <div id="rotate">Rotate</div>
        <div id="translate">translated 200px down, and 100px
                across.</div>
        <div id="rotate-skew-scale-translate">This div has
                all four types!</div>
</div>
```

You can see how the preceding code displays by loading this book's companion file, L7_22.htm, into your browser. To experiment with transformations on your own, try the following tasks:

✔ Change the float property to right. Look at what happens to the skews! Does this surprise you?

✔ Remove the float property altogether.

✔ Play around with the rotate value. Try values greater than 360deg.

Combining transitions and transform

When you combine transitions and transformations, you can create more complex CSS3 animations. The following CSS creates a box and spins it around a couple times:

```
<style>
#container div {
     height:100px;
     width:100px;
     border:1px red solid;
     margin:10px auto;
     text-align:center;
     -webkit-transition: all 3s ease-in-out;
     -moz-transition: all 3s ease-in-out;
     -o-transition: all 3s ease-in-out;
     -ms-transition: all 3s ease-in-out;
     transition: all 3s ease-in-out;
}
```

```
#container div:hover, #container div.spinme_effect {
    -webkit-transform:rotate(1080deg) scale(2,2);
    -moz-transform:rotate(1080deg) scale(2,2);
    -o-transform:rotate(1080deg) scale(2,2);
    -ms-transform:rotate(1080deg) scale(2,2);
    transform:rotate(1080deg) scale(2,2);
}
</style>
```

If you try this example in your browser, you see that the CSS transitions handle the animation of the transformation over time after you hover your mouse over the box.

Using CSS animations

CSS3 animations are an extension to CSS transitions. With CSS animations, you can animate without a line of JavaScript.

The best way to explain how to use CSS animations is with an example. If you want to follow along, you need to download a WebKit-compliant browser, such as Chrome or Safari. Neither the Opera nor Mosaic browser supports CSS animations yet.

The following CSS moves a butterfly image and the text Soaring Butterfly from the middle-left of the web page to the top and makes the butterfly image flutter. You can see the example animation in action by checking out this book's companion file, L7_23.htm, in a WebKit browser. Here's the style sheet that creates the animation:

```
#soar {
    position: absolute;
    top: 50px;left: 150px;
    height:166px;width:180px;
    background-color:transparent;
    background-image:url(blue_butterfly_2.gif);
    background-repeat:no-repeat;
    -webkit-animation-name:soaring-butterfly;
    -webkit-animation-duration: 2s;
    -webkit-animation-iteration-count: 4;
    -webkit-animation-timing-function: linear;
}
@-webkit-keyframes soaring-butterfly {
    from {
            -webkit-transform:translate(0px,450px);
    }
```

```
        to {
            -webkit-transform:translate(450px,0px);
        }
    }
```

The HTML looks like this:

```
<div id='soar' style="text-align:center;font-
        size:1.5em;">Buttertfly <br/>Soaring.</div>
```

Here's how the code works to create the animation:

- ✔ `position: absolute` starts the CSS. (Remember the position must be absolute for the `transform` property to work.)

- ✔ `-webkit-animation-name:soaring-butterfly` gives the animation a name. The name enables you to reference the animation with `keyframes` later in the code.

- ✔ `animation-duration` is the timeframe in which you want the animation to take place. The timeframe is measured in seconds.

- ✔ `animation-iteration` is the number of times you want the animation to take place.

- ✔ `animation-timing-function` takes the values in the following table. The default is `ease`.

- ✔ `keyframes`, in animation, are set reference points along a timeline. So, for example, if you wanted to move an object from point A to point B, but not in a straight line, you could insert `keyframes` along the path to indicate the path that the object should travel.

Value	What It Does
`linear`	The animation has the same speed from start to end.
`ease`	The animation has a slow start, then goes fast, and then ends slowly.
`ease-in`	The animation has a slow start.
`ease-out`	The animation has a slow end.
`ease-in-out`	The animation has a slow start and end.
`cubic-Bezier(<number>, <number>,<number>,<number>)`	Define your own values for a timing curve using numbers between 0 and 1.

To practice working with CSS3 animations, play around with the preceding code as follows:

- Experiment with the `keyframes` parameters.
- Remove the `animation-timing-function` and check out the result in a browser.
- Hack around with the other values and see what result you can get.
- Try your hand at making another animation using `skew`.
- In `L7_24.htm`, I combined the `keyframes` property with a JavaScript interval timer to create a flitting butterfly. Check it out and decipher the code. This, so to speak, can be your test!

That's all I have room for CSS3 animations here, but there's much more. I hope I've shown you enough to whet your appetite! For all the possibilities, visit the specification at `www.w3.org/tr/css3-animations`.

Summing Up

Congratulations! You've made it to the end of this course! If you've followed along and done the Practice exercises, you now know a lot about web programming on the client-side!

In this lesson, I covered the `<canvas>` element and animation. You learned how to

- Draw lines and shapes, including filling them and adding drop shadows.
- Draw text and load images on the `<canvas>`.
- Clip and scale these images. You also had a quick look at how to carry out manipulations at the pixel level.
- Use JavaScript, transitions, and transformations to create animations.
- Apply keystrokes and the x- and y- mouse coordinates to many different animations.

I hope all the examples have been helpful. A great way to continue your education is to use the examples to build your own site, modifying the examples as necessary. Look up similar examples on the web. My examples have been written with the aim of clarity in mind. On the web, you'll find that some very smart people have done a lot of amazing things. Many coders make one small area of the web their hobby, and they're always pushing the boundaries of what can and cannot be done. Sometimes, however, they forget that a lot of people aren't as smart as them! The examples I've given will help you understand their code!

Try-it-yourself lab

The best way to learn about the cutting-edge new features of HTML5 and CSS3 mentioned in this lesson is to experiment with them. To that end, try the following:

1. **Create a new document in your text editor and save it as** `Bezier.html.`

2. **Enter the following into the document (from earlier in this lesson):**

```
<!DOCTYPE html>
<html>
<head>
    <title>Bezier curve</title>
    <meta http-equiv="content-type" content="text/
        html;charset=utf-8" />
    <meta name="generator" content="Geany 0.20" />
</head>

<body>
    <canvas id='myCanvas' style='border:1px solid
        red;background-image:url(10px.png);height'
        height='300' width='500'></canvas>

    <script type='text/javascript'>
    window.onload = function(){

    var canvas = document.getElementById("myCanvas");

    var context = canvas.getContext("2d");

    context.moveTo(190, 120);
    context.BezierCurveTo(160, 260, 400,
        10, 400, 150);
    context.lineWidth = 10;
    context.strokeStyle = "black"; // line color
    context.stroke();
};
</script>
</body>

    </html>
```

3. **Open this document in a web browser to see how it draws a Bézier curve.**

4. **Adjust each of the numbers in the** `BezierCurveTo` **method, one at a time, and refresh the browser window to see what effect it has on the curve.**

Use the following as a guide:

```
context.BezierCurveTo(controlX1, controlY1, controlX2,
         controlY2, endX, endY);
```

5. **Change all the values to 0 and see what happens; then change one of the values at a time from 0 to something other than 0 and observe what happens each time.**

6. **Try different values until you can predict what effect a number change will have on the curve.**

After you're done with this lab, you have a much better understanding of Bézier curves than most web designers!

Know this tech talk

Bézier curve: A curved line that's described mathematically.

<canvas> element: Allows you to draw on the page using JavaScript and allows you to manipulate images at the pixel level.

color gradients: The transition of one color to another.

context object: A JavaScript `context` object of the `canvas`. It can either be 2D or 3D.

drop shadow: A shadow cast by an object lifted off a surface.

interval timer: Used in animation to time intervals between events.

global variable: Created outside of a function and can be used anywhere in a script.

local variable: Created inside of functions. They can be accessed only from within the function they're created.

radian: An angular measurement. The angle subtended by an arc the same length as the radius. A circle's circumference is 2 pi radians.

sliders: A complex object that changes a value as it slides along via a mouse pointer or keystroke.

transformation: An element transforms from one state to another.

transition: The time period over which a transformation takes place.

x- and y-coordinates: In Javascript, x- and y-coordinates are measured from the top-left corner.

About the CD

This appendix file contains information to help you get started using *For Dummies* eLearning. This course requires no installation.

System Requirements

For Dummies eLearning will provide all required functionality on the following Microsoft operating systems: Windows 7, Windows Vista, Windows XP, Windows 2000, and Windows 2003 Server.

The following browsers will be supported under Windows: Microsoft Internet Explorer 6.0 or higher, and Mozilla Firefox 2.x or higher.

To run a QS3 CD-ROM, the system should have the following additional hardware/software minimums:

- ✔ Adobe Flash Player 8
- ✔ A Pentium III, 500 MHz processor
- ✔ 256MB of RAM
- ✔ A CD-ROM or DVD-ROM drive

A negligible amount of disk space must be available for tracking data. Less than 1MB will typically be used. Your purchase of this *For Dummies* eLearning Kit includes access to the course online at the *For Dummies* eLearning Center. If you have purchased an electronic version of this book, please visit www.dummies.com/go/getelearningcode to gain your access code to the online course. If you borrowed this book from a library, you can use the course on the CD only. Follow the instructions for using the CD found later in this appendix.

Launch Instructions

Keep in mind that course functionality relies heavily on mini-windows known as *pop-ups* for delivering its content. Many web browsers have *pop-up blockers*, on the (mistaken) assumption that all pop-ups must be advertising that no one really wants to see. These browsers also let you enable pop-ups if you so desire. Please make sure to enable pop-ups before starting to use the CD or the course online. If you don't enable pop-ups, some pop-up blockers may restrict the course from running.

Setup instructions for Windows machines:

1. **Put the CD in the CD drive.**

2. **Double-click the My Computer icon to view the contents of the My Computer window.**

3. **Double-click the CD-ROM drive icon to view the contents of the *For Dummies* eLearning CD.**

4. **Double-click the `start.bat` file to start the *For Dummies* eLearning CD.**

   Your computer may warn you about active content. Click Yes to continue starting the CD. The CD may create new tabs in your browser. Click the tab to see the content.

The browser offers the option of using the lessons from the CD or from the website, as spelled out in the next sections.

Accessing the course on the website

When you launch your *For Dummies* eLearning CD, you have two options for accessing your eLearning course: Access Course(s) Online and Access Course(s) on CD. To access the course online, do the following:

1. **In the Activate Your FREE Online Course Now! section, click the Access Course(s) Online button.**

   Note: You will need the online course access key found behind the CD-ROM in this book to complete your online registration.

2. **In the new browser page that appears, click the blue <u>Here</u> link found in the sentence "Click here for the online course."**

   On the resulting *For Dummies* eLearning home page, notice the Access Key field for entering your personal access key.

3. **Enter your personal access key (found behind the CD-ROM in this book) into the Access Key field and then click the Send button.**

   You're brought to a Terms and Conditions of Use browser page.

> You only have to use the access key once. In fact, if you try to enter an access key after it has already been accepted, you'll end up getting an error code.

4. **Read through the terms and conditions of use for the online course, then click the Accept button.**

5. **On the Registration page, fill in the required personal information (including username and password); then click the Submit button.**

   You are brought to the My Courses page of the *For Dummies* eLearning website.

6. **In the My Courses page, click the link for the course you want to work on.**

   The course launches.

The opening page for your online course gives you a nice overview of the course. To actually get started, click the Content tab to see a list of course topics. Click to select any topic from the list. When the topic opens, it plays an introductory animation. To watch more animations on the topic, click the Next button (the arrow pointing right) at the bottom of the screen to play the next one.

If you want to switch to another lesson or another topic, use the list on the left side of the topic window to open a lesson and select a topic.

Some topics have an active tab for resources on the right side of the window. By default, Windows opens this content in a new window. If you have another compressed file manager installed, such as WinZip, your system may behave differently.

Here are some things to keep in mind when working with your online course:

- ✔ You can come back and resume your course as many times as you like over the six-month subscription period.

- ✔ Your online course "home base" can be found at `www.dummies elearning.com`. Whenever you want to return to your online course, just point your browser to that address. (You may want to use your browser's Bookmark feature to store this address for quick access later on.)

✔ After landing at the dummieselearning.com site, just enter your username and password in the appropriate fields in the upper right and then click the Login button to return to your My Courses page. (If you click the Remember Me check box, the dummieselearning.com site will store your username and password for you, so when you return, all you need to do is click the Login button to get to your My Courses page.)

✔ Once back at your My Courses page, you can click one of your courses and either start over from the beginning or pick up where you left off.

✔ For a quick overview of other online courses available from the dummieselearning.com site, click the Catalog tab on the site's home page to access the online catalog. From there, you can choose to purchase new courses.

Accessing the course on the CD

When you launch your *For Dummies* eLearning CD, you see a browser page that offers you *two* options for accessing your eLearning course (online or on CD). If you choose to use the CD version of the course, do the following:

1. **In the Activate Your FREE Online Course Now! section, click the Access Course(s) on CD button.**

2. **On the resulting Add User page, enter your username in the Add a New User Account field and then click the Add a New User Account button.**

3. **In the new page that appears, select your username from the Learner Name list and then click the Enter button.**

   You are brought to the home page of your *For Dummies* eLearning course. From here, you can choose a lesson (or topic within a lesson) to work with.

Whenever you want to return to the CD version of your eLearning course, just launch the CD, click the Access Course(s) on CD button, select your username from the Learner Name list in the page that appears, and then click the Enter button. (No need to add a new user account, in other words.)

After you enter your username, the eLearning course displays a list of topics similar to what you would see if you were working with the course online. Here, however, you select a topic from the list by clicking its Launch button. When the topic opens, it plays an introductory animation. To watch more animations on the topic, click the Next button (the arrow pointing right) at the bottom of the screen to play the next one.

As is the case with the online version of the course, if you want to switch to another lesson or another topic, use the list on the left side of the topic window to open a lesson and select a topic.

Troubleshooting

What do I do if the page does not load?

It is possible that you have a security setting enabled that is not allowing the needed Flash file to run. Be sure that pop-up blockers are off, ActiveX content is enabled, and the correct version of Shockwave and Flash are on the system you are using.

Please contact your system administrator or technical support group for assistance.

What do I do if the Add User window appears when the course loads and there are no names in the Learner Name list, but I have previously created a user account?

The course stores your information on the machine on which you create your account, so first make sure that you are using the *For Dummies* eLearning course on the same machine on which you created your Learner account. If you are using the course on a network and using a different machine than the one on which you created your account, the software will not be able to access your Learner record.

If you are on the machine on which you created your account, close the course browser window. Depending on the configuration of your machine, sometimes a course will load before accessing the user data.

If this still does not work, contact your network administrator for more assistance.

What do I do if I click on a Launch button but nothing happens?

This may occur on machines that have AOL installed. If you are using the course from a CD-ROM and you are an AOL subscriber, follow the following steps:

1. **Exit the course.**

2. **Log on to AOL.**

3. **Restart the course.**

What do I do if the Shockwave installer on the CD says that I have a more recent version of the plugin, but the software still says that I need to install version 8.5 or higher?

Download the latest version of the Shockwave plugin directly from Adobe's website:

www.adobe.com/downloads

If prompted to install Flash Player to view the CD's content, you can download the latest version from the same URL.

Index

Apple & Mac

iPad 2 For Dummies,
3rd Edition
978-1-118-17679-5

iPhone 4S For Dummies,
5th Edition
978-1-118-03671-6

iPod touch For Dummies,
3rd Edition
978-1-118-12960-9

Mac OS X Lion
For Dummies
978-1-118-02205-4

Blogging & Social Media

CityVille For Dummies
978-1-118-08337-6

Facebook For Dummies,
4th Edition
978-1-118-09562-1

Mom Blogging
For Dummies
978-1-118-03843-7

Twitter For Dummies,
2nd Edition
978-0-470-76879-2

WordPress For Dummies,
4th Edition
978-1-118-07342-1

Business

Cash Flow For Dummies
978-1-118-01850-7

Investing For Dummies,
6th Edition
978-0-470-90545-6

Job Searching with Social
Media For Dummies
978-0-470-93072-4

QuickBooks 2012
For Dummies
978-1-118-09120-3

Resumes For Dummies,
6th Edition
978-0-470-87361-8

Starting an Etsy Business
For Dummies
978-0-470-93067-0

Cooking & Entertaining

Cooking Basics
For Dummies, 4th Edition
978-0-470-91388-8

Wine For Dummies,
4th Edition
978-0-470-04579-4

Diet & Nutrition

Kettlebells For Dummies
978-0-470-59929-7

Nutrition For Dummies,
5th Edition
978-0-470-93231-5

Restaurant Calorie Counter
For Dummies,
2nd Edition
978-0-470-64405-8

Digital Photography

Digital SLR Cameras &
Photography For Dummies,
4th Edition
978-1-118-14489-3

Digital SLR Settings
& Shortcuts
For Dummies
978-0-470-91763-3

Photoshop Elements 10
For Dummies
978-1-118-10742-3

Gardening

Gardening Basics
For Dummies
978-0-470-03749-2

Vegetable Gardening
For Dummies,
2nd Edition
978-0-470-49870-5

Green/Sustainable

Raising Chickens
For Dummies
978-0-470-46544-8

Green Cleaning
For Dummies
978-0-470-39106-8

Health

Diabetes For Dummies,
3rd Edition
978-0-470-27086-8

Food Allergies
For Dummies
978-0-470-09584-3

Living Gluten-Free
For Dummies,
2nd Edition
978-0-470-58589-4

Hobbies

Beekeeping
For Dummies,
2nd Edition
978-0-470-43065-1

Chess For Dummies,
3rd Edition
978-1-118-01695-4

Drawing For Dummies,
2nd Edition
978-0-470-61842-4

eBay For Dummies,
7th Edition
978-1-118-09806-6

Knitting For Dummies,
2nd Edition
978-0-470-28747-7

Language &
Foreign Language

English Grammar
For Dummies,
2nd Edition
978-0-470-54664-2

French For Dummies,
2nd Edition
978-1-118-00464-7

German For Dummies,
2nd Edition
978-0-470-90101-4

Spanish Essentials
For Dummies
978-0-470-63751-7

Spanish For Dummies,
2nd Edition
978-0-470-87855-2

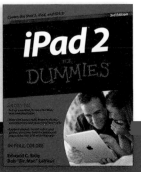

Math & Science

Algebra I For Dummies,
2nd Edition
978-0-470-55964-2

Biology For Dummies,
2nd Edition
978-0-470-59875-7

Chemistry For Dummies,
2nd Edition
978-1-1180-0730-3

Geometry For Dummies,
2nd Edition
978-0-470-08946-0

Pre-Algebra Essentials
For Dummies
978-0-470-61838-7

Microsoft Office

Excel 2010 For Dummies
978-0-470-48953-6

Office 2010 All-in-One
For Dummies
978-0-470-49748-7

Office 2011 for Mac
For Dummies
978-0-470-87869-9

Word 2010
For Dummies
978-0-470-48772-3

Music

Guitar For Dummies,
2nd Edition
978-0-7645-9904-0

Clarinet For Dummies
978-0-470-58477-4

iPod & iTunes
For Dummies,
9th Edition
978-1-118-13060-5

Pets

Cats For Dummies,
2nd Edition
978-0-7645-5275-5

Dogs All-in One
For Dummies
978-0470-52978-2

Saltwater Aquariums
For Dummies
978-0-470-06805-2

Religion & Inspiration

The Bible For Dummies
978-0-7645-5296-0

Catholicism For Dummies,
2nd Edition
978-1-118-07778-8

Spirituality For Dummies,
2nd Edition
978-0-470-19142-2

Self-Help & Relationships

Happiness For Dummies
978-0-470-28171-0

Overcoming Anxiety
For Dummies,
2nd Edition
978-0-470-57441-6

Seniors

Crosswords For Seniors
For Dummies
978-0-470-49157-7

iPad 2 For Seniors
For Dummies, 3rd Edition
978-1-118-17678-8

Laptops & Tablets
For Seniors For Dummies,
2nd Edition
978-1-118-09596-6

Smartphones & Tablets

BlackBerry For Dummies,
5th Edition
978-1-118-10035-6

Droid X2 For Dummies
978-1-118-14864-8

HTC ThunderBolt
For Dummies
978-1-118-07601-9

MOTOROLA XOOM
For Dummies
978-1-118-08835-7

Sports

Basketball For Dummies,
3rd Edition
978-1-118-07374-2

Football For Dummies,
2nd Edition
978-1-118-01261-1

Golf For Dummies,
4th Edition
978-0-470-88279-5

Test Prep

ACT For Dummies,
5th Edition
978-1-118-01259-8

ASVAB For Dummies,
3rd Edition
978-0-470-63760-9

The GRE Test For
Dummies, 7th Edition
978-0-470-00919-2

Police Officer Exam
For Dummies
978-0-470-88724-0

Series 7 Exam
For Dummies
978-0-470-09932-2

Web Development

HTML, CSS, & XHTML
For Dummies, 7th Edition
978-0-470-91659-9

Drupal For Dummies,
2nd Edition
978-1-118-08348-2

Windows 7

Windows 7
For Dummies
978-0-470-49743-2

Windows 7
For Dummies,
Book + DVD Bundle
978-0-470-52398-8

Windows 7 All-in-One
For Dummies
978-0-470-48763-1

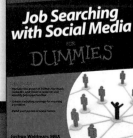

End-User License Agreement

READ THIS. You should carefully read these terms and conditions before opening the software packet(s) included with this book "Book". This is a license agreement "Agreement" between you and John Wiley & Sons, Inc. "WILEY". By opening the accompanying software packet(s), you acknowledge that you have read and accept the following terms and conditions. If you do not agree and do not want to be bound by such terms and conditions, promptly return the Book and the unopened software packet(s) to the place you obtained them for a full refund.

1. **License Grant.** WILEY grants to you (either an individual or entity) a nonexclusive license to use one copy of the enclosed software program(s) (collectively, the "Software") solely for your own personal or business purposes on a single computer (whether a standard computer or a workstation component of a multi-user network). The Software is in use on a computer when it is loaded into temporary memory (RAM) or installed into permanent memory (hard disk, CD-ROM, or other storage device). WILEY reserves all rights not expressly granted herein.

2. **Ownership.** WILEY is the owner of all right, title, and interest, including copyright, in and to the compilation of the Software recorded on the physical packet included with this Book "Software Media". Copyright to the individual programs recorded on the Software Media is owned by the author or other authorized copyright owner of each program. Ownership of the Software and all proprietary rights relating thereto remain with WILEY and its licensers.

3. **Restrictions on Use and Transfer.**

    (a) You may only (i) make one copy of the Software for backup or archival purposes, or (ii) transfer the Software to a single hard disk, provided that you keep the original for backup or archival purposes. You may not (i) rent or lease the Software, (ii) copy or reproduce the Software through a LAN or other network system or through any computer subscriber system or bulletin-board system, or (iii) modify, adapt, or create derivative works based on the Software.

    (b) You may not reverse engineer, decompile, or disassemble the Software. You may transfer the Software and user documentation on a permanent basis, provided that the transferee agrees to accept the terms and conditions of this Agreement and you retain no copies. If the Software is an update or has been updated, any transfer must include the most recent update and all prior versions.

4. **Restrictions on Use of Individual Programs.** You must follow the individual requirements and restrictions detailed for each individual program in the "About the CD" appendix of this Book or on the Software Media. These limitations are also contained in the individual license agreements recorded on the Software Media. These limitations may include a requirement that after using the program for a specified period of time, the user must pay a registration fee or discontinue use. By opening the Software packet(s), you agree to abide by the licenses and restrictions for these individual programs that are detailed in the "About the CD" appendix and/or on the Software Media. None of the material on this Software Media or listed in this Book may ever be redistributed, in original or modified form, for commercial purposes.

5. **Limited Warranty.**

    (a) WILEY warrants that the Software Media is free from defects in materials and workmanship under normal use for a period of sixty (60) days from the date of purchase of this Book. If WILEY receives notification within the warranty period of defects in materials or workmanship, WILEY will replace the defective Software Media.

(b) WILEY AND THE AUTHOR(S) OF THE BOOK DISCLAIM ALL OTHER WARRANTIES, EXPRESS OR IMPLIED, INCLUDING WITHOUT LIMITATION IMPLIED WARRANTIES OF MERCHANTABILITY AND FITNESS FOR A PARTICULAR PURPOSE, WITH RESPECT TO THE SOFTWARE, THE PROGRAMS, THE SOURCE CODE CONTAINED THEREIN, AND/OR THE TECHNIQUES DESCRIBED IN THIS BOOK. WILEY DOES NOT WARRANT THAT THE FUNCTIONS CONTAINED IN THE SOFTWARE WILL MEET YOUR REQUIREMENTS OR THAT THE OPERATION OF THE SOFTWARE WILL BE ERROR FREE.

(c) This limited warranty gives you specific legal rights, and you may have other rights that vary from jurisdiction to jurisdiction.

6. Remedies.

(a) WILEY's entire liability and your exclusive remedy for defects in materials and workmanship shall be limited to replacement of the Software Media, which may be returned to WILEY with a copy of your receipt at the following address: Software Media Fulfillment Department, Attn.: *HTML5 eLearning Kit For Dummies,* John Wiley & Sons, Inc., 10475 Crosspoint Blvd., Indianapolis, IN 46256, or call 1-800-762-2974. Please allow four to six weeks for delivery. This Limited Warranty is void if failure of the Software Media has resulted from accident, abuse, or misapplication. Any replacement Software Media will be warranted for the remainder of the original warranty period or thirty (30) days, whichever is longer.

(b) In no event shall WILEY or the author be liable for any damages whatsoever (including without limitation damages for loss of business profits, business interruption, loss of business information, or any other pecuniary loss) arising from the use of or inability to use the Book or the Software, even if WILEY has been advised of the possibility of such damages.

(c) Because some jurisdictions do not allow the exclusion or limitation of liability for consequential or incidental damages, the above limitation or exclusion may not apply to you.

7. U.S. Government Restricted Rights. Use, duplication, or disclosure of the Software for or on behalf of the United States of America, its agencies and/or instrumentalities "U.S. Government" is subject to restrictions as stated in paragraph (c)(1)(ii) of the Rights in Technical Data and Computer Software clause of DFARS 252.227-7013, or subparagraphs (c) (1) and (2) of the Commercial Computer Software - Restricted Rights clause at FAR 52.227-19, and in similar clauses in the NASA FAR supplement, as applicable.

8. General. This Agreement constitutes the entire understanding of the parties and revokes and supersedes all prior agreements, oral or written, between them and may not be modified or amended except in a writing signed by both parties hereto that specifically refers to this Agreement. This Agreement shall take precedence over any other documents that may be in conflict herewith. If any one or more provisions contained in this Agreement are held by any court or tribunal to be invalid, illegal, or otherwise unenforceable, each and every other provision shall remain in full force and effect.